The Idea of the English Landscape Painter

THE IDEA OF THE ENGLISH LANDSCAPE PAINTER

Genius as Alibi in the Early Nineteenth Century

KAY DIAN KRIZ

Published for
THE PAUL MELLON CENTRE
FOR STUDIES IN BRITISH ART
by
YALE UNIVERSITY PRESS
NEW HAVEN AND LONDON

Designed by Gillian Malpass
Set in Linotron Bembo by Best-set Typesetter Ltd., Hong Kong
Printed in Hong Kong through Worldprint Ltd

Library of Congress Cataloging-in-Publication Data
Kriz, Kay Dian, 1945–
The idea of the English landscape painter:
genius as Alibi in the early nineteenth century / Kay Dian Kriz.
Includes bibliographical references and index.
ISBN 0-300-06833-6 (cl : alk. paper)
1. Landscape painting, English.
2. Landscape painting – 19th century – England.   I. Title.
ND1354.5.K75   1997
758′.1′094209034—DC20   96-43187
CIP

A catalogue record for this book is available from
The British Library

Frontispiece: Augustus Wall Callcott, *The Pool of London* (detail), RA 1816. Trustees
of the Bowood Settlement, Calne, Wiltshire.

In memory of Brian Kriz

Contents

facing page Cooke after Turner. Detail of Figure 35.

Acknowledgments

IN A BOOK DEVOTED TO DEMYSTIFYING the notion of individual genius it seems particularly appropriate to affirm once again the communal nature of the scholarly enterprise that produces the single-authored text.

My professors at the University of British Columbia, colleagues at Brown University, and other friends and scholars in Britain and North America were crucial in the development of various stages of this project. Particular thanks go to Ann Bermingham, Edward Hundert, Coppélia Kahn, Paula Krebs, Evie Lincoln, Laurie Monahan, Dietrich Neumann, and Maureen Ryan for reading and commenting perceptively on various portions and versions of the manuscript and to Bibiana Obler for proofreading parts of the final draft. I also benefited from many lively and provocative conversations about the project with Claire Buck, Peter Funnell, Barbara Rofkar, Thomas Prasch, Ann Pullan, Linda Smeins, and Toby Smith.

Four scholars deserve special mention for the huge intellectual debt I owe them. I have learned an enormous amount about the politics of British culture and landscape painting from Andrew Hemingway, who generously shared with me the penultimate draft of his dissertation when I first came to London, and took the time to offer a rigorous critique of the finished version of my dissertation. Over the past ten years I have been honored and enriched by the friendship of Rose Marie San Juan, who has read and commented on various drafts and portions of the text, and supplied constant support and encouragement. Beyond this, I am also grateful to her for providing me with a model of scholarship, based on her strong commitment to a fully historicized, politicized, and theorized account of visual culture, that continues to inspire my admiration and highest esteem. As my advisor, and one of my first teachers at UBC, Serge Guilbaut is largely responsible for impressing upon me the value of examining the highly complex and often vexed relationship between culture and politics. I thank him for his wisdom, patience, wit, and forthrightness. My largest debt of gratitude is to David Solkin. He was generous to a fault with his time, unfailing in his support, and unsparing in his criticism – in other words, the ideal advisor. His impact not simply on this project, but on my way of thinking about visual culture in general, is greater than he can ever know.

This project could not have been completed without the generous financial support I received during my graduate studies at the University of British Columbia through the I. W. Killam Foundation and the Tina and Morris Wagner Foundation. Sabbatical funding from Brown University made it possible for me to complete the

facing page Girtin. Detail of Figure 27.

major revisions to the text. The Paul Mellon Centre for Studies in British Art not only funded a year's research in 1988–89, but its staff, including Kasha Jenkinson and Evelyn Newby, gave me the kind of practical guidance (from finding a school for my daughter to helping me gain access to archives) that contributed enormously to the success of my first major research trip to London. I would like especially to thank Michael Kitson, then Director of the Centre, present Director Brian Allen, and Kim Sloan (now at the British Museum) for their generous and ongoing support. I have also benefited from the sound advice of my editor, Gillian Malpass and the thoughtful criticism of the readers for the manuscript at Yale University Press.

Finally, I would like to thank my children, Ken and Michelle, who have literally grown up with this project and have been models of patience and support, and my parents for their constant love and encouragement. I suspect that my scholarly interest in landscape has much to do with early and fond memories of the sight and smell of my mother's oil paintings of California mountain scenes, "in process" in our living room.

Introduction

We are almost led to describe it [J.M.W. Turner's *Snowstorm: Hannibal and his Army Crossing the Alps*] as the effect of magic, which this Prospero of the graphic art can call into action, and give to airy nothing a substantial form. . . . All that is terrible and grand is personified in the mysterious effect of the picture; and we cannot but admire the genius displayed in this extraordinary work.[1]

Repository of Arts, June 1812

[Thomas Girtin's] views of many of our cities, towns, castles, cathedrals, etc, were treated by his pencil in a manner entirely his own; a depth of shadow, a brilliancy of light, and a magical splendour of colour characterized his drawings, and displayed a vigour of inherent genius that promised to raise the art [of watercolour] to the highest summit of excellence. In the works of too many artists we perceive only the labour of the hand, but in Girtin the hand was obviously directed by a superior mental power and capacity.[2]

[W.H. Pyne?]
Repository of Arts, February 1813

THESE PAEANS TO TURNER AND GIRTIN, published in a fashionable women's magazine, invoke many of the qualities that continue to be associated with the Romantic landscape painter. In his representation of the Carthaginian army's stormy Alpine passage (Figure 1), Turner, the modern Prospero, dazzles the viewer through his painterly transfiguration of the most ethereal features of the landscape – clouds, snow, and wind – into a sublime image of nature's savage power.[3] As the critic emphasizes in the concluding lines of this passage, this sublime exchange between the viewer and Turner's image not only produces awe in the face of nature, but awe before the genius of the painter. Girtin, working in the medium of watercolor, also is seen to perform magical acts, transforming the mundane subject matter of topography into visual displays that reveal as much about the artist's "inherent genius" as they do about the sites represented.

To the degree that we as modern readers and viewers accept as natural and self-evident the judgments contained in such accounts, we confirm ourselves as the cultural heirs of a tradition of genius that has attempted, rather successfully, if the popular and scholarly literature on artists such as Turner is any indication, to

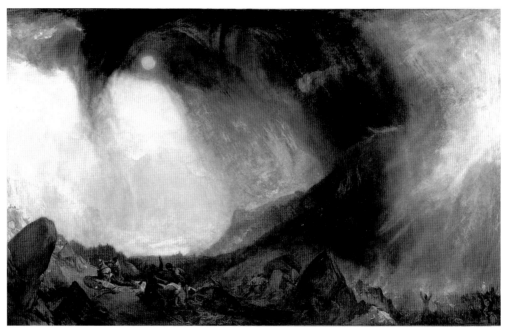

1   J. M. W. Turner, *Snowstorm: Hannibal and his Army Crossing the Alps*, RA 1812. Oil on canvas, 57.5 × 93.5 in. Clore Gallery for the Turner Collection, Tate Gallery, London.

transform active viewers into passive admirers of a magical creative power. As a result of this transformation, genius simultaneously represents an ideal of the autonomous creative individual so valued in Western society and yet offers this ideal in the form of a model that viewers cannot hope to emulate, to understand, or to criticize. The force of genius lies in the seemingly intuitive way in which it manifests itself in works of art – we gaze at a painting and immediately experience it not as merely a landscape, but a Turner landscape or simply a "Turner." This book undertakes an analysis of the historical circumstances that gave rise to this phenomenon of the native landscape genius in the decades after 1800; it is a task that requires "denaturalizing" the domestic landscape so compellingly represented by native geniuses and also questioning the naturalness of those private feelings which still are seen to mark our uniqueness as individuals.

An examination of the critical discourse on landscape painting at the turn of the nineteenth century offers firm evidence that the above-quoted tributes to Turner and Girtin are not simply pronouncements on genius. More broadly, they articulate a highly interested position within an extended and often heated debate about the social function and cultural identity of the native English artist in the years around 1800. While unquestionably there were individuals alive in England at the turn of the century who were called artists, an examination of contemporary writings on art reveals that what it meant to *be* an artist, and within that general category, what it meant to be an artistic genius, were very much in dispute.

Consider, for example, this statement by Girtin's teacher, Edward Dayes, made in the context of an essay on drawing first published in 1802: "The artist is a true logician: not content with producing effects, he is ever inquiring after causes founded on visible demonstration, to exhibit them in his work."[4] For Dayes the artist is no magician transforming base matter into spectacular displays of color and light, but a rationalist seeking to discover and record the "essence" of nature through systematic inquiry. As we shall see, Dayes promotes this artistic ideal both as an alternative to the notion of the genius governed by imagination and in vehement opposition to a contemporary anti-type that featured prominently in writings on art and culture – the artist as a man of commerce, whose vulgar, flashy pictures pander to the specious demands of a market in luxury goods.

Four years earlier, a critic reviewing the Royal Academy exhibition of 1798 for the *London Packet* employs the term "genius" ironically in expressing a preference for the classically ordered, delicately hued landscapes of Joseph Farington (e.g., *A View of Skiddaw and Derwentwater*, Figure 2) over the productions of "those enthusiastical geniuses of the age who have yet to learn how to contemplate nature with a correct eye." He advises these misguided "geniuses" to study Farington's works, which display "no fanatical flourish of outline or gaudy diversity of tint, but everything is legitimate."[5] "Enthusiastical," "fanatical," "legitimate": during the 1790s these terms were highly charged, occurring most frequently in political and religious attacks on those forms of popular radicalism that variously combined millennialism, a visionary evangelicalism, and a radical political utopianism.

2   Joseph Farington, *View of Skiddaw and Derwentwater*, *c.*1780. Watercolor over pencil, 19.3 × 25.9 in. Yale Center for British Art, Paul Mellon Collection, New Haven.

Although this melding of religious enthusiasm with popular radicalism enjoyed a resurgence in the years after the French Revolution, many middle-class English radicals and reformists sought to distance themselves from such "visionaries." On the other hand, Edmund Burke and other counter-revolutionary writers attempted to equate all forms of English radicalism with French Jacobinism and with that earlier form of English "fanaticism" that provoked the regicide of Charles I.[6] Appropriating this politically charged rhetoric, the *London Packet* critic insinuated that "fanatical" artistic geniuses – identifiable by their unnatural, gaudy landscapes – were threatening to wreak the same revolutionary havoc within the domain of English culture that French Republicans and their English counterparts were attempting within the political realm.

Such different deployments of "genius" in the passages cited above attest to its "multi-accentuality" – that is, to the ability of the term "genius" to signify a range of positive and negative values within intersecting discourses on high art, nationalism, commerce, and politics.[7] But, equally importantly, such differences also testify to a significant reworking of the visual codes by which both "the natural" and "the native genius" were figured in certain forms of domestic landscape painting in the decade and a half which separates the *London Packet* review of Farington and the *Repository*'s panegyrics to Turner and Girtin. This book is concerned with tracking precisely those cultural discourses that addressed such shifts in the visual rhetoric of landscape painting occurring between 1795 and 1820.

What follows, then, is decidedly *not* a history of the idea of the native landscape genius as a coherent entity that "evolves" gradually over the course of the eighteenth century or, alternatively, "emerges" suddenly around 1800 in some vaguely defined response to the development of the "modern sensibility." Indeed, this account takes issue with such a notion of history by demonstrating that artistic identity was produced in the same way as other forms of subjectivity: in and through difference. Hence, I employ the term "artistic subject" to denote the artist as a category – defined by nationality, social status, gender, wealth, education, moral codes, and so forth – as distinguished from artists as living persons. In adopting the term "subject position" I wish to emphasize the contingent and relational nature of a particular notion of the artist; such a subject is defined by its position in representation, social practices, and institutions relative to other conceptions of the individual.[8]

Michel Foucault's analyses of the manner in which human subjects are formed through discourse and discursive practices have been crucial to my formulation of subjectivity. However, the usefulness of his work is limited to the extent that he tends to focus upon the mechanisms by which individuals become "subjected" within systems of power, and devotes less attention to the ways in which individuals resist, support, or change those systems.[9] In the course of this study, it will be necessary to attend to this complex interaction of individuals and systems of power. For landscape painters such "systems" were highly diverse, encompassing modes of patronage, institutions involved in teaching and displaying art, and various attempts to codify methods of viewing and representing the natural landscape. We will encounter artists like Turner, Girtin, and Augustus Wall Callcott, whose success derived largely from their ability to participate actively in the recasting of cultural identities through their manipulation of these institutions and systems of representation. But we will also examine artists such as James Barry and Edward Dayes, whose inability or unwillingness to modify their principles and practices was instrumental in their professional failure.

This book profits from and in many ways is a response to recent studies of late eighteenth- and early nineteenth-century British landscape imagery by John Barrell, Ann Bermingham, Stephen Daniels, Andrew Hemingway, and Michael Rosenthal.[10] These scholars have analyzed the various ways in which representations of cultivated land and uncultivated nature promote a particular vision (usually an ordered and harmonious one) of British society at this time. Bermingham, Rosenthal, and Barrell have examined how agrarian landscapes articulate visually those class relations that pertain to landed society, while Hemingway has explored the relationship of naturalist landscape painting to the urban and provincial middle class. These important studies have contributed enormously to our understanding of how various types of property relations and social practices are mediated by images of the land. They do not, however, attempt to explain what is peculiarly English about English landscape painting – that is, they do not consider how this particular genre of painting was able to articulate a form of identity which was perceived in terms of nationality that was embedded within various class formations. Stephen Daniels's recent book, *Fields of Vision: Landscape Imagery and National Identity in England and the United States*, considers, as the title indicates, the diverse ways in which English landscape painters have sought to "picture the nation" via sites, industries, and activities that have nationalist implications.[11] However it is one thing for an image to represent a specifically "English" form of landscape and quite another for an image to be seen to embody its producer as an ideal of Englishness. This latter process is what I am attempting to analyze via a particular notion of genius – characterized by boldness, imagination, independent-mindedness, sensibility, and manliness – that certain segments of the cultural elite came to identify as "essentially" English.

Many of the landscapes under consideration here could be seen to fall within the category of "English naturalism" that Andrew Hemingway has recently analyzed with regard to its role in the articulation of a modern, urban, middle-class consciousness: Girtin's townscapes, Copley Fielding's brilliant sunset views of the beach at Hastings, Callcott's coastal scenes, and Turner's images of the Thames evidence as much concern for those effects of light, atmosphere, and climate that are specific to a given season, place, and time of day as Constable's paintings of the Stour Valley, or John Sell Cotman's scenes of Norfolk. And indeed, many of the issues addressed here – concerning sources of patronage, the nature of the public for art, the status of landscape painting within the academic hierarchy of genres, and the definition of what is natural, unnatural, and ideal, to name but a few – impinge upon a wide range of domestic landscape imagery, including those works grouped under the rubric of naturalist painting. The signal feature of the artists I will be dealing with is not only their attention to "natural" effects, or even their choice of subject matter (a tendency towards non-agricultural sites possessing widely known poetic or historical associations). In fact, many of the artists discussed here depicted sites that had few such "elevating" literary associations, while, conversely, scores of

their contemporaries produced "naturalistic" views of such poetically and histori-
cally charged subjects as castles and ruined abbeys without being acclaimed for their
genius and originality. What distinguishes the artists discussed here is first their use
of high-key color, highlighting, and other visually arresting effects in order to
represent local conditions of light, atmosphere, and climate; and secondly, the
special relationship that contemporary commentators perceived to exist between
the pictures manifesting these painterly effects and their creators. Specifically,
certain qualities of the artist's character were seen to be embodied *in and through* the
work produced. The quote from W. H. Pyne that introduces this discussion makes
the point quite clearly: "In the works of too many artists we perceive only the
labour of the hand, but in Girtin the hand was obviously directed by a superior
mental power and capacity." As this quote suggests, it was not only "imaginative
geniuses" such as Turner and Girtin who were embodied (if that term can be
applied to something so pointedly "disembodied" as a "mind") in their works, but
also other painters ("too many" by Pyne's reckoning) like the Alsatian Philippe de
Loutherbourg, whose pictures, according to a critic writing for the *Repository of
Arts*, "always bring the painter too much to our mind; and instead of dwelling on
the majesty of the scene and partaking of the sentiment intended to be conveyed
by the composition, we can think of nothing but the dexterous touch and fine
execution of the artist."[12] A major part of this investigation, then, will be determining what painterly techniques prompted such varied assessments of these artists,
and what those assessments signified not only for the artists involved but also for
their viewers.

This study focuses on the production of English identity, rather than British
identity, in spite of the fact that many of the "domestic" landscapes produced by
the artists considered here represent geographical sites in Wales and Scotland.
Recently Linda Colley has asserted that the period under consideration here was
one in which cultural, religious, military, economic, and political forces served
variously to "produce" a unified British identity in contradistinction to a foreign
Other (Catholic France); she emphasizes that this newly forged national identity
was superimposed upon, but did not obliterate, Englishness, Scottishness, and
Welshness.[13] This study of English landscape painting demonstrates just what a
complex and conflicted process this was by showing how certain notions of Englishness sometimes reinforced the idea of Britishness and at other times promoted
regional differences. For example, the production of an English school of landscape
painters (and they were more commonly referred to in these terms, rather than as
the "British" school) was usually portrayed as a cultural achievement which
brought honor to Britain among its cultural and political rivals on the continent.
However, those qualities of "mind" such as originality and independent thinking
that writers so frequently touted as distinguishing domestic artists from their continental counterparts were invariably labeled as English, even when they were
ascribed to men like Irish artist James Barry or the Welsh-born landscape painter
Richard Wilson.[14] If, as Colley persuasively argues, the association of Scottishness
with the physical prowess and courage necessary to protect and administer the
nation's colonies enabled the Scots to identify themselves as leaders in the forging
of a British imperium, then, I would argue, the interlinking of Englishness with

intellectual prowess and creativity enabled the dominant elite in England (from landowning peer to the middle-class businessman) to validate its position as preserver of civilization, culture, and a market system dependent upon individual enterprise.

It would be misleading, however, to imply that all sectors of the propertied elite and intelligentsia were in agreement about what constituted national character (either British or English) or shared the same opinions about what type of art best represented that character. This book is as much about the conflicts that arose around the production of national identity as it is about the successful forging of consent. One such conflict concerned the ability of the various academic genres of painting to represent the diverse interests and values of a patriotic assemblage of private individuals. Those landscape painters who became identified as native geniuses were able to capitalize on opportunities that arose as the result of the limitations and/or inadequacies of history painting. Therefore, in Chapter 1 I begin an investigation of the issue of genre – specifically the claims made for the social function of history painting and "lesser" genres such as landscape. History painter James Barry's project for the Society of Arts and topographical draughtsman Edward Dayes's essays on painting provide focal points for a discussion of the relationship of genre to debates around the articulation of national character and the need to reform the public taste for art in England. The following chapter continues this examination of the social function of various genres of painting by analyzing contemporary debates on private versus public patronage and related discussions concerning the ability of seemingly "private" genres, such as landscape, to instantiate moral values and national character. Connoisseur and collector Richard Payne Knight's defense of painting as a purely private art form, concerned with visual sensation rather than moral or intellectual ideas, is considered here as a highly controversial and well publicized critique of academic history painting.

Chapter 3 explores the complex relationship between professionals and amateurs working within the genre of landscape painting. Women amateurs and domestic tourists (of both genders) were targeted as major sources of support for the very idea of an English school of landscape painting; but for the English school to claim national and international prominence, amateur and professional production had to be distinguished both in theory and in practice. Attempts to define and secure a boundary between the amateur and the professional can be identified in such writings for amateurs as William Gilpin's essays on the picturesque and instructional manuals for drawing and painting landscapes. These texts are discussed in concert with paintings by professional artists such as Thomas Girtin.

The theory of academic practice had little to offer in the way of professional validation of the landscape painter as an individual capable of acting in the public interest. Chapter 4 sets out to determine the impact of associationist psychology on the construction of the imaginative genius within critical discourse of landscape painting. After discussing two important texts on associationist aesthetics, I examine *Views in Sussex* (1820), which consists of engravings after watercolors by Turner and a descriptive text by Ramsay Reinagle, as a case study of how the landscape genius was constituted in the historical circumstances of post-war Britain.

Representations of genius and imagination elicited expressions of anxiety and disapproval as well as acclaim. The final chapter surveys art criticism generated by the exhibited works of Callcott, Turner, Copley Fielding, and others in order to assess not only the nature and significance of their success, but also the limits of that success. Considering this criticism together with other writings on the power of the imagination will help us to understand the degree to which the native genius had to be controlled lest its "excesses" threaten the stability of the very community which it was supposed to inspire and embody.

As noted at the outset, this exploration of artistic subjectivity is not only important in and of itself, but also because it enhances our understanding of viewers as social subjects. In the decades around 1800 the viewing public for painting comprised wealthy collectors who were variously categorized in terms of their knowledge, liberality, and motives, and a more extensive middle-class public of men and women whose ability to respond to the vision of nature created by the "mind" of genius was seen as tied to their personal sensibility and private interests, rather than their capacity for liberal learning or public largesse. The success of the "native genius" lay in its ability to accommodate many of the "private" and "public" interests of these various sub-classes and social groups.

Given the vexed relationship that was perceived to exist between commerce and the serious artist, we will pay particular attention to the way in which genius was able to negotiate the economic demands of the marketplace without compromising its viability as a social ideal of the independent-minded English subject. In other words, how native genius came to serve as an alibi – as a claim to be somewhere other than where it was: not in the marketplace, vying for profit and fame, but in the purified and disembodied realm of the artistic imagination.

Chapter 1

The Crisis of the English School
and the Question of Genre

The progress of the British school may be thus estimated: – To be retrograde in grand historical and poetical composition; to be increasing in correct drawing and chaste coloring; eminent in portrait; and beyond competition in landscape.[1]

Monthly Magazine, July 1810

SO WIDELY ACCEPTED IS THE CLAIM that England achieved international pre-eminence in the sphere of landscape painting in the early 1800s that scholars seldom trouble to document it. My purpose in quoting the above passage from a review of the Royal Academy exhibition of 1810 is not to restate the obvious, but rather to emphasize that for contemporary viewers the "triumph" of English landscape painting was perceived and discussed in relationship to concerns about the state of domestic painting in general. While this may seem no less obvious, scholarship on English landscape painting has tended to focus on artistic transformations solely within that genre, rather than consider new forms of landscape painting as one response to a broader crisis in visual representation.[2] It was this crisis, I will argue, which provided the opportunity for certain landscape painters to produce works that were seen to embody mental powers and moral qualities associated with a particular ideal of Englishness.

As the passage from the *Monthly Magazine* suggests, the crisis was most visibly manifest in history painting, the most prestigious and publicly oriented genre within the academic hierarchy. Contemporary art criticism and commentary devoted to what Morris Eaves usefully terms "English school discourse" at the turn of the nineteenth century registers a broadly based concern that history painting had failed to live up to its mandate to represent those universal ideals and values which bind together the body politic.[3] This problem of embodying the public through visual representation was inseparable from ongoing attempts to sustain the body of the artist. Throughout the late eighteenth and early nineteenth centuries there was an acute disjunction between the practical needs of living artists to engage with the market via exhibiting institutions, private patrons, dealers, publishers, and the like, and the ideological imperatives of those discourses which defined the artist as an ideal of the creative individual. This ever widening gulf between the private needs of individual artists and the ideal of the artist is inextricably linked to the issue of genre: while a painter devoted to the "lowly" genre of portraiture could gain publicity as a financially successful artist, academic discourse dictated that only the history painter was accorded the prestige of a public artist. We shall see that another "inferior" genre, landscape painting, offered new possibilities for defining both artistic and communal identity in ways which were both foreclosed and enabled by the discourses of academicism.[4] But first it is necessary to examine the nature of the dilemma facing those who maintained a commitment to some form of history painting.

In his well-known study of English academic theory John Barrell argues that history painting as *the* public genre was conceptualized via a political model of civic republicanism in writings by prominent academicians such as Joshua Reynolds, James Barry, and Henry Fuseli.[5] According to this thesis, history painting was highly esteemed insofar as it was qualified to address individuals in their capacities as public men – that is, as citizens involved in governing.[6] It was not only the didactic subject matter – heroic episodes from history, literature, and the Bible – which engaged such a public and thus distinguished history painting from the lower genres of landscape, still life, portraiture, and "comic" genre painting. Crucially, the highest genre could address such a public because its production and appreciation involved the same processes of intellection which qualified these men as citizens – namely the ability to recognize and abstract the general from the particular. In politics this meant being able to discern the public good through a broad survey of those limited, private interests which, taken together, constitute the social field. In history painting these mental powers involved discerning those ideal and general forms which underlie the local and particular features found in nature.

However, more was required for successful history painting than fulfilling a set of aesthetic criteria. Such works had to be displayed in spaces invested with political and religious authority in order to serve both as moral exemplars for a British public and as signs of Britain's cultural prominence to governing elites on the continent. In England at this time such access to public space was severely circumscribed: George III's patronage of public painting was largely restricted to commissioning from Benjamin West a series of paintings and stained-glass window designs for Windsor, projects that were terminated in 1801 when the artist fell out of favor with the monarch. The attitude of the English Church to history painting was made clear in 1773, when a group of academicians offered to decorate St. Paul's Cathedral with large-scale paintings. The plan was rejected out of hand by the Archbishop of Canterbury and the Bishop of London who objected that such images would be idolatrous.[7]

Earlier in the century, as David Solkin argues, British artists, theorists, and entrepreneurs sought to address this long-standing lack of official patronage by recasting the notion of public painting in accordance with a society that was conceptualized spatially and ideologically in terms of commercial values, private interests, and relations of economic dependency. Solkin demonstrates that in the first three-quarters of the century artists such as William Hogarth, Edward Penny, and Joseph Wright were able to modify history painting and mobilize other genres (such as the conversation piece and genre painting) in order to represent those social values and consensual relations befitting a market society.[8] The Society of Artists was the institutional embodiment of these consensual values, manifested in its refusal to acknowledge the hierarchy of genres in hanging works on display (that is, in refusing to grant history painting pride of place) and its inclusion in exhibitions of prints and other objects that would be denied high art status by the Royal Academy. However, the Royal Academy's success in supplanting the artistic authority of the Society of Artists in the early 1770s served to reassert the prestige of traditional history painting based upon historical and literary subject matter and the idealized human figure.[9]

Although the Academy was unable to secure for its members a wealth of large-scale public commissions, its schools and exhibitions did facilitate the production of "historical" pictures well into the nineteenth century. Possessing themes drawn from the Bible, the classics, and British history and literature, these works appeared briefly at the exhibitions of the Royal Academy and British Institution before decorating the walls of country estates and town houses. Historical pictures also circulated in the form of single-sheet prints, print sets, and book illustrations, and were the featured attractions of single artist shows (such as Copley's private exhibition in 1781 of the *Death of Chatham* and Haydon's touring exhibition of *Christ's Triumphal Entry into Jerusalem* in 1820).

Throughout this period artists and critics continued to bemoan the deplorable state of the English school, despite the continuing promotion of history painting by Royal Academicians and by the Directors of the British Institution, who offered a prize for the best history painting displayed in their annual exhibition. Barrell has argued that this sense of crisis was occasioned by the inability of a "public" genre of painting to represent a commercial society defined in terms of private interests, speculation, and specialized forms of knowledge and labor. However, I shall argue that in the decades following the French Revolution there was an increasingly vocal demand for a native school of painting which represented not simply commercial society but a particular ideal of English "character" which in its specificity could not be accommodated by the generalizing aesthetic of history painting.[10]

We will consider these post-revolutionary demands in the chapters to follow. But since concerns about national identity and the status of the English school did not emerge *de nouveau* with the advent of the French Revolution, it will be useful to examine first the dilemma facing would-be "liberal" artists in the 1780s. A major cycle of paintings by academician James Barry for an important civic space in London, the Great Room of the Society of Arts, largely completed by 1783, provides dramatic testimony to the nature of the crisis within history painting and offers a vantage point from which to consider the reasons for its intensification by the turn of the century.

In 1777 James Barry offered to provide the Society for the Encouragement of Arts, Manufactures, and Commerce with a cycle of history paintings for the central meeting room of their new premises in the Adelphi. The Society had been established in 1754 as a private association to promote the economic advancement of art, industry, and commerce in Britain. The heterogeneous nature of the Society's membership, which included noblemen, merchants, professional men, and finan-ciers, was symbolically and legally underscored by the fact that the institution was literally disembodied, for it lacked a charter of incorporation.[11] When James Barry proposed to undertake the project at cost, he was faced with the dilemma of how to represent this assemblage of private individuals, dedicated to a commercial ideal of national progress, by means of large-scale, didactic paintings which would confirm his reputation as a liberal artist.

The scarcity of commissions for history paintings undoubtedly explains Barry's willingness to enter into a financially unpropitious contract with the Society.[12] The project had initially been offered in 1774 to ten well-known artists including Barry and Academy President Joshua Reynolds. Rather than pay the artists a fixed sum, the Society planned to subsidize an exhibition after the project was completed; the profits from the exhibition would then be given to the artists. Such an arrangement placed the artists in the position of financial speculators, a role which accorded well with the entrepreneurial Society, but not with academic artists, whose self-identification as professionals demanded that their fees be set in advance. Not surprisingly, the artists refused the offer, objecting that "the mode of Raising Money by Exhibition would be disreputable to them."[13] Despite this collective refusal, Barry favored the arrangement; three years later he offered to undertake the entire decorative scheme on essentially the same financial terms as the original proposal. Although the Society paid for the materials needed for the project, it refused to pay his living expenses; the artist subsisted on what he could borrow and the meager earnings he obtained through the sale of prints.[14]

The hardships Barry sustained in order to produce the Adelphi cycle could only have intensified his campaign to gain public support for a national school of history painting. A prominent member of the Royal Academy, and from 1782 to 1799 its Professor of Painting, he was committed to a universalist aesthetic. This point was made emphatically in his lectures to the Royal Academy where he distinguishes "a *beautiful* which is positive, essential, and independent of national or temporary institutions or opinions" from local notions of "false beauty,"

> which have a kind of occasional currency under the terms *ton, fashion*, or *mode*; and like particular languages, are ever fluctuating and unstable, always different amongst the different nations, and in the different ages of the same nation.

This false beauty, he cautions, may please those who commission art, "and [may] consequently be advantageous to what we may call our interest, yet it must lose us the admiration of men of sound judgment in all times."[15]

Visual representations of the particular, the local, and the national are accorded here the status of temporary fashions and directly associated with the private inter-ests of both the artist and his employer. Thus, while the artist was committed to a national school of painting he did not endorse the notion that its function was to represent some form of distinctively English character. For Barry, as for Reynolds and other traditional history painters, the true public for the liberal artist was an international constituency of discerning males whose disinterested judgment was the ground for their identity as public men. Only an artist who wins the esteem of such a civic body, then, could secure a reputation which transcends time and place.

As Barrell has noted, the patriotic fervor of these academicians was the opposite of nationalism:

> Their hope that higher art will be restored in Britain is to them a *properly* patriotic hope, because it is also a civic hope. By its style, England would win a legitimate contest for distinction, and become an exemplar of civic culture by which all the nations of Europe will benefit. If higher art is restored elsewhere than in Britain, that also will be an occasion for rejoicing, hardly qualified by the regret that the palm was not won by the English school. For in competitions for civic excellence, when one nation wins, they all win.[16]

The six large canvases Barry produced for the Society of Arts (see Figure 3) reveal the extent to which this "patriotic," but anti-nationalist theory of history painting informed his artistic practice.

Official and personal accounts of the Society of Arts confirm that foreigners and domestic commentators alike identified the private and voluntary nature of its undertaking as a feature which distinguished the Society from its publicly funded continental counterparts.[17] However, a visitor viewing Barry's "Progress of Human

3   A.C. Pugin and Thomas Rowlandson, *The Great Room of the Society for the Encouragement of Arts.* Aquatint in *The Microcosm of London,* vol. 3, London, 1809. Brown University Library, Providence, RI (photo: Brooke Hammerle).

4   James Barry, *Orpheus*, 1777–84. Oil on canvas, 142 × 182 in. Royal Society of Arts, London.

Culture" in the Society's Great Room would have been hard pressed to determine how this much-praised voluntary institution could advance modern British society beyond the idyllic state represented in the three history paintings of Greek culture which initiate the series. Even in the first work of the series, *Orpheus* (Figure 4), which depicts the Greek hero addressing a group of "primitive" men and women dressed in animal skins, peace and harmony reign supreme. Displaced onto the bodies of animals (a tiger attacking a horse) and reduced to a background detail, the brutal conflicts commonly associated with humankind in a state of barbarism do not disfigure the classically proportioned bodies of the hero and his enraptured audience, nor disrupt the harmony and balance of the landscape.[18]

Social harmony is also emphasized in the second picture of the series, the *Grecian Harvest Home* (Figure 5), in which young men and women are shown dancing around a sculpture of nature deities. As Barry's own referencing of Virgil's *Georgics* in his published description of the work makes clear, the composition celebrates not only agrarian abundance, but an ideal of rural peace, social harmony, and virtue. In his composition Barry represents this rustic perfection via the dance itself, which features classically proportioned bodies, clad in simple garments connoting "antiquity," moving gracefully in concert with each other and the rhythm of

5 James Barry, *A Grecian Harvest Home*, 1777–84. Oil on canvas, 142 × 182 in. Royal Society of Arts, London.

nature. Since the genre of history painting was based upon an aesthetic which posited classical culture as a universal standard for human beauty and human behavior, it was ideally suited to represent such a homogenized vision of Greek culture, purged of racial, ethnic, and class differences.

However, Barry encountered serious difficulty when he attempted to depict via the historical genre the specifically modern features of British society in the picture which hangs on the wall opposite his *Grecian Harvest Home. Commerce, or the Triumph of the Thames* (Figure 6) sets out to represent the contributions British commerce has made to the "Progress of Human Culture." In this composition the artist juxtaposes the nude, classicized forms of Father Thames and a group of Nereids bearing him aloft in procession, with the clothed and particularized figures of British navigators. The end-product is an unhappy mixture of allegorical and historical figures, all of whom appear ill-suited to their aquatic environment. Indeed some prominent contemporary viewers were inclined to laughter and dismay at the artist's depiction of the renowned musicologist Dr. Charles Burney, who is shown playing a keyboard of Barry's design while wading chest high in the river next to a coyly smiling Nereid.[19] Within the context of the cycle Burney might be seen as Orpheus's contemporary musical counterpart, but he cuts a

6   James Barry, *Commerce, or the Triumph of the Thames*, 1777–84. Oil on canvas, 142 × 182 in. Royal Society of Arts, London.

pathetic figure compared to the artist's rendering of the Greek hero whose music transformed an entire race.

In his published *Account of a Series of Pictures in the Great Room of the Society of Arts, Manufactures and Commerce at the Adelphi* (1783), Barry asserts that some of the tensions registered in the delineation of the figures were consciously intended to express the problematic nature of commercial society itself:

> if some of those Nereids appear more sportive than industrious, and others still more wanton than sportive, the picture has the more variety and, I am sorry to add, the greater resemblance to the truth; for it must be allowed, that if through the means of an extensive commerce, we are furnished with incentives to ingenuity and industry, this ingenuity and industry are but too frequently found to be employed in the procuring and fabricating such commercial matters as are subversive of the very foundations of virtue and happiness.[20]

That the female body serves here to figure the moral corruption wreaked by commercial society is consistent with the gendering of anti-commercial discourse. It distinguished a republic of stoic, virtuous landowners from a commercial society softened by luxury and given over to sensual pleasures that led to the emasculation of men and the sexual corruption of women.[21] There was a long tradition of using paired female figures to represent virtue and vice, as in Benjamin West's *Choice of Hercules* (Figure 7), which was a popular subject for artists in the eighteenth century.[22] But unlike Vice in the *Hercules*, Barry's "sportive" Nereids represent not a choice to be rejected, but a moral threat that inheres *within* the fabric of British commerce itself. Beyond the ideological difficulties presented by an attempt to extol the cultural and material benefits of British commerce while criticizing its moral effects, such a procedure violates a basic tenet of history painting, which is to represent a single, unified "expression" through a composition which should possess variety, but not ambiguity.[23] The ambiguity of the *Commerce* threatens to undermine Barry's claims to competence as a liberal artist, and also puts into question the viability of academic history painting as a genre capable of representing the type of national enterprise which the Society of Arts was so strongly promoting.

7 Benjamin West, *The Choice of Hercules*, 1764. Oil on canvas, 40 × 48 in. Victoria and Albert Museum, London.

On the other hand, Barry's group portrait of the Society's most highly esteemed members, *The Distribution of Premiums in the Society of Arts* (Figure 8), did address the institution and its public via a genre and a visual rhetoric consistent with those private interests, distinctions of rank, and divisions of labor which were seen to enable British commerce to prosper. In this portrait private interests are inscribed not only at the level of form and content (through details of facial feature, gesture, accessories, dress, and the like) but also via bravura technical displays. William Pressly rightly observes that Barry's brushwork and use of color is strikingly different in this image than in his other works for the series. The viewer's eye is attracted to the foreground figures which evidence the artist's use of high-key color, dramatic color contrasts, and vigorous brushwork. These painterly effects were associated with those virtuoso displays of skill (or "manner") which any competitive artist had to deploy to distinguish himself from others. And in fact, as Pressly notes, Barry would appear to be offering this display of painterly virtuosity as a challenge to the work which originally hung to the left of his group portrait in the Great Room, Reynolds's portrait of Society President Lord Romney (Figure 9). Viewers would have been induced to engage in such a comparison of the two works since Barry's own representation of Romney is prominently featured to the left of the Prince of Wales in the foreground of his picture (Figure 10).

That the artist was willing and able to engage in such displays of his individual manner without apparent censure lies in the nature of portraiture as a genre in which the private interests of both sitter and artist can be represented. And in fact

8   James Barry, *The Distribution of Premiums in the Society of Arts*, 1777–84, with portions added in 1789 and 1801. Oil on canvas, 142 × 182 in. Royal Society of Arts, London.

Barry's financial interests were directly served in the production of the *Distribution of Premiums*, for it led to his obtaining separate portrait commissions from several of the men who appeared in it, including Lord Romney.[24] Nonetheless, Barry had never intended to paint portraits as a livelihood; his primary interest remained in promoting himself as a history painter. To that end he included in the background of the *Distribution of Premiums* a painting of St. Michael and a sculpted relief of Venus rising from the sea based upon two of his own historical works as examples of the type of art worthy of the Society's esteem and its public's patronage.[25] *Venus Rising from the Sea* was executed as an oil painting in 1772, but remained in the artist's possession, circulating only as a print. The *Fall of Satan*, which features the figure of St. Michael, circulated as an etching; according to the inscription on the print, the composition was intended for the (stillborn) project to decorate St. Paul's (seen in the background of the *Distribution of Premiums*).[26] As public art these two works exist only as simulacra within the frame of a portrait.[27]

Among the six canvases in the Great Room *The Distribution of Premiums* most directly represents the patriotic goals and interests of the Society's members. For

Barry, however, it could not bring Britain the cultural prestige which he associated solely with the category of historical painting. He made this point quite clearly in the section of his Adelphi series essay devoted to this particular painting:

> Were we to continue multiplying portraits for a century longer, were we to arrive at even so great a degree of mechanical excellence in this way it could make no alteration in the opinion of Europe; we should be still, as we have been, a scoff and a bye-word amongst nations.[28]

For Barry, as for so many of his artistic contemporaries in the 1780s and 1790s, the problem of genre lay at the heart of a nationalist discourse around the international status of the English school. So interlinked was history painting with the authority of academies in England and throughout Europe, that attempts to promote a national school continued to focus on that most prestigious of genres.

Artists were not the only cultural producers involved in the promotion of

9   Joshua Reynolds, *Robert Marsham, Second Baron Romney*, 1770. Oil on canvas, 90 × 56 in. Royal Society of Arts, London.

10   James Barry, detail of *The Distribution of Premiums in the Society of Arts* (Figure 8).

Frontispiece to the European Magazine Vol. 46.

SHAKSPEARE GALLERY

Engraved by S. Rawle

The Alto Relievo in the front of the Shakspeare Gallery, Pall Mall.

Published by I. Asperne, at the Bible, Crown & Constitution, Cornhill, 1. Aug.ᵗ 1804

11   S. Rawle, *View of the Shakespeare Gallery*, frontispiece, *European Magazine* 46, 1804. Engraving. Brown University Library, Providence, RI (photo: Brooke Hammerle).

history painting. In the 1790s publishers John Boydell, Thomas Macklin, and Robert Bowyer each launched ambitious schemes to market domestic history painting through the medium of the reproductive print.[29] There was nothing new in engraving historic pictures for distribution as single-sheet prints and in illustrated folios, but these projects were far more elaborate and ambitious than anything that had gone before. The most well-known of these schemes was Alderman John Boydell's Shakespeare Gallery. Briefly, this project involved commissioning from domestic artists scores of paintings based on Shakespeare's plays; these works were publicly exhibited at a specially constructed gallery beginning in 1789, with more pictures added over the years (Figure 11).[30] The financial success of the enterprise depended not on the Gallery but upon the sale of engravings of the pictures, which were issued serially in folio with letterpress and also as smaller illustrations in a new luxury edition of the plays.[31] Similar projects combining the exhibition and engraving of pictures based upon British literature and history were undertaken by Thomas Macklin, who opened the Poets' Gallery in 1790, Henry Fuseli, whose Milton Gallery was conceived in the same year, and by Robert Bowyer, whose Historic Gallery (1792) co-ordinated with the production of an illustrated edition of David Hume's *History of England*. These enterprises were marketed as patriotic, commercial endeavors to promote English history painting at home and abroad, but with the collapse of the foreign market for prints after the French Revolution and the onset of the Napoleonic wars, they could not sustain themselves through an appeal to a domestic market and by 1805 all of them had ended in failure.[32] But the problematic nature of these publishing ventures for history painters was evident long before the collapse of continental markets. From the outset the process of translating history painting into a less expensive, more marketable commodity called into question the high-minded claims of professional "liberality" which the title "Royal Academician" implied. Whereas engravers were repeatedly denied admission to the Royal Academy because of their so-called artisan status, publishers and print-sellers were, except in rare cases, loath to acknowledge financially the self-proclaimed professional superiority of academic painters over engravers. Sven Bruntjen has observed that because of the time-consuming procedures involved in the production of prints, engravers routinely were paid higher fees than the painters whose canvases were so highly touted in the promotions for these projects.[33] Thus, while the circulation of reproductive prints could gain academic history painters publicity and some income, the commercial relationship which artists entered into with publishers and engravers profoundly affected their ability to sustain their identities as aesthetically autonomous creators producing serious public art for a disinterested community of viewers.

Despite the failure of English artists to find sources of public patronage and to command the type of public space necessary for historical painting in the grand style, the discourse of history painting, as manifested in published writings on the theory and practice of academic art, displayed a remarkable resilience. The Academy lectures of Henry Fuseli were first published in 1803, those of Barry and John Opie in 1809, while Reynolds's *Discourses* went through several editions during this period. Although these four academicians had important disagreements about the way in which public art could function in contemporary England, they were united in their belief that the cultural prestige of individual artists and the nation remained tied to the fate of history painting.[34]

For instance, in his diatribe against the English obsession with portraiture, Barry considers how the genre of landscape painting suffers from the dominance of portraiture over history painting:

> Even in the painting of landscapes where more genius and intent of mind can be shewn [than in portraiture], and where some of our artists have possessed first rate abilities, is it not more probable that these excellent artists will not obtain the full credit they deserve, until the curiosity and attention of the world shall be excited by our success in the higher species of art?[35]

By the late 1820s it would become clear that the answer to this question was no – that English landscape painting could command a degree of foreign attention and admiration that history painting never did. Yet in the 1790s and early 1800s, impelled by the seductive claims of academic discourse, certain artists and writers continued to produce and/or advocate a form of landscape painting which conformed to a set of aesthetic protocols and artistic conventions designed primarily for the genre of history painting.

One such artist was Edward Dayes, whose writings and art signal an acute, at times even painful awareness of the disjunction which existed between his lowly professional status as a producer of landscapes and the academic ideal of the history painter. Trained as a topographical draughtsman, Dayes eked out a meager living making sketches and watercolors of picturesque sites and historical monuments; many of these were engraved and circulated in publications geared to the tourist and antiquarian markets.[36] Although never a member of the Royal Academy, he showed landscapes and the occasional portrait there throughout the 1790s and in 1798 exhibited four watercolors of historical subjects.[37] These stiff and pedantic drawings generated little discernible interest among an audience increasingly unwilling to support the more accomplished works of well-known specialists in historical art.

Perhaps it was this lack of public interest in his historical pictures that prompted Dayes to turn to writing as a vehicle for his artistic ideas. In any event, beginning in 1801 he published a series of ten essays on painting in the *Philosophical Magazine*.[38] The essays have been neglected in art historical scholarship, probably because of their singular lack of originality. It is this very fact, however, that commends them to our attention. For these essays restate and affirm, with a few important modifications, the principles of academic practice set down in their most authoritative form by Joshua Reynolds a quarter of a century earlier.[39] I would argue that in his endorsement of academic art Dayes, like Reynolds and Barry, was chiefly concerned with advancing his own status as a professional artist. But unlike these academicians, the topographer was acutely aware that this status was jeopardized by contemporary practices in landscape painting as well as by the continuing lack of patronage for history painting. For not only was Dayes frustrated in his attempts at history painting, but he was also evidently dismayed at the growing success of young landscape artists such as his student Thomas Girtin, who had achieved before the age of twenty-five what Dayes had failed to gain at forty – critical acclaim and numerous commissions from leading members of the landed aristocracy and gentry. According to Richard and Samuel Redgrave's biography of Dayes, included in their *A Century of British Painting*, Dayes was openly jealous of the younger artist.[40] Despite the highly subjective nature of the Redgraves' biographies, this account is compatible with Dayes's posthumously published attack on Girtin's character in "Professional Sketches of Modern Artists." In a brief, but damning description of his former student, Dayes wrote:

> This artist died November 9th, 1802, after a long illness, in the twenty-eighth year of his age. Biography is useful to stimulate to acts of industry and virtue; or, by exhibiting the contrary, to enable us to shun the fatal consequences of vice. While our heart bleeds at the premature death of the subject of this paper, it becomes equally an act of justice to caution young persons against the fatal effects of suffering their passions to overpower their reason, and to hurry them into acts of excess, that may, in the end, render life a burthen, destroy existence, or bring on a premature old age. Though his drawings are generally too slight, yet they must ever be admired as the offspring of a strong imagination. Had he not trifled away a vigorous constitution, he might have arrived at a very high degree of excellence as a landscape painter.[41]

Moral character and artistic prowess are here interlinked: Girtin's strong imagination, Dayes insinuates, is connected to his passionate and implicitly vice-ridden nature.[42] Conflict between the two artists may also be inferred from the fact that Girtin was apprenticed to Dayes, but did not serve out the full term of his contract. While there appears to be no evidence to support stories circulating decades after the deaths of both artists that Dayes had Girtin jailed for breach of contract, some strain between student and teacher may have precipitated the early termination of Girtin's apprenticeship.[43] In the light of this inconclusive, but highly suggestive evidence, it is worth considering the extent to which Dayes's essays on art served not simply as a restatement of academic theory, but also as a defense of his own idealized self-image as a virtuous, and supremely rational, liberal artist against the artistic anti-type of the irrational, imaginative genius, embodied in the person of (the late) Thomas Girtin.[44]

Although most of these essays deal with the general practice of painting, the topographer Dayes begins his series with a discussion of landscape. It is evident from the opening sentence of his first essay, "On the Principles of Composition as Connected with Landscape Painting" (1801), that the same intellectual, moral, and aesthetic principles which underwrite history painting are to be applied to this lower genre: "The principles that govern this branch of composition, extend to every other connected with the art of painting, whether the subject be history, or otherwise."[45] He concludes the essay by exhorting landscape artists to respect this universal theory of painting in order to "endeavor to create a nature of our own, if possible, more dignified and noble than the one that strikes our senses: we should feel an enthusiasm in our pursuits not to be satisfied with a perfection short of divine" (p. 202). This is a goal scarcely less ambitious than that marked out by the most zealous advocate of history painting. The emphasis is upon representing an ideal of nature that exerts a morally elevating influence on the producers as well as the viewers of landscapes.[46] Dayes repeatedly cautions his readers that this state of perfection is not to be discovered and represented by a direct encounter between the unschooled imagination and external nature, but only by a mind, disciplined by reason and conditioned by a careful study of past art (pp. 191–2).

The relationship between nature as ordered by art and virtuous behavior is clearly articulated in a later essay on drawing:

> To have a just relish for what is elegant and proper in painting, sculpture, and architecture, must be a fine preparation for true notions relative to character and behaviour. Should such a one be overpowered by passion, or swerve from his duty, we need not fear but he will return on the first reflection, and with a redoubled resolution not to err a second time: for he cannot but observe, that the well being of nature, as well as of the individual, depends on regularity and order; and that a disregard of the social virtues will ever be accompanied with shame and remorse. (pp. 258–9)

This passage pointedly recalls earlier eighteenth-century treatises on taste by writers such as the Third Earl of Shaftesbury, George Turnbull, and Lord Kames.[47] Like them Dayes forcefully represents the underlying order of nature as an active moral power capable of bringing the passionate individual back to his "true" identity as a social subject. In the context of essays directed to the polite readers of the *Philosophical Magazine*, such a social subject conforms to the ideal of the "man of taste" – an individual belonging to the landed or professional classes who devotes part of his leisure to a serious study of the arts. An essay on drawing provides an appropriate context specifically to address the concerns of this social subject, since drawing was a common amateur practice.[48] Although he briefly notes the utilitarian benefits of drawing, Dayes is primarily concerned with demonstrating that the process of study involved in acquiring mastery of drawing "improves the reasoning faculty," "harmonizes the temper," and "regulates moral conduct" (p. 258). The cultivation of such moral and intellectual qualities is not presented as a matter solely of private enrichment, but is seen to impinge upon the well-being of the nation. Hence, the gentleman who travels is advised to educate himself about the arts so that he may enrich the "national stock of knowledge," upon his return.

Dayes's essays, then, constitute an individual subject who conforms to the eighteenth-century ideal of the cosmopolitan. While he addresses this individual as a national, that is, English subject, the moral qualities, intellectual faculties, and forms of knowledge which characterize such a being were regarded as supranational, yet gender specific. That the subject position of the cosmopolitan was coded as masculine is clear from Dayes's reference to women in his essays: in a footnote praising the amateur practice of Sir George Beaumont (the most well-known amateur and connoisseur of his day) and Sir Richard Colt Hoare (a prominent antiquarian and collector), he addresses women readers for the first and only time in his writings:

> While we are recommending to gentlemen to learn to draw, it must not be understood, that we wish to deprive the ladies of the pleasure and advantage that must result from their practising an art that stands, perhaps, before all others for improving our taste, particularly in such things as are connected with decoration. (p. 259n.)

Relegated to a place on the margins of his text, and to a private, marginal, and artisan practice, that of decoration, women are thus effectively excluded from Dayes's operative subject positions – the liberal viewer and professional artist. In so doing Dayes endorsed the socially dominant view that only men possessed reason and the power of abstract thought, and had the capacity and need for a long and studied engagement with "high" culture (notably the artistic and literary classics of antiquity and the Renaissance).[49]

Like Reynolds before him, Dayes believed that for this notion of the cosmopolitan viewer and liberal artist to prevail, the power of individual artistic imagination and genius had to be de-emphasized and regulated.[50] As President of the Royal Academy, Reynolds's professional identity depended upon upholding the institutional authority of that body. Academic rules and instruction rooted in the study of past art could make no claim upon the development of an artist if genius and imagination – commonly understood as inherently and arbitrarily endowed upon particular individuals – were accepted as the necessary and sufficient qualifications for the professional mastery of painting. Reynolds's strategy was to submit imagination and genius to the rule of law by invoking tradition and "nature" (in its general guise) as the ultimate artistic authorities.[51]

We have seen how Dayes also invokes ideal nature and tradition (represented by the old masters), as a means of regulating the encounter between the individual and external nature. He also seeks to diminish the power of the artistic imagination by de-emphasizing its creative role and emphasizing its function as merely a storehouse of images which serve as raw material for the reasoning artistic mind to process. The imagination is involved in selecting these images, but he cautions that this selection is only part, and a lesser part at that, of the process of artistic production.

Combining these images to form a unified composition is the key operation: "Imagination is shown in the production of materials, but to arrange them requires the soundest judgment" (p. 197).

That the power of the imagination must be circumscribed even in the rather mundane function Dayes assigns to it is evident in a later discussion of style and its necessary components and constraints:

> But unless all this [compiling of imagery by a "lively fancy"] be accompanied by a good judgment, the imagination will riot at the expense of reason, and we shall never possess a sound and accurate style. Hence it is that we often confound genius with an active imagination, not recollecting that excess is not its character. (p. 270)

It is fair, I think, to read this injunction against excessive imagination as a response to up-and-coming young artists such as Turner and Girtin. As early as 1798 these artists were garnering praise for their boldness and originality. In that year, the critic for the *Monthly Mirror* claimed that Turner's works "discover a strength of mind which is not often the concomitant of much longer experience; and their effect in oil or on paper is equally sublime." He goes on to remark that "Girtin's productions . . . though not so softened as Turner's . . . display so much daring and vigorous execution, that a sedulous attention to the finishing would perhaps be injurious to the effect."[52] John Taylor, writing Royal Academy reviews of the 1799 exhibition for both the *Sun* and *True Briton*, was also suitably impressed by his first sight of a Girtin watercolor, declaring that his *Beth Kellert [Beddgelert], North Wales*

12   Thomas Girtin, *View of Mynnydd Mawr, North Wales*, 1798. Watercolor, 11.4 × 17 in. British Museum, London.

13   J. M. W. Turner, *Harlech Castle from Twgwyn Ferry, Summer's Evening Twilight*, RA 1799. Oil on canvas, 34.3 × 47 in. Yale Center for British Art, Paul Mellon Collection, New Haven.

(see Figure 12)[53] "exhibits all the bold features of genius."[54] He also praised Turner's oil, *Harlech Castle* (Figure 13), in the same exhibition for its originality, and his watercolor view of Caernarvon Castle for its ability to "make its way immediately to the imagination of the spectator."[55] These young artists were also reaping financial rewards for their genius. Joseph Farington records in his *Diary* that John Julius Angerstein paid Turner forty guineas for the latter work, more than the artist would have asked.[56]

In the face of public and private acclaim for these bold, imaginative geniuses who were transforming Dayes's chosen genre of topographical landscape painting the older artist stages an appeal to reason, secured by its origins in universal human nature, as means of fixing an absolute standard of taste. In a passage worth quoting at length he declares:

> taste is not an imaginary something, depending on the accident of birth, but arises from, and is immediately connected with, a sound judgment. Were there not in art, as in every thing else, a standard of right and wrong, all opinion must be capricious; but to acquire just notions, we must habituate ourselves to compare and digest our thoughts, be well read in human nature, as connected with the characters, manners, passions, and affections of man; this, with some knowledge of the human mind, will, in time, enable us to distinguish right from wrong, which constitutes the true principles of taste. . . . Real truth does not

depend on opinion; it is immutable, fixed, and permanent, and in it must be sought whatever is grand and beautiful. Apparent truth depends on fashion, and like that, is fluctuating and uncertain; it may be considered as a sort of impostor, for though it carries the appearance of science, it is far from having any true connection with it. (p. 205)

In this text Dayes, again following Reynolds, sets out a contrast between "apparent" and the "real" truth upon which sound judgment and taste are based.[57] It is revealing to note those words which take on a pejorative cast as Dayes draws out the chimerical qualities of "apparent truth": imaginary, accident, opinion, fashion. These terms all connote that which is fleeting, insubstantial, outside the bounds of reason, and thus beyond control. Their frame of reference lies not solely in the domain of art and aesthetics, but in the realm of the social and the economic. There, accidents of birth can confer power, if not taste, while opinion, fashion, and fantasy drive a commercial market that feeds on the fluctuations of insatiable popular demands.

Dayes is unwilling to accept that reasoned aesthetic judgments could arise from debates among self-interested individuals. For him, an aggregation of private individuals speaking in their own interests produces collective fantasies, not critical judgments. This conclusion is borne out in his essay on beauty in which the potential excesses of the private imagination and the collective fantasies forming opinion are reduced to equivalence: "Fancy, or opinion, will go but a little way towards illustrating a subject that seems to influence on some universal principle, and to affect all persons, and at all times" (p. 214).[58]

Such an insistence on defining an artistic practice which addresses a supranational public via universal principles and ideal forms severely circumscribes the degree to which the individual's private character can be inscribed in public works of art. In his essays on manner and watercolor technique Dayes addresses, perhaps more directly than anywhere else in his essays, the problem of regulating the artist's own character as it is made visible in his paintings. Following Reynolds he defines manner as

> expressive of certain peculiar marks that invariably characterize the works of each individual. . . . So far is a new manner from being a mark of genius, as some assert, that, could perfection in painting ever be attained, it would be unaccompanied by any peculiarity whatever. (p. 262)[59]

The writer is concerned here primarily to discourage contemporary artists from slavishly imitating the manner of any particular master – a danger deriving not only from the emphasis academic discourse itself places upon copying the old masters, but also from the desire of some English artists to cash in on the popularity of seventeenth-century continental paintings (old masters and their imitators) which were flooding the London markets during the Napoleonic wars.[60] Thus Dayes cautions students, when copying, to select works that exhibit a manner which is "purest" and the least "vicious" – that is, which exhibit the least singularity. To ignore this advice is to give up one's independence, and thus one's claim to be a liberal artist, "for the arts cannot be liberal in the hands of those who want spirit to think for themselves" (p. 262).

The independent-mindedness of a liberal artist is not displayed through the cultivation of his individual manner, for as Dayes notes in the passage just cited, the ideal artist would have no discernible manner at all. Such a procedure not only produces an object, nature, which is perfect, but an artistic subject which is transparent. That is, the private personality of the subject is repressed – rendered transparent – in order that it should not act as a medium which distorts the "truthful" representation of nature.[61] Dayes acknowledges that such perfection is not attainable, and thus, "every artist, of necessity, will have a manner; but in proportion as he succeeds in approaching perfection will his manner become more pure" (p. 264). Although he does not explicitly set out what a mannerless style would look like, he is clear about its antithesis: "the word *manner* may be applied to color, light and shade, and penciling [i.e., brushwork]" (p. 262). Reynolds, it should be noted, offered a broader definition of manner as an effect which arises from poor judgment in selecting the objects of representation and a failure to use just proportions in drawing figures.[62] For Dayes, then, manner is more specific and relates precisely to what he terms, in his watercolor essay, execution or "touch" – those manipulations of color, light, and brushwork which produce a brilliant, eye-catching surface. Such effects were what distinguished the landscape productions of the young "geniuses" Girtin and Turner from those of artists like Dayes who relied upon outline and comparatively muted color. Dayes's association of effects with singularity was a commonplace at the turn of the century. What was disputed was whether that singularity was to be viewed as a form of commercial self-promotion or as an innate quality of the individual which allowed him to express the true character of nature. Before considering further Dayes's views on this issue, it is worth examining briefly his general conceptions of landscape, and especially landscape watercolors, as set down in his final essay and in a watercolor which follows the precepts of that essay.

Within the parameters of an academic practice outlined by Dayes, it is not only the personality of the artist which is effaced, but also the genre of landscape and the medium of watercolor. Nowhere in his essay on landscape painting and his final essay on the coloring of landscapes (where he specifically refers to watercolors rather than oils) does he offer an endorsement of that genre and medium comparable to his spirited defense of art in general. In his first essay on landscape one can discover modest claims for what he terms "pastoral" landscape promoting a domestic ideal (p. 199). And in his essay on "Grace" he includes a passing reference to his own practice of topography: "Equally interesting [as the pastoral painter], though in a less degree meritorious, stands the simple representer of nature; he acquires a new character as a topographer, provided he attach fidelity to his representations" (p. 226). Clearly these statements do not amount to a defense of landscape in academic terms. Rather they support the absolute exclusion of artists who (like himself) work in genres such as landscape from the elevated ranks of their profession, since such faithful imitations of external nature represent the antithesis of a universal art based upon generalized, idealized forms. Throughout the essays there is a persistent tension between Dayes's acknowledgment of the lowly status of landscape painting and his continued insistence that it attempt to conform to the very academic standards which it is unqualified to meet.

This tension is registered in the essay on watercolor where technical advice regarding the mixing and application of watercolor pigments is accompanied by recommendations that students copy monochrome prints of works by past masters such as Claude, Wilson, Gainsborough, Titian, Cuyp, and Rembrandt, known primarily for their oils (p. 282).[63] The techniques he recommends are restricted to firm underdrawing in black-lead pencil, and then either "dead colouring" the surface or laying in the shadows with Prussian blue, and working up the picture from dark to light through a series of washes (pp. 301–2). In the 1790s Girtin and Turner had employed these methods, learned from Dayes, in their watercolors; by the turn of the century, however, they were using other techniques, such as scraping and stopping out, which had generated widespread interest, if not universal approval.[64]

The visual impact of such techniques becomes evident when we compare two river views of Durham, Dayes's *Durham Cathedral and Prebends Bridge* (Figure 14, 1791), with Girtin's later *Durham Castle and Cathedral* (Figure 15, c.1799).[65] Dayes's drawing was produced by the techniques the artist himself recommends in his essay on watercolor. First the outlines are carefully drawn, followed by a controlled laying in of shadow "with a soft or tender colour." Blue sky and clouds are represented by unbroken areas of color, laid in with the subtlest modulations. The manner of arranging the light and shade is both "broad and simple" in order to avoid a distracting and confusing surface "flutter." Thus the principal light evenly illuminates the bridge and cathedral towers, and sets up a rationally ordered play of shadows over the bridge, water, and foliage below the towers. This organization of surface effects is in accordance with long-standing academic strictures that there be one major light in a composition, with no more than two others subordinate to the first (see Dayes, pp. 289–90). Throughout this essay Dayes emphasizes the need to produce a harmonious effect by avoiding strong contrasts, which indeed he does achieve here – the starkest contrast is confined to the darkened foreground – a standard landscape device which serves to frame and focus the scene.

Girtin's view capitalizes on just those active surface effects which Dayes endeavors so assiduously to avoid. Interspersed throughout the composition are three dark masses of trees and bushes and another dark mass in the central buildings by the bridge. It is difficult to speak of a "central" light – is it to be found in the bold sweep of the clouds or the complex of architecture atop the hill? Instead, the entire composition flickers with areas of light, broken both by the dark masses and lesser shadows as well as by the many dot-like touches scattered across the roofs and walls of the buildings.

Such a comparison could be made between works by Girtin or Turner and any number of landscape artists of Dayes's generation whose oils and watercolors depended upon underdrawing and local color more than painterly surface effects achieved by broad washes and loose brushwork. Differences in execution and visual impact are perhaps most obvious in scenes that attempt to dramatize the effects of a storm, sunset, or fire. A case in point is Paul Sandby's night view of Caernarvon Castle (Figure 16, 1795), which features a cloud-streaked sky illuminated by moon-

14 Edward Dayes, *Durham Cathedral and Prebends Bridge*, 1791. Watercolor and ink over pencil, 10.5 × 15.8 in. Anonymous Gift, Museum of Art. Rhode Island School of Design, Providence, RI. (photo: Del Bogart).

light and a fire burning within the castle precinct. The doubled effects of the conflagration and full moon are registered in the clarity with which people and objects can be discerned in a night scene: clouds are distinguishable from smoke, and neither obscures the characteristic silhouette of the castle towers, the diminutive forms of people on shore, and the rising hills in the background. The more permanent and solid features of the landscape – landforms, architecture, water, and trees – appear to be tightly drawn and "tinted" rather than painted. Superimposed on this structure are the more loosely applied daubs and dashes of pigment that constitute the ephemeral elements of the scene – clouds, smoke, reflections. It is precisely this way of distinguishing "earthly matter" from atmospheric effects that is rejected by up-and-coming artists like Girtin and Turner. Girtin's *Durham Castle and Cathedral* and Turner's sunset view of Harlech Castle, which received such critical acclaim in 1799, threaten to dissolve the difference between earth, air, and water, to the point that light and air become the most palpable features of the landscape.

What, then, was at stake for the artists involved in this inversion of the traditional hierarchies that ordered both art (which privileged drawing over painterly effects) and nature (where landforms, not atmosphere, constituted the essence of a place)? Some contemporary writers such as W. H. Pyne heralded the achievements of this

15   Thomas Girtin, *Durham Castle and Cathedral*, *c*.1798. Watercolor, 16.3 × 21.5 in. Victoria and Albert Museum, London.

new generation of landscape painters in terms of their superior technique and "superior mental power and capacity."[66] How and why superior mental powers should be associated with such techniques will be considered at length in the pages to follow. What concerns us at this point are the terms in which opposition to such innovations were framed. Dayes's *Essays* are useful in this regard, since they comprise one of the most sustained contemporary accounts of such opposition.

As we have seen in his discussion of "manner," bold, painterly effects are, for Dayes, the visible signs of artistic individuality; and an overweening interest in individual "touch" or execution is dangerous. "Though execution is an excellence," he writes, "it is an excellence of an inferior kind; its fascinating power ought to be guarded against, and the artist concealed as much as possible, otherwise he will lose more than he will gain" (p. 285).[67] The physical transparency of watercolors is not to be subverted and manipulated into bold effects, for it is precisely that transparency which permits the artist to remain hidden and protected from a fascinating power. Dayes elsewhere defines this fascination as the lure of material rewards and popular acclaim:

> To paint for what is termed effect, may answer the purpose of the idle, the ignorant, and those who make a trade of the art, but will not satisfy the discerning. The only apology the artist can offer is, that he must fish with such

16   Paul Sandby, *Caernarvon Castle*, 1795. Watercolor, 36.6 × 54 in. Photograph reproduced with the Kind Permission of the Trustees of the Ulster Museum, Belfast.

baits as will take: unfortunately, he does not live to paint, but paints to live. (p. 206)[68]

This was the central dilemma facing artists who attempted to fashion their practice on the basis of academic rules and precepts. Such principles ignored the private functions of works which adorned the walls and occupied the portfolios of private homes, and discounted the needs of artists who had to compete in a commercial market for luxury goods in order to survive. For within the academic paradigm, the subject position of the liberal artist and that of the artist as economic participant in the market were mutually exclusive. It was this unwillingness to recognize how untenable a theory of art had become that failed to engage with the inextricable links between cultural production and a capitalized economy, which doomed at the outset both Dayes's attempts at history painting and his attempts to regulate and elevate the practice of landscape painting via the precepts of academic discourse. The inability or unwillingness to accommodate the needs and desires of contemporary viewers had consequences which were far from "academic" for individuals whose living depended upon the sale of their work. Becoming despondent about his straitened finances, Dayes neither lived to paint nor painted to live, but committed suicide in 1804.[69]

Chapter 2

Of Old Masters, French Glitter, and English Nature

Every person interested for the fine arts, or concerned for the reputation of his country, must perceive with more than regret at the present moment a growing disregard to the fate of the one, which cannot fail materially to affect the splendour of the other. All patriotic interest in the cultivation of British genius appears to be at an end; those who should be the patrons of artists have ceased to be even their employers.[1]

Martin Archer Shee
Rhymes on Art, 1805

THE FAILURE OF MAJOR FIGURES like Barry and minor artists such as Dayes to gain fame and fortune as liberal artists did not prevent others from continuing vigorously to promote history painting in Britain in the decades following the French Revolution. Rather than defending the ability of history painting to represent local (i.e., national) interests, advocates like academician Martin Archer Shee revived the complaint, raised by Hogarth and others nearly a century before, about the lack of patronage for domestic art.[2] Although it is the arts in general that are invoked in the above passage from Shee's widely read and reviewed *Rhymes on Art* (1805), it was lack of government sponsorship of history painting that was the key issue, not private support for the "lower" and more popular genres of portraiture and landscape painting.[3] Analyzing the arguments employed in the debate over public patronage will allow us to understand how traditionally held public ideals such as "English liberty" were reworked to accord with the interests of a community of private individuals. This transformation was central to the production and reception of the landscape genius as an embodiment of English character.

Shee's poetic paean to the fine arts appeared in 1805, the same year that lotteries were held to dispose of the history paintings which formed John Boydell's Shakespeare Gallery and Robert Bowyer's Historic Gallery. Morris Eaves argues that this conjunction of events was not purely accidental – that in fact the failure of Boydell and other publishers to promote history painting through commercial galleries and the market for engravings provided the occasion for artists and writers such as Shee and Prince Hoare (whose *Inquiry into the Cultivation and Present State of the Arts of Design in England* appeared the following year) to campaign for government funding for the arts.[4] These appeals often played on a combination of anti-commercial and anti-Gallic feeling. For example, Shee makes clear reference to the commercial schemes of Boydell, Macklin, and others when he warns that if British culture is "to be overrun by a mob of mercenary sentiments, we shall have escaped to little purpose the disorganization of one revolution, to be reserved to suffer under the degradation of the other."[5] The first revolution to which Shee refers is of course the French Revolution. By invoking the specter of a "mob" of mercenaries (rather than republicans) and the social disorder associated with the French Revolution, the writer was attempting to defame what he perceived to be an internal enemy – those commercial interests involved in the commodification of high art. Throughout *Rhymes on Art* Shee uses similar rhetorical strategies in order to appeal to his public as a national community which is defined by its difference from a French anti-type.

The tone is set for this way of constructing English identity against a French stereotype early in *Rhymes on Art*. On page two of the poem the author asserts that "the taste of the French has undergone a revolution as well as their government, and with as little advantage to the one as to the other." While in politics the French have "proceeded from servility to licentiousness," in art the move has been in the opposite direction: "they have exchanged the fire, and the flutter of meretricious extravagance, for the frost, and phlegm of timorous detail." Shee goes on to characterize the art of David and his school as "dry, sapless," and possessed of a "statue-like insipidity." Implicit here is a causal connection between the nature of a nation's political institutions and quality of its public art. Later in the poem he expresses the hope that such an interrelationship will work to Britain's advantage:

> Let us hope, that it is reserved for Great Britain to prove that the purest system of civil freedom, is creative of the noblest powers of intellectual excellence. – Let us hope, that the liberal policy of our princes and our statesmen will excite and second the genius of their country; that we may shortly see the arts and sciences revolving in planetary splendour round the enlivening sun of British liberty.[6]

Shee was not unique in mobilizing anti-French stereotypes in the service of a particular cultural agenda. Both Linda Colley and Gerald Newman have shown that anti-Gallicism was a salient feature of nationalist discourse throughout the eighteenth century, taking on a new power and pervasiveness after the Revolution, when France came to embody not simply a foreign power, but an enemy espousing (ir)religious and political ideologies antithetical to the principles of a Protestant monarchy.[7] As is apparent in Shee's not-so-veiled attack on Boydell and other cultural entrepreneurs, anti-Gallicism functioned not only to discredit England's cross-Channel enemy; even more importantly, it was marshalled by factional interests within English society as a means of discrediting their domestic rivals.[8]

Given the power of such nationalist rhetoric, it is not surprising to find Shee's opponents in the patronage debate also appealing to British patriotism via anti-French sentiments. And it is worth emphasizing here that the patronage issue *was* a debate and not simply a spontaneous outpouring of support for the English school during a time of nationalist fervor. In fact Shee's and Hoare's polemics for public support of the arts represented the loser's side of the controversy over artistic patronage which continued throughout the early decades of the century. It is a curious feature of the art historical literature on this period that while this failure to gain public support for painting is repeatedly acknowledged, scant attention has been paid to the case presented by the winners of the debate – those vaunting the benefits of private patronage or a "free" market competition for art.[9]

Throughout the early nineteenth century supporters of state funding for history painting either implied or boldly asserted that public patronage of the arts was a sign of good government and strong national character. A case in point is Robert Hunt, art critic for the anti-ministerial, reformist weekly *Examiner*, who in his reviews of the annual exhibition of the Royal Academy frequently linked the corruption of the current government with its failure to support domestic artists, especially history painters. His review of the Royal Academy exhibition of 1810 begins with the assertion that the lack of public support of history painters "reflect[s] disgrace on the sordid government of this country, but not on its genius. . . . It is insulting to the genius, the understanding, the patience, and wasted industry of the British people for government to plead necessity while lazy noblemen and court-sycophant commoners meanly receive many thousands without giving a shilling's value in return".[10] In countering such claims, other writers readily agreed that forms of artistic patronage were a measure of political or national character; but made the point that private patronage or free market competition in the arts should be seen as a sign of English independent-mindedness. For example, in *A Visit to Paris in 1814*, writer and newspaper editor John Scott pointed out sharp distinctions between English and French character as displayed in their divergent forms of art patronage.[11] Scott introduced the terms by which this Anglo-French comparison would be articulated in the opening section of the book, noting that the English love of travel "shews a freedom and custom, as well as a power to think, – a bold and independent disposition . . . and feeling certain of commanding respect." The French, on the other hand, are represented as lacking the public curiosity of the English, and are indifferent to the past, even their own revolutionary history.[12]

The French state's long-term involvement in cultural projects provides Scott with further evidence of the difference in the two national characters. After reviewing a number of government projects – commissions for public sculpture, "self-willed" and "extravagant" buildings, and fêtes that "put one in the mind of those at Versailles" – Scott reminds his readers that these have all arisen from the "indisputable mandate of a Louis or a Napoleon."[13] He then goes on to contrast this cultural authoritarianism with the much more liberal state of affairs in England:

> The public of England have been accustomed to look to themselves – to their own spirit and opinion, – for their own comforts, luxuries, and ornaments. Little, or nothing, is performed by the English executive government, but the details of state business, – and it seems safest to entrust it with no power, and to enter no expectations beyond this. . . . When the people originate what they enjoy, it is but reasonable to conclude that the people's welfare will be consulted, – but in France it is directly the reverse – The French people have been accustomed to look to themselves for nothing; their rulers have given them every thing of which they boast.[14]

While Scott professes respect for the aristocracy and a belief in the present social and political order, he joins a host of other bourgeois intellectuals in identifying independent-mindedness with a broad public which includes the literate middle class.[15] What is striking in the above passage is the manner in which English liberty and spirit is manifested: namely, in the ability of private citizens to form their own opinions and choose their own luxuries and "ornaments." For Scott implies that there is a connection between this independently minded public and a state which does not intervene in the circulation of luxury goods. Thus interlinked, public opinion and a *laissez-faire* economic policy become synonymous expressions of the English individual's independence from authoritarian control.

Scott's formulation of an English public for art bears a complex relationship to the ideals of the public instantiated in academic discourse. Crucially, the qualities of intellect and personal autonomy are central to both formulations. However, the notion of aesthetic and economic disinterest which underpins such academic productions as Reynolds's *Discourses* and Barry's history paintings no longer forms the ground for Scott's ideal of personal autonomy. For him, concepts of aesthetic and economic disinterest are abandoned in favor of the individual's "freedom" to act on his/her private interests in acquiring luxury commodities without the intervention of a central state authority.

Whereas Scott's attack on public patronage rested largely on the independent character of the English public for art, other arguments appealed to the benefits afforded artists by rigorous competition in the marketplace. This argument was, for example, proffered in response to Prince Hoare's *Inquiry into the Cultivation and Present State of the Arts of Design in England* in an article published in 1807 in *Le Beau Monde*. The writer disputes Hoare's contention that the arts in England are unsupported, and further insists that artists are harmed by liberal patronage, not its lack. Rather than give artists commissions, public and private patrons should allow works to enter into "public" competitions provided by exhibitions at the Royal Academy and British Institution and commercial displays at private galleries. Artists would then feel they deserved the remuneration they received. He concludes:

> we therefore entreat our countrymen, as they value their own happiness, as they hope for the continual prosperity and independence of Britain, to refrain in every practicable instance, from giving commissions for works of art. Let every professor then, as he certainly will, bring his works to public competition and sale.[16]

National prosperity, happiness, and – once again – independence, are presented here as the benefits to be reaped from a cultural market in which artists compete freely for financial rewards and public acclaim.

Seven years later a writer in the conservative *New Monthly Magazine* mounted an even more vigorous defense of this free market in cultural production; in the process he also defined the characteristics of the producer and consumer within such an economic system.[17] In a letter to the editor, the anonymous writer "Claudius" explains that "the high prices which speculative men are disposed to give for works of merit are strong excitements to renewed efforts." Beyond monetary rewards, he adds, "the writer and the painter feel their independence without being shackled by the arbitrary dictates of great men upon whom they are dependent for bread."[18] Whereas financial speculation was invariably considered the plague of the commercial system by anti-war reformers and other critics of governmental corruption, this writer invokes it as the spur to artistic independence, which is presented here as synonymous with aesthetic excellence.

This economic argument is bolstered by a political argument which invokes a comparison between English support of the arts and continental patronage. "True patronage," "Claudius" writes, "consists rather in facilitating the production of meritorious works by encouraging the purchase of them, than in taking their authors under the protection of royal and noble personages, which is, at the very best, but little more than a splendid state of servitude." He continues by noting that a free market system is appropriate for English artists and patrons because "in this island men of distinguished abilities ought to be left to the vigour of their minds, and to the application of their powers, according to the bent of nature, without being cautioned or directed by the caprice of an illustrious patronage."[19] Whereas for Reynolds, Dayes, and Barry, capriciousness was a quality which defined the masses, unschooled in matters of taste, here it is the patronage of "illustrious" individuals which is represented as a form of servitude and as driven by caprice. Only the independence and competitiveness offered by a free market system can preserve those qualities of intellectual vigor which mark the productions of English genius.

What kind of art would be able to thrive in such a competitive environment? State support was lacking for large-scale historical works designed to hang in the chambers of government, public institutions, and churches. The obvious alternative lay in small-scale paintings – landscapes, genre scenes, and portraits. The question then becomes whether it was possible or even desirable for such works, which were so closely identified with private, luxury consumption, to mediate some form of national character. In seeking an answer to this question it will be useful to consider other spaces, beyond those of church and state, that were available for the open display of English painting, and what specific demands those spaces were seen to exert on the works that hung on their walls.

Modern English paintings achieved the highest public visibility when they occupied sites within the metropolis in which luxury goods were sold, promoted, and displayed. These included auction houses, emporiums, private commercial galleries, the public exhibition spaces of the Royal Academy and British Institution, and the not so private mansions and town houses of "Society," whose routs, dinners, and assemblies were reported in the "fashionable life" columns of the press.[20] These were sites of luxury consumption, an activity which extended from the upper classes through an increasingly prosperous middle class and which, as Neil McKendrick, Colin Campbell, and others have emphasized, reached unprecedented dimensions by 1800.[21] McKendrick has noted that the luxury of the English raised a "deafening chorus of comment" from Russians, Germans, and other foreign visitors.[22] But it is domestic comment on the spaces of consumption that concerns us here – how the spectacle of luxury consumption was made to signify in public discourse.

As luxury commodities, paintings entered into an arena of competition that took

EXHIBITION OF WATER COLOURED DRAWINGS,
OLD BOND STREET.

London. Pub. 1st Sept. 1808, at R. Ackermann's Repository of Arts 101 Strand.

17 A.C. Pugin and Thomas Rowlandson, *Exhibition of the Society of Painters in Watercolours.* Aquatint in *The Microcosm of London*, vol. 3, London, 1809. Brown University Library, Providence, RI (photo: Brooke Hammerle).

on an explicitly spatial dimension with the establishment of public exhibitions in the 1760s. By 1806 the Royal Academy, the British Institution, and the Society of Painters in Water–Colours all provided spaces in which artists could exhibit their wares annually. An engraving from the *Microcosm of London* in 1809 depicts the first exhibition of the Society of Painters in Water–Colours (Figure 17); the pictures are shown set in heavy gilded frames and hung close together, blanketing exhibition walls from floor to ceiling.[23] In such an exhibition situation, it is not surprising that some artists should choose to heighten the visibility of their works through the use of bold effects and brilliant coloring in order to attract viewers' attention. In one of his lectures to the Royal Academy, John Opie, Professor of Painting at the Academy from 1805 to 1809, made such a connection between painting for effect and the circumstances of an exhibition: "In a crowd, he that talks loudest, not he that talks best, is surest of commanding attention; and in an exhibition, he that does not attract the eye, does nothing." Opie went on to deplore such practices, urging artists to paint "for eternity," not for fashion and the contemporary acclaim of "corrupt and incompetent judges."[24]

Such practices may have prompted changes in the exhibition sites themselves. In 1807 a commentator on the state of the arts, writing in the short-lived *Beau Monde*, speculated that the (much-hated) red walls of the new British Gallery might serve "perhaps as a precaution against too vivid colours, which a desire of attracting notice has introduced into the school of painting." The same writer vigorously promoted an open market for the sale of paintings rather than public or private commissions.[25] He did not acknowledge that he had placed artists in an untenable position by advocating a "free" competition in art while disapproving of an exhibition style designed to accommodate the demands of such a system.

An economically successful artist had to be able to produce works which held their own in the spaces of display within private homes as well as in public exhibition sites.[26] Some idea of the general trend in the contemporary taste which governed the decoration of recently built and refurbished London town houses can be ascertained from those interiors, furnishings, and decorative ornaments which have survived, as well as from visual and written accounts. Typical of such accounts are the descriptions of Montague House, redecorated in the 1780s by the society hostess, Elizabeth Montague. The house included a room decorated entirely in brightly colored feathers and a "great room" with a barrel-vaulted ceiling, elaborate stucco ornaments, gilded Corinthian capitals, and lavish furnishings. The *St. James Chronicle* in 1791 enthused: "the curtains are of white satin fringed with gold; the chandeliers and large looking-glasses are superb; and the whole is an assemblage of art and magnificence which we have never witnessed in a private room."[27]

This emphasis on brilliant reflective surfaces, color, and light was enthusiastically endorsed by the Prince Regent, whose admiration of the lavish decorations that marked the Bourbon court at Versailles was evident in the plans for the remodeling of Carleton House, conducted under the auspices of Walsh Porter.[28] A colored engraving from 1819 of the crimson drawing room (Figure 18) suggests the overall effect achieved from the rich glowing color of the walls, the heavily gilded ceiling, and the immense crystal chandeliers which, when lit for evening entertainments, would be reflected in huge mirrors occupying the wall spaces between the windows. Such splendor was reproduced to varying degrees in other remodelings, such as those completed at Grosvenor House in 1808 and at Devonshire House a decade later.[29]

The taste for brightly colored paintings, which could compete visually on the walls of private homes and exhibition halls, was identified by some as a particularly "English" phenomenon. This taste was manifested in the preferences English collectors displayed in acquiring old masters. In 1803 picture dealer William Buchanan advised his agent in Italy, James Irvine, to seek out works by artists such as Titian, Rubens, Ostade, and Berchem that displayed "bravura and breadth of light."[30] Such partiality for virtuoso displays of painterly effects was nearly synonymous with a preference for landscapes and other works in the "lower" genres. The point was made forcefully by Buchanan, who repeatedly advised Irvine to be on the lookout for "grand Landscapes" by Rubens, Claude, Poussin, and Rosa as well as smaller "common" landscapes by Dutch and Flemish landscape painters.[31] He judged altarpieces and other works in the grand style to be bad investments, observing that "the Historical does not really appear to be so well understood or at least so much relished in this Country."[32]

As a picture dealer Buchanan found it necessary to identify and accommodate an "English" taste in art in order to be financially successful, but he was not impelled to adduce the national character from such a practical assessment. Such character judgments can be inferred, however, from the comments of some of Buchanan's contemporaries. One such individual was Prince Hoare, Secretary for Foreign Correspondence at the Royal Academy and staunch advocate for the state support of history painting. While Hoare shared Buchanan's judgment about the English penchant for paintings displaying "boldness and force of colour, and of light and shade; and richness of effect," his opinion of this state of affairs was decidedly mixed. He declared in his *Inquiry into the Requisite Cultivation and Present State of the Arts of Design in England* that "our painting is like our drama, libertine in method and combination, but animated and forcible in effect."[33] Given the centrality of the notion of "English liberty" in nationalist discourse, such a statement could be taken to imply that contemporary taste manifests an English desire for liberty which threatens to become excessive. For while this taste is characterized by positive, masculine qualities of vigor and force, it evinces a "libertine" lack of control in precisely those areas of composition and conception that were the special province of academic training.

A very different notion of the relationship between the possession of a particular taste in painting and national character was posited by those vaunting the cultural activities of wealthy collectors such as Thomas Hope, the Marquis of Stafford, Francis Baring, and Lord Egremont. In 1806, for example, the ultra-nationalistic and conservative *True Briton* published the following description of a gala hosted by the daughters of the prominent banker and merchant, Sir Francis Baring:

> The unbounded wealth of Sir Frances Baring, acquired by the most honourable and extensive mercantile concerns, is a theme not confined to this country but discussed throughout Europe. It cannot, therefore, occasion surprise, that the *Cornu-copiae* was liberally discharged. Every apartment in the house exhibited a profusion of the most costly and well-chosen Ornaments. . . . In the Anti [*sic*] Drawing Room, the Connoisseur was delighted with a collection of Paintings by the most approved Masters, truly valuable and *unique*, and highly creditable to the discernment of SIR FRANCIS in the beauties of the Fine Arts. . . . [In attendance were] the most distinguished ornaments of the *Haute Ton*, who were not more dazzled by the riches, than they were delighted by the attention, and gratified by the hospitality of the BRITISH MERCHANT.[34]

A plenitude of dazzling ornaments, human and otherwise, is presented here as a sign of both personal and national wealth, of virtue, and of pride. This physical display would have taken on a heightened significance in the years between 1806 and 1819 when the government suspended the gold standard in order to facilitate

18   T. Sutherland after C. Wild, *Crimson Drawing Room at Carleton House*. Colored engraving in *The History of Royal Residences of Windsor Castle, St James Palace, Carlton House and Frogmore*, vol. 3, London, 1819. Brown University Library, Providence, RI (photo: Brooke Hammerle).

increased financing of the war with France.[35] During a time in which bank notes were no longer convertible into gold upon demand, visible demonstrations of the wealth of private individuals and the royal family was proffered as evidence of continued national prosperity.

The *True Briton*'s paean to Baring constituted an ideal of Britishness characterized by a cosmopolitan taste for fine paintings and other "costly and well-chosen Ornaments," the commercial acumen necessary to possess (not merely to appreciate) these goods, and the liberality to "share" them with (i.e., display them to) the cream of English society. While there is a strongly nationalistic tone to the passage, there is no attempt to identify Baring's collecting habits or preferences in art as English.[36] The banker's discernment in collecting "the most approved Masters" qualifies him as a man of [good] taste, not as a man of "English" taste, despite the fact that his particular attachment to Dutch painting conforms to his dealer Buchanan's account of an English preference for landscapes, genre scenes, and other non-historical pictures, notable for their "bravura and breadth of light."[37]

Baring's "patriotic" cultural activities extended beyond opening his town house to the *haut ton* (and the press), for in 1805–6 he was also involved in the establishment of the British Institution for Promoting the Fine Arts in the United Kingdom.[38] Unlike the Royal Academy which was governed by artists, the British Institution was directed by a committee composed of connoisseurs and collectors whose wealth derived from banking, commerce, and land. As its name suggests, the new institution professed to be a patriotic enterprise committed to the promotion of British art and artists, primarily by providing domestic artists with another venue (an annual exhibition) in which to display and sell their wares. Early on, however, the Directors of the Institution revealed that their ambitions went beyond merely providing modern artists with another showroom. They also offered artists enrolled in the Institution's "British School" (established in 1806) an opportunity to advance their study by copying directly from old master paintings.[39] From the beginning it was clear that the Institution's criteria for artistic excellence among modern British painters were set by the works of the old masters, especially those northern masters which formed the greater part of the collections of its Directors and Governors. Thirteen of the sixteen owners providing old masters for copying in the first British School were Governors of the Institution; and out of the twenty-three masterworks that went on display that first year, twelve were Dutch or Flemish.[40]

Although the Institution enjoyed wide praise for its patriotic support of British artists, it also was the target of criticism, frequently from academicians who feared that the Institution was undermining the teaching and authority of the Royal Academy. For example, Martin Archer Shee expressed his concern that the Institution was promoting small-scale Dutch art over historical painting in the Italian tradition in his *Elements of Art*, which was published in 1809 as a sort of sequel to the popular *Rhymes on Art*. He complained that those genres most associated with northern painting – portraits, landscapes, and "familiar scenes" – are "commodities that suit the market" rather than works which can "exercise a moral influence over the minds and manners of man."[41] English artists, he claimed, were already too devoted to this type of painting ("the peculiar taste of the country has necessarily driven them into that direction"), and he went on to argue that the function of the British Institution was "not to co-operate with that Taste, but to correct it."[42] For Shee, a strong proponent of the Academy and of academicism, non-historical paintings were no more than commodities. Hence, it would be indefensible for an institution formally dedicated to fostering a native school of painting to promote such commodities/paintings, which, possessing only exchange value, were incapable of morally elevating the individual and the nation. Underlying such a critique is not only a concern about paintings that cannot inscribe "moral values," but the fear that genres other than history painting, the focal point of academic training and traditional source of the academic artist's claims to professional status, could come to represent the interests and values of such a culturally prestigious national establishment as the British Institution. Were this to be the case, then certain types of non-historical painting could legitimately be seen to mediate positive values of the nation at large, rather than to represent a "peculiar taste," which had to be eradicated.

Objections to the British Institution's promotion of foreign masters grew over the next decade. In 1815 the Institution mounted its first old master exhibition, consisting of paintings, not surprisingly, from the Dutch and Flemish schools. The

Directors aroused the ire of the Royal Academy by running this exhibition concurrently with the annual exhibition of the Royal Academy. The Royal Academicians so resented the Institution's support of "foreign competition" that they refused, almost unanimously, a special invitation by the BI Directors to a private evening viewing.[43] This gesture of disapproval was accompanied by an acerbic attack on the British Institution which was published serially in the *Morning Chronicle* and as a pamphlet entitled *A Catalogue Raisonnée [sic] of the Pictures Now Exhibiting at the British Institution* (1815).[44] The attack was aimed mainly at the Directors, who, it was alleged, had only a superficial understanding of ancient pictures, yet set themselves up as arbiters of art. Such a role was unsuitable for such men since they came "to the judgement seat unprepared with any information at all drawn from the contemplation or study of nature. . . .Their ONLY standards are old pictures."[45]

Such a judgment was supported by a review of old master copies made by domestic artists on display at the British School two years earlier, in 1813. Appearing in the *Morning Post*, which was a vigorous supporter of the Institution and the Prince Regent, its titular President, the review discusses two landscapes, a *Death of Regulus*, copied by William Marshall Craig from the original by Salvator Rosa, and William Westall's copy of Aelbert Cuyp's *A Fête on the Water at Dort*. What is striking about the reviewer's comments is that they are restricted to praise for the original masterworks and their British owners. After duly noting Rosa's felicitous union of historical figures with the grandeur of his landscape, the reviewer concludes that "Lord Darnley may feel proud to be the possessor of such a performance." Similarly the remarks on the second copy are confined to praise for the rich color and sunny calm of Cuyp's harbor scene.[46] For the reviewer, then, the English artistic producer becomes not virtuously "transparent" (in the sense of displaying liberal disinterest by repressing all signs of personal manner) but totally absent. The copy functions as a sign of judgment, sensibility, and intellect only for the "old master" or "modern collector."

At the heart of the debates around the efficacy of the British Institution in promoting a national school of painting was another controversy – one which centered on the significance and desirability of collecting, promoting, and emulating old pictures by continental masters. The Institution claimed that in giving domestic artists access to original old masters it was (merely) supporting and supplementing the type of education advocated by the Royal Academy, and thus fostering a successful national school of historical painting.[47] Contrary to the Institution's stated commitment "to produce those intellectual and virtuous feelings, which are perpetually alive to the welfare and glory of the country," the anonymous author of the *Catalogue Raisonnée* alleged that the Institution's Directors promoted old masters in a fashion that was neither disinterested nor patriotic, but in fact a self-serving ploy to promote their own collections over and above works by modern artists. Among the various fears raised by the Institution in this writer and other partisans of the Academy was the concern that for the first time what had previously been (regretfully) identified as a "peculiar" and even "libertine" "English" taste for foreign landscapes and genre painting featuring brilliant effects of light and color was now being institutionalized in a self-declaredly patriotic, prestigious, and powerful cultural establishment, symbolically presided over by the Prince of Wales and governed by some of the nation's most powerful merchants, bankers, and landowners.

Not surprisingly, English landscape painters responded in various ways to these controversies concerning the role of old master painting, the public function of the "lesser" genres, and the (re)formation of "English" taste. In their attempt to compete in a market fueled by a fascination with foreign paintings and other luxury goods, many domestic artists found themselves in the midst of these public debates; and frequently they, like the collectors of old masters, were accused of promoting their financial self-interest over the artistic needs of the nation. A common complaint lodged against both portrait and landscape paintings was that their colors were too gaudy and their highlights too brilliant. We recognize these characteristics as precisely those which were seen by some artists, dealers, and critics as defining a particularly English taste for certain genres and schools of foreign art. Although portrait painters such as Thomas Lawrence were consistently criticized on this basis, this critique was subsumed into the broader allegation that portraiture as a genre pandered to the personal vanity of individuals rather than representing those commonly held ideals which distinguished and elevated the national character.[48] In fact the most fully elaborated attacks on such eye-catching effects were directed toward landscape painting in language that testifies to the increasing importance of that genre as a site for the production of national identity.

One of these attacks on landscape painting occurred in the rather curious context of a popular poem, *Walks in a Forest* (1794) by the Anglican clergyman, Staffordshire landowner, and amateur artist Thomas Gisborne.[49] The poem is structured around the theological notion of *concordia discors*, a harmonious disposition of discordant elements. This concept was frequently invoked in the eighteenth century as a means of representing social inequality as divinely ordered social diversity.[50] Gisborne draws an analogy between the harmony of external nature, exemplified by the forest, and a divinely ordered human society in which "harmonious though dissimilar, all conspire to swell the sum of general bliss."[51] Following a passage in which the forest is described as "one congenial mass, brilliant but chaste, with every dye that stains the withering leaf/Glowing yet not discordant," Gisborne interjects this stern advice to landscape painters:

> Hither come,
> Ye sons of imitative art, who hang
> The fictions of your pencils on our walls,
> And call them landscapes; Where incongruous hues
> Seem their constrain'd vicinity to mourn; Where gaudy
>   green with gaudy yellow vies,
> And blues and reds with adverse aspect glare.
> Here deign to learn from nature: here though late,
> Learn the peculiar majesty which crowns
> The forest, when the slowly passing clouds
> Triple preponderance of shadow spread,
> And separate the broad collected lights
> With corresponding gloom.[52]

Gisborne defends the rules of academic practice (which dictate a "triple preponderance of shadow" compared to light in a composition) as being an observable feature of the "forest," which here represents both external nature and, metaphorically, the social order.[53] Gisborne's use of "majesty" and "crown" in the passage serves to displace onto the forest the royal character of its owner – for much of Britain's forests were the property of the king, including the forest in which Gisborne's own estate was located.[54] Against this (literally) noble harmony of nature Gisborne opposes the "fictions" called landscapes which are unnatural precisely because they make discord visible. The vocabulary of social conflict is used to describe the juxtapositioning of "incongruous" and "adverse" colors which "vie" with each other, "mourning" their constrained proximity. This passage functions neither as aesthetic criticism couched in political language nor as a political attack on revolutionary disorder via an artistic metaphor. Landscape painting is presented here as an active participant in the *production* of social disorder at a moment of crisis – this was the year after the French king and queen had been executed, and counter-revolutionary reaction in Britain was at its height.[55] The inclusion of a critique of landscape painting in such a text testifies to the growing importance of the landscape artist as a producer of such potent symbolic representations of national order in a period of social upheaval throughout Europe. Whereas the ideal history painter had been identified in academic discourse as a supra-national subject who represents universal truths through forms divested of national prejudice, the landscape artist in the 1790s and the decades thereafter is figured as a national subject, in both his public and his private character.

The importance of the landscape painter as a national subject was reaffirmed the following year, 1795, in a vehement attack on contemporary landscape painting by the reviewer for the *Morning Post* when that journal was profoundly anti-court and anti-ministerial. These remarks occurred in the context of a review of Paul Sandby's topographical watercolors. Favorably disposed to the works, the critic had even more praise for Sandby himself, whom he hailed as a pillar of the Academy while expressing the regret that he had so few pictures in the exhibition.[56] In the following passage he explains that Sandby's presence is necessary because landscape painting is in need of reform:

> There is a taste spreading abroad for gaudy hues, glittering effects and mechanical fopperies dazzling to weak-sighted connoisseurs and unfledged students – with the meretricious ornaments of a courtezan, they lure the idle and inexperienced, while unobtrusive modesty has no attraction. If this extravagant perversion of all taste is not checked and exposed – if we are not brought back from the delusive mazes of eccentric art, into the plain, but unfrequented road of nature, the worst consequences may be prophesied to the Arts. We shall quickly be precipitated from the eminence to which we have attained, and degenerate into all the vices of French frippery and affectation, to the utter exclusion of Nature, Simplicity and Truth.[57]

This text employs a constellation of tropes to connect a painterly play of surface effects and brilliant color with illicit sexual desire, fantasy, display, artificiality, and French taste. Dazzlingly delusive, such effects are not only capable of seducing the "idle and inexperienced," but threaten to pervert the general taste, precipitating moral and cultural decline. Although the passage targets "unfledged students and weak-sighted connoisseurs," its references to idleness, extravagance, and ornament conjure up a wider public of fashionable pleasure-seekers, whose property holdings were unspecified and whose elevated class status was no longer a guarantee of their good taste. Significantly, this decline is represented as a falling away from national eminence and a falling into the character of another nation. To embrace the gaudy and artificial in art is to abandon one's social and national identity by taking on the vices and affectations of a debased Other – an Other which, as we have seen, was at this moment almost invariably characterized as French.[58] Although the critic does not refer to specific French painters in this passage, it is clear that he has in mind pre-revolutionary artists such as Watteau, whose brilliantly colored canvases adorned many English collections, rather than contemporary post-revolutionary artists such as David, whose paintings enjoyed a notoriety eclipsed only by his revolutionary activities.[59] The *Post* critic has strategically mobilized not simply *the* anti-French stereotype, but the stereotype of French art most suited to the critique he is making of English painting and taste.

What is of course suppressed in the *Post*'s indictment of fashionable landscape painting is the fact that the attraction to gaudy colors and glittering effects was an English phenomenon, in part the consequence of a highly competitive environment, be it the exhibition hall, the Stock Exchange, or the ballroom. Such self-display instead is read as an abandonment of one's "natural" (modest, moral, English) social identity and the taking on of another which is not only foreign but self-interested. For the *Post* critic's use of sexualized and feminized metaphors is consistent with a civic humanist construction of the subject as a citizen who suppresses his sensuous needs and desires. This arises from the fact that liberal "disinterest" signified not only economic independence but, as John Barrell argues, a form of masculinity which is desireless.[60] Within the parameters of such a discourse, it is only in their character as private individuals that male viewers could be seen as susceptible to seduction by pictures possessing the "meretricious ornaments of a courtezan." If such paintings are figured as female, then gaudy color and painterly effects assume the status of ornaments or make-up applied by the artist, who becomes identified as a pimp – the lowest form of "merchant" within the commercial sphere.[61]

Although neither Thomas Gisborne nor the *Post* critic named specific artists and works in their censure of landscape painting and English taste, we can gain some sense of the works in question, for art critics repeatedly identified spotty effects, gaudy colors, and surface glitter with a few individuals, especially Julius Caesar Ibbetson, Francis Bourgeois, Richard Westall, and Philippe de Loutherbourg.[62] Ibbetson's small (7.4 × 10 in.) cabinet picture, *Sand Quarry at Alum Bay* (Figure 19, *c*.1792) is indicative of this type of work.[63] Its intimate size invites a type of extended private viewing which would have afforded connoisseurs, as history painter Benjamin Haydon disdainfully put it in 1808, the "delight in cocking their nose[s]" close to its active, fractured surface.[64] The cliff on the right is represented as an intricate array of frothy projections, indicated by rough, irregular brushstrokes. Following the general form of the cliffs below, the clouds appear as a series of

19   Julius Caesar Ibbetson, *Sand Quarry at Alum Bay*, *c*.1792. Oil on wood panel, 7.4 × 10 in. Tate Gallery, London.

separate daubs, picked out with highlights. The fragmentation of forms is further carried into the representation of the water. Its surface is broken by the highlights of the whitecaps, laid on in a thin, nervous line, which thickens and intensifies at the water's edge. There the brilliant white of the foam contrasts sharply with the dark rocks of the foreground. Water, land, and sky vibrate with the activity of the artist's brush – an activity which led some critics to characterize his manner as "spotty."[65] One of the artist's harshest critics, the reviewer for the *London Packet*, attributed this mode of execution directly to the pressures of the market. Writing of Ibbetson's *Miners Setting out to Encounter the French* exhibited at the Royal Academy in 1798, he declares: "It appears to be a work of haste, painted for sale."[66] Broken surface effects, then, could connote a slapdash manner, provoked by the need to produce quantity, not quality, while also serving to draw viewer attention away from less eye-catching visual displays.

More popular and financially successful than Ibbetson, Richard Westall began exhibiting watercolors and oils at the Royal Academy in the 1780s. By the 1790s his sentimentalized rustic genre pieces, literary subjects, and titillating mythological scenes were garnering much the same type of criticism as Ibbetson's landscapes. Typical of the rustic landscapes which Westall was producing in the mid- to late 1790s is *A Storm in Harvest* (Figure 20), which was exhibited at the Royal Academy in 1796 and purchased by connoisseur Richard Payne Knight.[67] The scene depicts a group of agrarian laborers, under a bower of trees, anxiously waiting out a passing rainstorm. The central figures are illuminated by a strong light from the left which bathes the woodland setting in a luminous yellow ochre glow. The subsidiary lights, picking out the branch in the upper left and the distant vista visible through the trees below it, combine with a feathery handling of the foliage and an overall emphasis on a coiling and twisting line to produce an active, flickering pictorial surface. Although it seems clear that Westall was drawing upon the rustic genre scenes of Gainsborough, this connection was rarely made in the press.[68] Most critics avoided any association between Westall's work and that of other English artists, choosing rather to insist on the foreign quality of his manner.

While popular with George III and connoisseurs such as Horace Walpole and Payne Knight, in the years around 1800 Westall provoked consistent criticism from artists such as John Constable and Paul Sandby, prominent connoisseur and amateur George Beaumont, and a number of art critics writing for periodicals with diverse political and cultural views.[69] Published accounts praising Westall's art were rare and brief. While the critic for the *True Briton*, writing in 1798, praised his watercolors for their "powerful impulse and elegant controul," most favorable accounts of his oils tended to ignore his use of color and light effects. Even Payne Knight, who was Westall's most important patron, and who mounted the most fully elaborated defense of this painterly style, as we will see shortly, was remarkably restrained in his praise. He tacitly acknowledged the criticism that Westall's *Grecian Marriage* (1796) received on its exhibition at the Royal Academy when he insisted that the work possessed the "utmost purity and dignity of heroic character and composition, embellished and not impaired by the most rich and splendid harmony of colouring."[70] In his treatise on taste he praised Westall's selection of a theme from "common life" as the subject of *A Storm in Harvest*, describing it as "affecting and full of pathos," but made no specific reference to its mode of execution.[71] More frequently, however, Westall's work was criticized as being affected rather than affecting – of appealing to the vanity and base appetites of viewers rather than their higher sensibilities.

In a review of 1796, Anthony Pasquin connected the artist's production of brilliantly hued watercolors directly to the demands of competition within an exhibition space:

> Mr. Westall's drawings appear to more advantage in the Exhibition, than they do out, which is derived from their gaudiness of tinting. . . . There is nothing more certain, than that a picture chastely coloured, may be ruined in character by being placed next to a glaring composition, in such an assemblage.[72]

To characterize coloring as chaste was to invoke the discourse of sexuality as a means of regulating artistic practice, which, along with the gendering of color and painterly effects, had long been a common tactic in aesthetic and critical writing.[73] By means of this regulatory move, excessive coloring was doubly condemned as

20   Richard Westall, *A Storm in Harvest*, 1796. Oil on card, loosely mounted on canvas, 23.8 × 31 in. Private collection (photo: Angela Lloyd-James).

both aesthetically offensive and immoral. Such a rhetoric of sexual and moral contamination is further mobilized here to suggest that the good character of a picture can be "ruined" when placed next to one that is "unchaste." This language of contamination recalls the remarks of the critic for the *Post* (who may well have been Pasquin) a year earlier, that likened "gaudy hues, glittering effects and mechanical fopperies," to the "meretricious ornaments of a courtezan." The art critic for the conservative *St. James Chronicle* seems to have concurred in this negative assessment of Westall's rustic landscapes for he accused the artist of being a "disgusting mannerist," in a review of his *Peasant's Return* of 1800.[74] An excessive manner, as we have seen from the writings of Reynolds and Dayes, was the visual evidence not only of the self-interested artist who "shows himself," but also of a debased viewer, who is defined by a love of sensuous display, rather than by social sensibility and intellect. Such a concern about the character of the viewers of Westall's paintings was voiced privately by the writer C.R. Leslie, who in a letter

21   Richard Westall, *The Bower of Pan*, RA 1800. Oil on canvas, 57.5 × 65.3 in. Manchester City Art Galleries, Manchester.

of 1812 supposed that Westall's showy style appealed to those "who are not in the habit of thinking when they look at a picture."[75] This same criticism was also made publicly, by the predictably antagonistic Anthony Pasquin, who, in reviewing Westall's *Hesiod Instructing the Greeks* (RA, 1796) declared that "this is such an effort, as no person, possessing taste and knowledge, can regard with satisfaction; yet it involves that trickery and finery which is so captivating to vulgar minds."[76] Other critics writing about Westall's work in the period between 1795 and 1810 similarly implied, or openly asserted, that the artist's work was predicated upon an insensitive, unknowing viewer.[77]

Taking exception to this general censure was the critic for the *True Briton*. Writing in 1800 in regard to Westall's *Bower of Pan* (Figure 21), which depicts the god accompanied by a trio of nude, nubile women taking their ease in a luridly colored "bower" of flowers and foliage, the critic praised its "rich, voluptuous, and splendid scenery," and went on somewhat defensively to observe that if some viewers find the coloring too gaudy, then they should observe that it is not "mere Nature" being represented.[78] Such a tentative defense was abandoned a few years later, in 1807, when critic John Taylor, writing for the same newspaper, harshly attacked a similar painting of richly "embowered" nude females by Westall, his

22   Richard Westall, *Flora Unveiled by the Zephyrs*, RA 1807. Oil on panel, 30 × 23.4 in. Private collection (photo: Courtauld Institute of Art).

Flora Unveiled by the Zephyrs (Figure 22).[79] He complained that "it has all the *spangle* and *catching light* of Watteau's work," and then warned young artists,

> who are too readily smitten by *dazzling professional witchery*, that, of all the style of painting, the *French* is the lowest and most contemptible. It has nothing of *nature* to please the eye, nothing of *sentiment* to gratify the mind: its *frippery* and *tinsel* please Frenchmen alone.[80]

Again, the move to identify brilliant effects with an unnatural and dangerously feminized (pre-revolutionary) French taste is here opposed to a notion of (manly) Englishness, ultimately based upon sensibility and intellect. Young artists who adopted such foreign techniques jeopardized their ability to address an English public (these effects "please Frenchmen alone") – and therefore risked alienating themselves from their true character as national subjects.

The linking of glittering style and high-key color with the foreign, the fashion-able, and debased modes of knowledge featured directly in political discourse as well. An anonymous volume, *Political Essays on Popular Subjects, Containing Disser-tations on First Principles; Liberty; Democracy and the Party Denominations of Whig and Tory* (1801), offered a Burkean defense of the English state against attempts to reform the constitution. Its author uses the language of contemporary artistic dis-course to condemn the "novel characteristics" of the present age:

> A general diffusion of the lowest species of knowledge, a dashing style of com-position, a tinsel sort of eloquence, together with a deficiency of solid thought, a want of logical precision, and an ignorance of original principles, mark the features of the times with colours too glaring to be mistaken, with foreign tints which shame the modest simplicity of nature, which disguise the genuine dignity of truth.[81]

Lest readers have any doubts about the origin of the unnatural "foreign tints" which disguise logical thinking and truth, the author went on to assert that the French Revolution sprang from false principles, unleashing abroad a "daring spirit of innovation."[82] What is striking about this passage, in our context, is the ease with which it appropriates the language of aesthetics and art criticism in order to attack the political precepts of post-revolutionary France. So strong were the associations of tinsel, glaring colors and "dashing" composition with a debased, vulgar, and foreign form of painting that these pejoratives could confidently be expected to call up unnatural and ephemeral modes of political knowledge – specifically those "leveling" principles which toppled the French monarchy. It is particularly ironic that the author appropriates pejoratives associated with pre-revolutionary rococo painting in attempting to discredit revolutionary political theories.

Since the period we have been considering here, roughly 1795 to 1805, corre-sponds to the interval in which British fears of a French invasion were the greatest and counter-revolutionary feeling and rhetoric was at its height, it is not surprising that attacks on a "gaudy" style of painting, and specious modes of political thought would be constructed as un-English (that is to say, French) by writers across the artistic and political spectrum. For an oppositional journal like the *Post* in the 1790s, such a critique of fashionable taste and vulgar knowledge was directed at a decadent elite that was incapable or unwilling to undertake the serious and prolonged study of art that was becoming associated with the educated sector of the upper middle class and patriciate. When presented in the context of more conservative publica-tions such as the *True Briton* and *St. James Chronicle*, however, this type of critique could serve as a way of distinguishing the superficial knowledge and philistine pleasures of an increasingly wealthy, but as yet culturally unsophisticated commer-cial middle class from the erudition of the traditional propertied elite. Attacking the debasement of taste which resulted from the corrupting power of monied interests, then, could serve the needs of diverse, even opposed, socio-political groups.

In the face of such searing criticism what kind of defense was possible? We have already had evidence that English artists and patrons continued to produce and purchase the brightly colored canvases that circulated as luxury commodities in the 1790s and the decades that followed. Is it possible that no defense of the moral and social value of such works was necessary, and that what they represented was an atomized private sphere where private interests and publicity replaced the republican ideal of public virtue? Arguably the most theoretically sophisticated and highly regarded response to this question was proffered by a powerful connoisseur, who, in the early 1800s, sought to banish ethics from the discourse of painting altogether.

We have seen that advocates for the Academy had a professional stake in promoting painting as a highly intellectual and moral activity, and consequently tended to devalue precisely those aspects of the art − color, dramatic light/dark contrasts, and other painterly effects − that were traditionally understood to appeal to the senses.[83] Not surprisingly, it was a man of profoundly anti-academic biases, Richard Payne Knight − Director of the British Institution, and Westall's liberal patron − who offered the most fully elaborated defense of painting as a practice concerned with the production of visual effects. It is perhaps not purely coincidental that the three texts which most fully articulate his position, a long aesthetic treatise and two extended book reviews, appeared between 1805 and 1815 − after the height of counter-revolutionary hysteria, hence after the period when critics were most apt to characterize painting for effect as anti-English. Whereas after the publication of *The Landscape* in 1795, Knight's aesthetics were linked to his alleged "republican" sympathies, his later defense of virtuoso effects was not attacked in such overtly political terms.[84]

Knight set out his theory of painting quite succinctly in 1814:

> Painting is an imitation of nature, as seen by the eye, and not, as known or perceived by the aid of other senses; and this consideration, if duly attended to, is alone sufficient to guide both the artist and critic to the true principles of imitation.[85]

Unlike academic theorists, Knight insists that painting should depict precisely those impressions which constitute the visual field. Artists should paint what they see, not what they know via the other senses or reason. Peter Funnell has analysed the various ways in which this emphasis on visuality was promoted in Knight's writings, especially the *Analytical Inquiry into the Nature and Principles of Taste* (1805) and the review articles (on the life and writings of Barry and James Northcote's biography of Reynolds) that appeared in the *Edinburgh Review* in 1810 and 1814 respectively.[86] Knight's preference for Rembrandt and other seventeenth-century Dutch (and Flemish) masters over Raphael and Michelangelo; his emphasis on "massing" to indicate foliage and other forms that appear visually indistinct at a distance; and his championing of the visual variety associated with the picturesque all testify to his belief that the imitation of visual sense impressions should be the primary goal of the painter.[87]

In his *Inquiry* Knight takes pains to connect his theory of painting with scientific theories of vision based upon empirical evidence and upon the writings of Scottish philosopher Thomas Reid.[88] The intricacies of these arguments do not concern us here; what is important is that Knight legitimizes through the discourses of empirical science and philosophical criticism those elements of painting (color, effects of light and shade, the broad brushwork necessary for "massing") which the theory of academic practice denigrated in favor of drawing and composition.[89] We have seen that these are precisely the painterly effects that enhanced the ability of pictures to compete visually for attention in private chambers or public galleries.

This mode of legitimizing "painting for effect" was new and extremely powerful. In making a connection between art and science Knight was able to capitalize on the growing authority of empirical science, which was replacing religion as the ultimate ground of truth. Of course we recognize this transformation as a major effect of Enlightenment philosophy which was disseminated throughout Europe during the eighteenth century. However, as David Simpson has recently argued, since the seventeenth century the discourse of empiricism had been identified by intellectuals in Britain as a particularly "British" mode of knowledge, which was often defined in opposition to a quintessentially French fascination with "theory."[90]

However, Knight was not the man to promote English painting as a morally elevating nationalist enterprise through his linking of (British) theories of vision to painting. Throughout his writings he repeatedly refuses to grant painting a didactic or moral function beyond potentially diverting viewers from sensual pleasures of a more morally dubious nature. The point was made most vehemently in Knight's attack on James Barry and his didactic history paintings for the Society of Arts:

> He [Barry] disdained every thing in his art that was meant merely to please . . . ; that is, he disdained the art itself, whose end and purpose is to please; for, as to conveying religious, moral, or political instruction in pictures, it is the most absurd of all absurd notions.[91]

Knight did believe that painting could engage the feelings and sympathies of viewers, but located the source of such emotional responses outside the visual field of the canvas. Following the principles of associationist psychology elaborated by a host of British philosophers, most importantly David Hartley and Archibald Alison, Knight maintained that "meanings" and "feelings" apparently generated by pictures were in fact the result of trains of associated ideas which the images stimulated in the minds of spectators.[92] A number of scholars have analyzed at length Knight's use of associationist psychology to critique Edmund Burke's theory of the sublime, which locates the source of terror and awe within the object viewed, rather than the mind of the viewer.[93] What is important to note here is the differential *status* which Knight accords viewers and artists based upon their differential *relationship* to painting. Artists were to concern themselves with developing techniques necessary to produce images that imitate what is perceived visually; viewers, on the other hand, could augment their purely visual responses to these images via the "meanings" and "feelings" that they brought to them based upon their own experience.[94] This means, of course, that a liberally educated connoisseur with a broad knowledge of art, literature, and history, would have been able to derive an enhanced (or more profound) aesthetic pleasure from contemplating paintings than "educationally disadvantaged" individuals of the unpropertied classes, or, arguably, artists themselves.[95]

As if to emphasize this disjunction between making and viewing, Knight urged artists to avoid engaging with philosophical or aesthetic theories. He warned them "not to confound *painting* with the *knowledge* of it; nor suppose that the ideas, with which they have furnished their heads, will communicate any kind or degree of technical skill to their fingers."[96] In disparaging German history painter Anton Raphael Mengs, whose artistic practice was said to be grounded in the philosophy of Plato and Leibnitz, Knight declared his works to be lacking

> that expression of feeling and sentiment – that spontaneous and seemingly fortuitous facility and felicity of execution, which is acquired by practice guided by taste, but can neither be learned nor limited by rule; and which, more than any thing else, distinguishes liberal from mechanic art, and the artist from the artisan.[97]

Thus is the liberal artist redefined as a man of feeling and practical knowledge, not as a classicist or theoretician. This description of artistic character was not unique to Knight; as we shall see in the following chapters, it was deployed by artists, critics, and other commentators on landscape painting throughout the early 1800s. Crucially, however, such an artistic subject was usually seen to have a more exalted social function than merely providing occasions for cultivated viewers to experience aesthetic pleasure.

Whereas academic constructions of the liberal artist depended upon preserving the traditional hierarchy of genres, Knight repeatedly undermined the supremacy of history painting. Not only did he make the common observation that in an age of increasingly private patronage, huge paintings of religious and historical subjects had no market; he also mounted a theoretical attack on their size.[98] Pictures should be no larger than the area the human eye could take in all at once, for, he reasoned:

> When the whole of a picture does not come within the field of vision . . . it is too large; since its effect on the mind must necessarily be weakened by being divided, and the apt relation of the parts to each other, and to the whole, in which the merit of all composition consists, be less striking when gradually discovered than when seen at once.[99]

Once again, then, Knight turned to a seemingly "objective" and "scientific" theory of vision as a way of discrediting the most esteemed artistic genre – a novel move at a time when the debates around history painting centered on the highly politicized issue of patronage. On the same basis the connoisseur defended small-scale landscapes and genre scenes as taking up subject matter, which although "common" compared to the elevated subjects of history painting, produced new and pleasurable visual impressions, and thus were worthy of artistic representation.[100]

Despite his championing of lower genres and the subjective responses of viewers, however, Knight remained a universalist – no more than Barry did he advocate the production of a specifically English form of painting that instantiates an equally distinctive English character.[101] Like Barry he cautioned artists to avoid fluctuating fashions in art, and insisted that artists should choose subjects and modes of representation that have natural and universal appeal: "the less these natural modes are connected with those of local and temporary habit, the more strong and general will be the sympathies excited by them."[102]

As a landed proprietor and man of taste, Knight promoted an aesthetic that was clearly designed to elevate the prestige of the connoisseur at the expense of the "liberal" artist. Andrew Hemingway has stated that

[Knight's] . . . man of taste was not the artists' ideal of a landed patrician, who manifested virtue by promoting a monumental and patriotic public art, rather he was an aesthete delectating over the finer points of cabinet pictures in rural retirement.[103]

However, we have seen that in the early 1800s Knight and like-minded collectors and connoisseurs did not restrict their cultural activities to "delectating" over pictures in private. On the contrary, many of these men were variously involved in a spirited debate on public patronage of painting, the establishment of the British Institution, and, in Knight's case, in mounting a "scientific" defense of painting based upon seeing rather than knowing. All of these activities served to unsettle the notion that the establishment of a nationally acclaimed school of painting was irrevocably harmed by the persistence of a taste (variously characterized by its detractors as English or French) for visually arresting, small-scale, non-historical paintings. While these conflicts about the interrelationships of public taste, the English school, and national character raged unabated throughout the early years of the century, they did more than generate angry words and ingenious theories. By the end of the first decade of the century landscape painters such as Girtin, Callcott, and Turner would be heralded by many commentators as producing a new type of bravura painting which was capable of competing visually in the cultural market-place, while embodying those aspects of imagination and genius that were central to a certain ideal of English character. It is to this artistic undertaking that we now turn.

Chapter 3

The Domestic Landscape as Contested Ground: Amateur Dabblers versus Native Geniuses

WE HAVE EXAMINED HOW CRITICS, patrons, and artists assessed the social value and function of history painting and lesser genres such as landscape in the decades around 1800. At a time when many people were touting the benefits of a "free" competition in painting, others were making equally vocal demands that paintings eschew their status as commodities and instantiate those qualities of the national community consonant with, but separate from, the ability to accumulate wealth. The nature of the dilemma in which artists were placed by these dual demands is clearly illuminated by Martin Archer Shee's *Rhymes on Art*. On the one hand, the writer celebrates the competitive spirit that stimulates the production of Britain's commercial power and wealth, for it was this relentless competition that also gave birth to the arts and sciences: "From the grand collision of mind operating, and operated on, in this unremitting contest of rival hopes, pretensions, and powers, are struck out those brilliant sparks of civilization, those electric lights of arts and sciences, which irradiate the otherwise sombre scene of our existence."[1] On the other hand, Shee condemns those lower genres of painting which operate most effectively within such an arena; for him landscapes, genre scenes, and portraits are no more than luxury commodities, and thus incapable of representing the highest values of the English school. Was there, then, a form of painting which could function within a commercial arena, while seeming to rise above it?

Clearly history painting could not. Payne Knight's solution involved demoting history painting from its elevated position within the academic hierarchy and promoting landscape and genre painting, which exploited most fully visual effects based on the painterly manipulation of color, light, and shade. The very fact that Knight's *Analytical Inquiry* was inspired by a vigorous and very public debate with fellow Whig landowner Uvedale Price over the picturesque, a term primarily associated with representing and viewing the domestic landscape, is indicative of the increasing prestige accorded the landscape genre within aesthetic discourse at this time.[2] But for Knight, demoting history painting was possible because he had abandoned ethics as a regulatory discourse for painting in favor of scientific empiricism: he had no interest in defending landscape painting as a genre capable of instantiating intellectual, moral, or political character.

Within the artistic and political climate of the Napoleonic war years, however, such a position was practically untenable; throughout this period there was a strong and persistent demand for a form of native painting that inscribed English character. While that character might not be based upon the heroic, universalist ideals associated with republican virtue, it equally could not be represented as immoral, unnatural, and feminine – "foreign" qualities which were frequently associated with the English artists Knight most admired.

If landscape painting were to provide the "fertile soil" in which new forms of English identity could take root, then it is reasonable that artists and cultural commentators should look to the past for models on which to base a school of English landscape painting. The likeliest candidates were Richard Wilson and Thomas Gainsborough, who died in 1782 and 1788 respectively. In the 1790s the two artists were acknowledged as the leading British landscape painters of the eighteenth century; at this time Wilson's work was widely copied and imitated, as was, to a lesser degree, that of Gainsborough.[3] The British Institution attempted to place these artists in a quasi-official foundational position in 1814 by including them in their "British Masters" exhibition (which also included Reynolds, Hogarth, and Zoffany). However, even in the 1790s, and certainly after that time, there were indications that, while the names Wilson and Gainsborough often figured in accounts promoting the English school, these two artists were problematic models for young professionals embarking on a career in landscape painting.

There were, for example, economic signs in the years immediately following Gainsborough's death that his landscapes were flagging in popularity. John Hayes has noted that they fared poorly in the Schomberg House sale conducted the year after his death, slightly better in the Christie's sale of 1792, and sold at prices averaging well under 100 guineas in sales held in 1797 and 1799.[4] Although Wilson's classicized views did not come close to competing with those of Claude (which ranged in price from 1,000 to over 6,000 guineas), his works consistently outsold Gainsborough's – a version of Wilson's *Destruction of the Children of Niobe*, for example, fetching over 800 guineas in 1806.[5]

However, the relative popularity of Wilson's historical landscapes and Italian views in the 1790s did not lead to his instatement as *the* native landscape genius in the years to follow – quite the contrary. David Solkin has noted that during his lifetime Wilson's British views of rural scenery and country houses fared far less well than his foreign views and classical subjects. He suggests that Wilson's attempt to imbue these scenes "with a strong dose of the Grand Manner" prevented them from appealing to an expanding artistic public who possessed little or no knowledge of classical art and old master painting.[6] This judgment is borne out in the criticism of Wilson's domestic subjects beginning in the early 1800s and continuing up to and beyond the major exhibition of his works at the British Institution in 1814.

Typical of this criticism is Edward Edwards's remark, in his *Anecdotes of Painters* (1808), that Wilson's "English views . . . were rather too much Italianized to produce a correct similitude to the scenes, from which they were drawn."[7] This view is echoed by the *Sun* critic reviewing the "British Masters" exhibition of 1814. He writes that many of Wilson's English views "are not congenial to the soil and climate of England. They partake too much of southern skies, and lose the character which ought to belong to them, to acquire that of another quarter of the globe."[8]

If Wilson's classicized view of British scenery appeared too foreign to serve as a suitable model for painters of the domestic landscape, Gainsborough's landscapes posed other problems. For many years, the most widely publicized and debated discussion of Gainsborough's painting was that which appeared in Reynolds's Discourse XIV.[9] Delivered four months after his death, this "critical eulogy" provides some insight into why Gainsborough did not easily conform to the ideal of the native landscape genius as it was formulated in the years to come.

Like writers who came after him, Reynolds made a stylistic division between Gainsborough's early landscapes, in which he is seen closely to imitate common nature, and his later works, produced in a more mannered style. In discussing the early works, Reynolds praised Gainsborough's imitation of natural objects, gained (in hallowed academic fashion) both through empirical observation and by the study of seventeenth-century Netherlandish landscape painting. However, Reynolds was quick to point out that Gainsborough's attention to empirical detail and to Dutch and Flemish painting was not combined with an "academical education" and travel to Italy – experiences that were crucial to an academic history painter's training. The implication was that by focusing on empirical observation and painterly technique at the expense of liberal learning, Gainsborough rendered himself unable to produce pictures that carried any elevated meaning. In a well-known comment, Reynolds notes that "if Gainsborough did not look at nature with a poet's eye, it must be acknowledged that he saw her with the eye of a painter; and gave a faithful, if not a poetical, representation of what he had before him."[10] While such a statement represented the highest form of praise a writer like Payne Knight could give to a painter (because he felt painting had no elevated moral or intellectual function), for Reynolds it consigned Gainsborough to the rank of a "humble," if highly successful, practitioner in a "lower rank of art."[11]

Commentators in the early 1800s generally praised the early landscapes in much the same terms as Reynolds. Edward Edwards writes that in these works, "every part is copied from the detail of nature, with simple effect and artless description, sometimes in the style of Rysdale [*sic*]."[12] While Edwards clearly intends this to be a positive assessment, he does not suggest that such "artless" productions required those qualities of imagination which, as we shall see shortly, were associated with the artistic genius. In reviewing the British Institution exhibition of 1814 William Hazlitt judges Gainsborough's early landscapes to be better than his late ones, but his observation that the former "are imitations of nature, or of painters who imitated nature" comes close to damning the painter with faint praise.[13] As hostile to the Academy and academic training as Knight, Hazlitt does not fault Gainsborough for his lack of "academical education."[14] But for Hazlitt, like Reynolds, the power of imitation alone is insufficient to imbue the artist or the native landscape he represents with a highly distinctive character.

Contemporary commentators were even less enthusiastic about Gainsborough's later landscapes. Reynolds locates the problematic aspect of these works in the random and sketchy brushstrokes that characterized them.[15] He acknowledges that these "odd scratches and marks" were frequently taken as evidence of manner and negligence, although he claims to be impressed by the visual impact of such a technique. He observes that

> this chaos, this uncouth and shapeless appearance, by a kind of magick, at a certain distance assumes form, and all the parts seem to drop into their proper places; so that we can hardly refuse acknowledging the full effect of diligence under the appearance of chance and hasty negligence.[16]

Edward Edwards uses the same backhanded approach in his highly qualified judgment of these same late works, declaring "their execution more indeterminate, and (if the expression may be allowed) more licentious than those of the former class."[17] As Sam Smiles convincingly argues, describing loose brushwork via pejoratives such as "uncouth," "negligence," and "licentious," conventionally used to assess human character, was a common tactic employed throughout this period to discredit landscape artists who adopted a painterly style.[18] Such techniques were taken as signs that the artist was a lazy, morally debased creature unfit to assume the gentlemanly title of liberal artist (or arguably, the upstanding, if less socially elevated position of the industrious artisan). Smiles observes that these attacks often were designed to enforce a distinction between the slovenly execution of some contemporary English landscape painters and the breadth and bravura that marked the grand-style painting of the old masters.[19] Preserving the "purity" of the old masters clearly is of the utmost importance to academician John Hoppner when, in an unsigned review from 1809, he charges that Gainsborough's works were "polluted by that extravagance of a style making pretensions to a higher character."[20] The problem is not simply that Gainsborough had attempted to elevate landscape painting beyond its assigned station in the hierarchy of genres:

> Its principal defect seemed to be, that it neither presented the spectator with a faithful delineation of nature, nor possessed any just pretensions to be classed with the epic works of art; for the first, it was, both in its forms and effects, too general; and for the last, not sufficiently ideal or elevated.[21]

For Hoppner, then, Gainsborough had overreached himself, producing extravagantly generalized works that represented neither common nor ideal nature.

Gainsborough's "generalization" also surfaces as a tacitly acknowledged problem in John Britton's enthusiastic account of *The Cottage Door* (Figure 23, 1780). Britton's description (along with an engraving) of the work appeared in his *Fine Arts of the English School*, a lavish volume, issued originally in parts between 1810 and 1812, that combined short essays with predominantly stipple engravings. Patriotically promoting British artists, sculptors, architects, and engravers, it was, in a scaled-down way, an enterprise similar to Boydell's.[22] Consistent with the nationalistic tone of the volume, Britton claims that Gainsborough's best landscapes "proved him to be a genuine English artist. They have a decided national character; and will never be mistaken for the landscapes of Wynants, Hobbima, Ruysdael, or Poussin."[23] However, when he turns to describing the *Cottage Door* it was the un-English and unnatural aspects of the characterization that claimed his attention:

> It has the true character of pastoral simplicity; but, like the eclogues of the poets, it heightens and exaggerates natural objects: the female figure is rather more

23   Thomas Gainsborough, *Wooded Landscape with Peasant Family at a Cottage Door and Foot-bridge over a Stream (The Cottage Door)*, 1780. Oil on canvas, 58 × 47 in. Henry E. Huntington Library and Art Gallery, San Marino, CA.

Arcadian than English, and the colouring and effects are more imaginary than real.[24]

Britton implies that in seeking to elevate his painting to the level of the poetic, Gainsborough had sacrificed what was English and natural.

As noted above, Gainsborough and Wilson were often invoked as "founding fathers" of the English school in discussions of domestic landscape painting in the early nineteenth century and beyond. Despite this fact, and the fact that certain aspects of their work were also praised, by the early 1800s the general pictorial solutions these artists had developed in attempting to elevate landscape painting beyond the level of topography had become highly problematic: neither Wilson's idealized Italianate vistas nor Gainsborough's "licentious" and "mannered" displays were able to satisfy the growing demand for representations inscribing the external "truth" and the internal "character" of English nature.

It could reasonably be argued that if Gainsborough failed to provide a viable model for ambitious young professionals working in the early 1800s, his broadly sketched views of English scenery did have an impact on amateurs through his influence on the formation of the picturesque.[25] This is not only the judgment of modern scholars, but that of the author (probably W.H. Pyne) of an 1813 essay on watercolor; he credits Gainsborough with inducing artists to look to the English countryside for subject matter, and with providing the "designs" that produced a "love of the picturesque" among artists and amateurs.[26] This linking of the picturesque with the practice of amateurs, however, presented a problem for those artists who sought to earn a living at landscape painting: in order to be recognized as professionals, they had to distinguish their practice from that of the growing numbers of amateurs engaged in sketching and painting picturesque views of English scenery.

Occupying, as it were, the middle ground between topographical painting (regarded as the lowliest sub-genre of landscape, related to surveying and map-making) and an increasingly irrelevant form of classically idealized landscape painting was the picturesque landscape, which drew from both traditions.[27] The most authoritative writer on the picturesque was the Whig landowner Uvedale Price. In an essay published in 1801, Price insists that beauty is universally recognizable, so a cultivated taste for pictures or natural scenery is not demonstrated by an appreciation of beautiful vistas or the representation of ideal forms. On the contrary, it is the ability to derive aesthetic pleasure from the "deformities" of common nature that distinguishes the man of taste.[28] An untrained viewer would undoubtedly react to a scene of hovels, dunghills, and ragged old women with disgust, whereas a connoisseur, schooled in the appreciation of old master painting, would be able to derive aesthetic pleasure from such figures and objects, based on the visual variety and contrast they afforded.[29] While Richard Payne Knight disagreed with his friend Price about the existence of the picturesque as a distinctive aesthetic category, we have seen that he, too, regarded a learned awareness of continental art as a precondition for a full appreciation of a landscape composed of such elements.[30] Such an educated awareness was, of course, predicated upon much the same social and economic criteria that defined the man of letters – the leisure and social access to education, travel, and the paintings themselves that only a substantial degree of wealth could provide.[31]

However, the picturesque was not a monolithic category, but a term associated with cultural practices ranging from landscape gardening and the appreciation of old masters to domestic touring and amateur sketching. These activities involved different aesthetic principles and engaged different publics.[32] While landscape gardening required the ownership of real property and the desire to effect "improvements" to that property, picturesque touring and sketching were based neither upon landed ownership nor on the leisure and education associated with it.

In the years under consideration here, roughly 1790 to 1820, the chief popularizer of this latter form of the picturesque was the Reverend William Gilpin, whose directives regarding picturesque sketching and viewing circulated as illustrated tour guides to domestic scenery. His essays and tours were designed to train tourists to see domestic scenery through the mediating structures of landscape painting, and then to translate this composed vision of nature into their own drawings. Far from being exclusively designed for the liberally educated connoisseur or the professional artist, such a practice, Gilpin writes in *Three Essays on Picturesque Beauty* (1792), is ideally suited to the bourgeois amateur. Whereas history painting and portraiture are too difficult to execute, "the art of *sketching landscapes* is attainable by a man of business; and it is certainly more useful; and I should imagine, more amusing, to attain *some* degree of excellence in an inferior branch, than to be a mere bungler in a superior."[33] Sketching landscapes, then, was an accessible cultural accomplishment for the man of business, who perhaps had the time to take a summer tour of the Lake District, Wales, or Scotland, but did not have the time or the motivation of the professional artist to take up the serious study of painting.

The type of drawing advocated by Gilpin can be found in graphic form not only in his tour guides and essays, published in the final decades of the eighteenth century, but also in prints after his drawings which continued to be issued in the nineteenth century.[34] Typical of Gilpin's many picturesque views of the Lake District is the oval pen and wash drawing (Figure 24) now in the British Museum.[35] The three figures looking across the lake provide a point of identification for the viewer, whose touristic gaze traverses the landscape in order to possess it visually, rather than inhabit it corporeally as either a proprietor or a laborer.[36] The composition is organized into a clearly delineated foreground, middle ground and brightly lit background, bracketed by side-screens of sketchily denoted trees. Although Gilpin preferred this format, derived from the compositions of Claude, other practitioners of the picturesque based their compositions on those of the Dutch masters, such as Ruysdael and Hobbema. Whether or not an identifiably Dutch or Italian model was followed, the format of a picturesque composition usually can be seen to conform to such a structure of well-marked planes receding into distance, framed at least on one side by trees, a road, or rock formations.

For Gilpin, as for Price, the hallmark of the picturesque is variety and contrast, discernible in this scene in the trees with their sinuous, intertwined trunks and clumps of foliage silhouetted against the sky. Enhancing the picturesque effect are the masses of the mountains and clouds, which take their shape from irregular blots of ink, applied in unmodulated shades of black and grey. This drawing boasts additional sources of contrast in the dramatic white highlights on the cliff in the center, the far shore of the lake, and the area of sky above the center mountain

24 William Gilpin, *View in the Lake District*, n.d. Pencil, india ink, and watercolor, 9 × 6.8 in. (oval). British Museum, London.

peak. The curvilinear pen strokes visible throughout the drawing have the air of being quickly laid down, and operate as a sort of glyphic shorthand designed to suggest rather than detail a mass of foliage or the irregular contours of a hillside.

Gilpin's emphases on massing, effects of light and shade, and irregular forms are consistent with an attention to visuality that marks the writings of another advocate of the picturesque, Richard Payne Knight. Like Knight, Gilpin does not claim that the act of viewing or sketching the native landscape has significant moral or intellectual value.[37] However, in his tours, aquatints of his drawings appear in tandem with written descriptions of the sites represented; and those descriptions frequently included moral and political judgments.[38] For example, in his Wye Tour, the section on Tintern Abbey contains two aquatints of the Abbey (Figures 25 and 26), an extended discussion of the picturesque and unpicturesque aspects of the site, and concludes with a lengthy account of the poverty of the local inhabitants: "They occupy little huts, raised among the ruins of the monastery, and seem to have no employment but begging; as if a place once devoted to indolence could never again

25   William Sawrey Gilpin after William Gilpin, *View of Tintern Abbey*. Aquatint in *Observations on the River Wye, and Several Parts of South Wales, etc. Relative Chiefly to Picturesque Beauty; Made in the Summer of the Year 1770*, London, 1782. Brown University Library, Providence, RI (photo: Brooke Hammerle).

26   William Sawrey Gilpin after William Gilpin, *View of Tintern Abbey*. Aquatint in *Observations on the River Wye, and Several Parts of South Wales, etc. Relative Chiefly to Picturesque Beauty; Made in the Summer of the Year 1770*, London, 1782. Brown University, Library, Providence, RI (photo: Brooke Hammerle).

become the seat of industry."[39] Although the huts and beggars are pointedly excluded from Gilpin's drawings, they appear in the text, not as signs of contemporary economic inequality, but as the living traces of an "indolent" Catholic past.

Ann Bermingham has recently stated that while Gilpin's tours were highly popular, his drawings were not: disillusioned tourists complained that Gilpin's picturesque sketches bore little resemblance to the actual sites depicted.[40] However, it would be a mistake to underestimate the impact of Gilpin, who popularized the notion that moderately circumstanced, literate, middle-class people were capable of making aesthetic judgments and were also capable of "realizing" those judgments in the form of sketches and drawings. Furthermore, Gilpin offered this public a model for sketching English nature that was relatively undemanding compared to the technical requirements of professional drawing instruction. Picturesque sketching, then, had the potential of aesthetically empowering a middle-class public, while devaluing the status of professional landscape painters to that of the casual tourist or the amateur dabbler. It is no wonder that, as Bermingham has shown, artists, engravers, and others invested in domestic landscape production were often quite vehement in their objections to Gilpin's enterprise.[41]

Of course Gilpin alone could not be credited with (or blamed for) for the increased activity of amateurs in sketching and painting the domestic landscape. The years around 1800 were marked not only by a growth in the number of domestic tourists, but also by a greater number of amateurs seeking various types of musical and artistic instruction – the latter from drawing masters and/or drawing manuals.[42] In a review of the watercolor exhibitions of 1810 a writer for the *Repository of Arts* alludes to this increased activity when he expresses concern over the quality of works on display. He explains that mediocrity was a signal feature of landscape painting, "because, to a certain degree, its requisites are within the reach of almost every capacity. A mechanical expertness in delineation, and a tolerable proficiency in colouring, may be attained by a course of lessons from a drawing-master." The critic goes on to encourage artists to persevere in their study and exert their mental powers.[43]

The technical accessibility of landscape was particularly troublesome for professional watercolor artists, since theirs was the medium of choice for amateurs. Complicating the relationship between watercolor artists and amateurs was the fact that the latter were not only producers of landscapes, but also consumers. They often purchased professionally made watercolors, patronized public exhibitions, and supported a small but vital watercolor industry which sold pigments, paper, brushes, drawing books, and the like. It is not surprising to find that the most extensive, and frequently the most enthusiastic, reviews of the work of professional landscape painters (in both oil and watercolor), such as Turner, Girtin, Callcott, and John Varley, were published in the *Repository of Arts* when one considers that its publisher was Rudolf Ackermann. The fashionable *Repository*, which began publication in 1809, targeted a polite female readership that formed the primary market for Ackermann's other art-related publications, and for the art supplies which were sold at his business in the Strand.[44] Within the micro-economy of Ackermann's enterprise, professional and amateur were locked in a symbiotic relationship. Professionals needed the financial support and publicity supplied by amateurs and the watercolor industry. Hailed as geniuses, a number of professional landscape painters were directly employed by Ackermann, more as artisans than artists, in the mundane task of supplying drawings for his illustrated books.[45] Amateurs were placed in an equally ambiguous, although less economically fraught relationship to professionals: they were encouraged to emulate and admire the great achievements of the newly emergent and triumphant English school of watercolor and yet tacitly discouraged from believing they could ever attain this level of genius themselves.

The existence of this double bind for amateurs was most pronounced in the treatment of female amateurs and perhaps most evident in exhibition reviews. Considering that the *Repository of Arts* solicited a female readership, one might expect exhibition reviews to highlight the productions of the women artists who displayed their work at the Royal Academy and the British Institution, as well as at exhibitions of the Society of Painters in Water-Colours (first exhibition, 1805), and the Associated Artists in Water-Colours (first exhibition, 1808). In fact the *Repository* gave *less* coverage to women exhibitors than did other periodicals.[46] In 1819, for example, the magazine published a five-page review of the British Institution exhibition; included was a one-and-a-half-page review extolling John Martin's *The Fall of Babylon*, another half-page devoted to a work by David Wilkie, and a concluding comment about women artists: "Miss H. Gouldsmith has some pleasing landscapes in this gallery and several other ladies have been equally successful contributers – We regret extremely that we have not room at present to enter into a detailed description of their works."[47] The message here is clear – within the public sphere of culture constituted by the periodical press, there is literally no "space" for serious discussion of work by either female amateurs or professional women artists.[48] One way of preserving the hierarchy which distinguished the male professional from the female amateur, then, was to restrict the discursive field in which women's productions could be discussed. What needs to be emphasized, however, is not only that male professionals had to distance themselves from women artists, but also that they *needed* them – as a crucial economic support, and as an "Other" against which a distinctively masculine, professional artistic subjectivity could be inflected. While women artists could not be lauded in the same terms as their male counterparts, it wouldn't do to ignore them altogether.

One sphere in which gender operated to distinguish professional from amateur subjectivity was in literary satires on the picturesque.[49] For example, in Chapter 18 of *Sense and Sensibility* (1811) Marianne, Jane Austen's exemplar of sensibility, feelingly describes a view of the surrounding countryside in picturesque terms. Her expressions of delight are countered by the "sensible" Edward's rejoinder; his pleasures, he insists, derive from wholly utilitarian judgments about the productivity of the timber and farms that fall within his gaze. Within the parameters of Austen's commentary on contemporary manners and morals, picturesqueness and utility are gendered signifiers of the undesirable extremes of sensibility – the former representing its excess, the latter its absence.

The picturesque could not only represent excessive sensibility, but could signify that equally feminized quality, capriciousness. In his comic opera *The Lakers* (unperformed, but published in 1797), the Reverend James Plumptre, an experienced and avid tourist, gently satirizes Gilpinesque drawing practices through the medium of a female character. Miss Beccabunga Veronica, a wealthy amateur botanist in search of a titled husband, has recourse to the picturesque to defend certain "renovations" she has wrought in a landscape she has drawn: "I have only made it picturesque. I have only given the hills an Alpine form, and put some wood where it is wanted, and omitted it where it is not wanted and who would put that sham church and that house into a picture? It quite *antipathizes*."[50] Feminine capriciousness is here conflated with and defended by a picturesque vocabulary and visual practice which had become the hallmarks of the tourist.

The identification of excessive sensibility and capriciousness as feminine traits that are associated with the amateur practice of the picturesque takes on heightened significance considering how closely these characteristics are related to "feeling" (or sentiment) and "imagination" – qualities that were seen to define a masculine genius for landscape painting. What kind of visual language could serve to distinguish imagination from caprice and an excessive sensibility excited by nature and "performed" before others from a sincere feeling for nature? This visual language would need to be readily distinguishable from that used in picturesque sketching and other types of amateur practice, while at the same time would have to compete successfully with the eye-catching effects so reviled by critics and so popular with consumers.[51] In order to identify with some specificity the formal strategies that were being developed by young professionals, let us consider one of Thomas Girtin's watercolor views of Kirkstall Abbey (Figure 27, 1800). As Lindsay Stainton observes, the artist has chosen for his subject a domestic tourist attraction with suitably picturesque features: an abbey replete with meandering river, variegated clumps of trees and brush, rural laborers and rustic cottages. But, as she goes on to point out, Girtin has represented this assemblage in a manner which would have been regarded as wholly unpicturesque.[52] A low viewpoint, so strongly recommended by Gilpin and so frequently employed at this time by both amateur and professional landscape painters, is eschewed here in favor of the panoramic view associated with topographical drawing.[53] However, Girtin's handling of incidental detail and atmospheric effects distinguishes his landscape from topographical drawings, picturesque sketches, and oil paintings. In the view of Kirkstall Abbey, foreground details are suppressed; similarly, the irregularities of the surrounding hills and the intricacies of the ruined abbey and rural dwellings are de-emphasized and subsumed into the sweeping movement of a panorama dominated by a storm-darkened sky. Although the range of colors in the work is severely limited, part of the drama and visual interest of the composition lies in the application of broad washes of color – blue, set against the gray and white of the clouds above, and the nearly monotone brown of the landscape below – punctuated by the brilliant white of the abbey, the sheen of the river, and the lights dappling the hills.

An examination of contemporary manuals designed to teach landscape watercolor and oil techniques attests to the fact that the techniques used in producing a picture like *Kirkstall Abbey* are precisely those which novices are encouraged to avoid. For example, in 1800 James Roberts published an *Introductory Lesson . . . in Landscape*, a watercolor manual that emphasizes drawing skills as the key to achieving success. Throughout the text he warns against the use of color for the first year or more.[54] This repeated warning may strike the modern reader as odd considering

27 Thomas Girtin, *Kirkstall Abbey*, 1800. Watercolor, 12.5 × 20.2 in. British Museum, London.

that this is not a drawing manual, *per se*, but one that purports to teach skills in watercolor painting. After the initial warning on page one, he reiterates the point on page two, asserting that "the student should be able to sketch with a vigor and freedom, before he bewilders himself with the seducing witchery of colours."[55] This rhetoric, as noted in Chapter 2, took its authority and currency from a highly politicized cultural discourse which invoked the specter of a foreign (read French) feminized taste that threatened to corrupt (manly) English art, especially landscape painting. Although Roberts does not condemn specific artists by name in his landscape manual, he does warn his readers against imitating "the flutter of the French school," which he describes as "unnatural and eye-piercing."[56]

William Gilpin also discourages his readers from attempting to produce highly colored watercolor drawings, despite his enthusiastic descriptions of the various color effects and tints that enhance the picturesque effect of natural scenery.[57] In *Three Essays on Picturesque Beauty* (1792) he notes that such activities are the precinct of the professional and can only bring frustration and failure to the amateur. While some gentlemen "who draw for amusement, go so far as to handle the pallet," he warned that "[p]ainting, is both a science and an art: and if so very few attain perfection, who spend a life-time at it, what can be expected of those, who only spend their leisure?"[58] Like Roberts, Gilpin regards color as technically difficult to control, although unlike the drawing master, he did not invoke moral or nationalist rhetoric in advising against its use by the young and inexperienced.

Beyond associating color and glittering surfaces with moral depravity and the art of England's military enemy and cultural rival, Roberts also stresses the extraordinary skill needed to employ color in producing naturalistic effects of sunlight, mists, and other atmospheric phenomena: it is difficult, he writes, "to seize upon the transient and ever-varying beauties produced by flying clouds and the various evanescent effects, which often elude the grasp, and mock the skill of the able professor."[59] Both Gilpin and Roberts are committed to the promotion of amateur practice, but their technical provisos are predicated upon a sharp division between the cautious, rule-bound amateur and the bold, knowledgeable professional.[60] Taken in this context, Girtin's *Kirkstall Abbey* could almost be said to form a compendium of effects and techniques to be studiously avoided by all but the most skilled professional.

It could be fairly argued, however, that the assertively anti-picturesque *Kirkstall Abbey* represents a loaded case. Girtin, Turner, and most other landscape painters at this time regularly used some compositional structures and devices associated with the picturesque (framing devices, low viewpoints, emphasis on irregular forms, and so forth). These techniques were, after all, central to the practice of landscape painting as it had developed over the seventeenth and eighteenth centuries. In addition, the market value of the term "picturesque," especially in the print trade, guaranteed its regular inclusion in the title of works like W. B. Cooke's *Picturesque Views of the Southern Coast of England* (issued in parts between 1814 and 1826). This collection included engravings after drawings by Turner which radically reworked, rather than wholly rejected picturesque conventions.[61] Nonetheless, when the landscapes of Turner, Girtin, Callcott, Fielding, and other critically acclaimed painters of the early 1800s were evaluated by art critics or other artists, the term "picturesque," with its connotations of amateurism, was rarely used, regardless of whether the criticism was positive or negative.

Changes in the professional practice of landscape painting eventually affected amateur practice as well. Around 1800 several instructional manuals appeared which de-emphasized drawing in favor of color. However, this new emphasis on color seemed guaranteed to produce pictures that would look wildly out of date by contemporary professional standards. One of the most successful authors and publishers of such guides to color was Carrington Bowles: his *Art of Painting in Water Colours* went through eighteen editions by 1818 and his *Art of Painting in Oil* was in its ninth edition in 1817. In the former work, Bowles's instructions focus on the mixing of pigments, not on the use of new types of paper, pigment, and techniques (high-keyed washes, scraping, stopping out) which were transforming professional watercolor practice.[62] Likewise his advice to amateur oil painters remained rooted in what he perceives to be the old master tradition. In *The Art of Painting in Oil* he recommends that "landscapes should be painted on a sort of tanned-leather coloured canvas."[63] The enterprising amateur is then cautioned to refrain from using high-key color, but to "incline to the middle teint [rather] than to the very high lights."[64] Denying any distinction between contemporary British painting and that

28   [After David Cox?], *Kennelworth Castle, Warwickshire*. Aquatint in *Ackermann's New Drawing Book of Light and Shadow*, London, 1812. Yale Center for British Art, Paul Mellon Collection, New Haven.

of the old masters so prized by British collectors, such a manual, then, teaches amateurs to paint pictures which look as if they are two hundred years old.

Considering his investment in modern forms of domestic landscape painting and the technology that supported it, one might expect Rudolph Ackermann to promote these new techniques to amateurs. And indeed, *Ackermann's New Drawing Book of Light and Shadow* (1812) was ostensibly designed to teach novices how to produce those atmospheric effects increasingly heralded by writers and critics in works on landscape painting. However, the crude aquatints of standard picturesque subjects that are reproduced in the book would have offered little aid to the aspiring amateur wishing to produce a work possessing subtle nuances of shading or dramatic illumination. The emphasis is upon the juxtapositioning of landscape elements simplified into schematized masses of unmodulated gray. Thus in the view of Kenilworth Castle (Figure 28), the rules of atmospheric perspective are illustrated (or more accurately, belabored) in placing the uniformly darkened ruins nearest to the viewer against the lightly tinted, less distinctly rendered parts of the castle complex that are most distant. Augmenting these heavy-handed atmospheric effects are the sharply delineated shafts of light that stream down from the clouds in wide, unmodulated bands.[65] The text accompanying the plates sheds no further light on how to execute the subject; technical directions are cursory and vague.

The book, in fact, functions less as a how-to manual than as a paean to professional English watercolorists.[66] The introduction sets the tone by tracing a history of watercolor from Thomas Hearne and Paul Sandby to Richard Westall, whose works are described as "elegant and masterly."[67] Since that time, the author continues, "a constellation of geniuses has arisen; of whom were Girtin, whose works were distinguished by a force of colouring which astonished . . . and Turner, who has united in his drawings every excellence that powerful genius and fine feeling could accomplish."[68] The distinctions between terms such as "elegant" and "masterly" (the first being commonly associated with the manners and polite accomplishments of genteel society) and those used to describe these newer artists and their work – "force," "excellence," "powerful genius," and "fine feeling" – are distinctions of type rather than degree. Turner and Girtin are not simply more elegant and masterly than Westall and Sandby, but possess both a sublime and a masculine intellectual force and a sensibility (that did not veer into feminine excess) which increasingly came to characterize the native genius.

Although the term "genius" was occasionally applied to women artists, when intended to convey the sense of singularity (having a particular genius "for" a given type of endeavor), as it is used by the author of Ackermann's *New Drawing Book*, it is taken to mean a specifically masculine creative power. This point is underscored by a passage that follows the above-cited account of the stellar appearance of genius in the English firmament:

> It is with feelings of national exultation, that we can ascribe, in a great degree, this improvement in so elegant a department of the fine arts, to our lovely countrywomen. It is to the cultivation of the study of drawing in watercolours, by the enlightened ladies of our time that the best artists have owed their encouragement; and the patronage of the fair sex has thus produced an epoch in art which will be a lasting honour to the country.[69]

Women support national genius by studying, encouraging, and patronizing the work of "the best artists," who, according to the list of names the writer goes on to supply, are all men. This promotion of women as consumers rather than producers of art is consistent with the accounts of women artists published in Ackermann's *Repository* examined above.[70] Not only does such a position deny female creativity; taken as a general principle, it also seeks to exclude women from participating actively and directly in the production of national identity.

Pronouncements about the characteristics that define the professional landscape painter were not confined to artists working in watercolor. This point is forcefully made by William Hazlitt in connection with Thomas Gainsborough, who then, as now, was known primarily for his work in oils. We have already noted that Hazlitt's opinion of Gainsborough's painting, published on the occasion of the "British Masters" exhibition of 1814, accords generally with the views of many of his contemporaries: he prefers the artist's earlier works which "are imitations of nature, or of painters who imitated nature" to the later pictures "which are flimsy caricatures of Rubens."[71] Although he voices mild praise for some of the early landscapes, Hazlitt is not inclined to think highly of any artist whose signal accomplishment is imitating others – as is quite apparent in the conclusion of the essay. Here he levels his harshest criticism by claiming that Gainsborough did not exhibit the character of a professional but that of a gentleman amateur:

> He was to be considered, perhaps, rather as a man of taste, and of an elegant and feeling mind, than as a man of genius; as a lover of the art, rather than an artist. He pursued it, with a view to amuse and sooth his mind, with the ease of a gentleman, not with the severity of a professional student. He wished to make his pictures, like himself, amiable; but a too constant desire to please almost necessarily leads to affectation and effeminacy. He wanted that vigour of intellect, which perceives the beauty of truth; and thought that painting was to be gained, like other mistresses, by flattery and smiles.[72]

Reynolds had labeled Gainsborough's late style "uncouth," a term that rendered a social and moral judgment in terms of strangeness and incivility. Hazlitt, on the other hand, does not accuse Gainsborough of baseness or barbarity, but of a form of affectation and negligence located firmly in the (over)refined aristocratic sphere of the gentleman. In fact, Hazlitt's remarks are as much an attack on the ideal of the leisured gentleman as on Gainsborough. The radical essayist identifies the gentleman as lacking in discipline, industry, and intellectual power. Divested of any notion of virtue (public or otherwise) and intellectual superiority, the gentleman as man of taste and amateur lover of art is presented as an idler, given over to elegant pleasures and amusements that soothe rather than actively engage his mind. He is a courtier who attempts to "win" painting, personified as a mistress, through the devices of flattery. This indolent, effeminate creature, Hazlitt tells his readers, has nothing in common with genius, which achieves success in painting by the manly application of a powerful intellect, a keen perception, and a professional's willingness to study.

The polarities which Hazlitt sets up between the professional (middle-class) genius and the leisured (aristocratic) amateur take both their language and social relevance from contemporary debates in which Hazlitt himself was involved regarding the social utility of the leisured classes as consumers. As a response to Napoleon's blockade of British ports, the British government passed in 1806 the Orders in Council. The Orders placed severe restrictions on foreign trade that proved far more injurious to manufacturers than to agricultural interests. In seeking the repeal of the Orders, the trade and manufacturing interest contrasted their own productivity with the unproductivity of landowners, who were merely consumers of luxury goods. In response, writers such as William Spence reiterated the defense of luxury consumption by the landed interest as a crucial activity, productive of national wealth.[73] Hazlitt entered into this debate in 1807 in an essay attacking the writings of Thomas Malthus, who, in elaborating his controversial theory of population and agricultural production, defended the importance of landed proprietors in stimulating domestic manufacture by their luxury consumption.[74]

Hazlitt's *Extracts from the "Essay on Population" with a Commentary and Notes* contained a lengthy diatribe against consumption by the rich, linking it directly to the impoverishment of the laboring classes.[75] He concluded by asking: "Have not the government and the rich had their way in every thing? Have they not gratified their ambition, their pride, their obstinacy, their ruinous extravagance? Have they not squandered the resources of the country as they pleased?"[76] The essayist's remarks on Gainsborough were far less heated than these angry interrogatives, but their underlying intent was remarkably similar. The wealthy leisured gentleman could no longer provide a model for serious artists to emulate; genius was the self-conscious antithesis of that effete and corrupted ideal – productive, studious, and manly.

Despite the fact that Rudolph Ackermann was a conservative who vigorously opposed the radical views expressed by Hazlitt, his publications support the basic association of genius and professionalism propounded by Hazlitt. As is evident in the *Repository*, deference is paid to the landed aristocracy and nobility, but their engagement with high culture is constructed *in the same way* as that assigned to upper middle-class women – primarily as that of consumers and enthusiasts. Within the domain of production, they participate only as amateurs, lacking the professional expertise either to produce paintings of "national" significance or to pronounce upon them publicly.[77]

Following his paean to English geniuses the author of *Ackermann's New Drawing Book* goes on to detail the changes that these male artists introduced in the production of landscape watercolors: "The incidents of light and shadow being admitted to constitute a very material part of the beauty of a landscape, the improved state of landscape painting may be attributed to the mode of practice of the artists of our day." Referring to practices which marked both topographical and classical landscape painting, he observes that formerly there was an overemphasis on outline and linear accuracy. But now artists such as Turner, Girtin, John Glover, William Havell, and John Varley "judiciously sacrifice the minutiae of details to the general effect, or sentiment of the subject."[78] Genius here is associated with specific techniques – the use of light and shade, rather than outline – in order to communicate a general "sentiment" to the viewer.

Although the "breadth" achieved through painterly effects had long been praised in academic discourse as a way of producing feeling and expression, these effects were always to be deployed in a manner which would enhance, not replace, the delineation of form through outline and subtle modeling. It was necessary for form and line to predominate over color and light to ensure that the meaning of the representation would be fixed and unambiguous. The point was made forcefully by Henry Fuseli, who declared in a lecture before the Academy in 1801 that

> languages perish; words succeed each other, become obsolete and die; even colours, the dressers and ornaments of bodies, fade; lines alone can neither be obliterated nor misconstrued; by application to their standard alone, discrimination takes place, and description becomes intelligible.[79]

To allow color and light effects to dominate drawing would result in the effacement of both the physical object represented and its expressive character. The resultant composition would be little more than an ornamental surface, incapable of registering anything beyond the (self-interested) "manner" of the artist himself.[80]

Academic discourse does allow for this type of "ornamental" practice in the case of "uninteresting" and "negative" subjects (the terms are Fuseli's) such as portraiture, low-life scenes, and common landscape paintings.[81] These pejoratives appear in Fuseli's notorious attack on landscape painting in his Academy lecture on "Invention."[82] He labels as "uninteresting"

> that kind of landscape which is entirely occupied with the tame delineation of a given spot: an enumeration of hill and dale, clumps of trees, shrubs, water, meadows, cottages, and houses; what is commonly called views. These, if not assisted by nature, dictated by taste, or chosen for character, may delight the owner of the acres they enclose, the inhabitants of the spot, perhaps the antiquary or the traveller, but to every other eye they are little more than topography.[83]

Such a form of painting is problematic because it requires no more than the imitation of common nature, and therefore accords the artist a mechanical role – the production of "map-work" as Fuseli terms it in the continuation of this passage. He explains that the interest accruing to this class of painting "depends entirely on the manner of treating; such subjects owe what they can be to the genius of the Artist."[84] Paintings of "common" landscapes could provide the site upon which a certain type of genius could display itself – where the artist could reveal his "character" through displays of a personal manner.

This tenet of academic discourse in England is all too frequently overlooked in discussions of early nineteenth-century landscape painting. That English landscape painting could serve as a site for the inscription of a new form of individual identity in large part derives from the fact that within the parameters of academicism landscape painting was *already* designated as the place where the "personal" could be inscribed, not only via the choice of subject matter, but also through a self-declaredly individual "manner." That said, within academic discourse such productions of genius could not claim to have anything but a private function, since the objects depicted were deemed incapable of addressing a public (whether constituted as a "universal" republic of taste or a national community of citizens).[85]

In his remarks on landscape Fuseli makes no distinction between picturesque views and those more "naturalistic" studies which emphasized atmospheric effects. However, he does indicate that landscapes displaying character and/or taste have the potential to transcend the category of topography. Nonetheless, Turner was so disturbed by Fuseli's remarks that he requested John Britton to publish a rebuttal to them in his *Fine Arts of the English School*, which included an engraving of Turner's *Pope's Villa at Twickenham* (Figure 29; 1812).[86] The publisher acquiesced, including his comments in the context of a paean to Wilson in which Britton disparages Fuseli's comments and then goes on to defend the representation of particular locales. Although he agrees with Fuseli that artists who copy nature indiscriminately are unworthy of notice, he also insists that

> the artist who, like Wilson and Turner, after having chosen a scene for pictorial representation, can portray all the local features of that scene, and at the same

Clafs t. Painting   for "the Fine Arts of the English School"

29   John Pye (with figures by Charles Heath) after J. M. W. Turner, *Pope's Villa at Twickenham*. Copperplate engraving in *Fine Arts of the English School*, London, 1812. British Museum, London.

time embellish them with the most favourable effects of light and shade, sun, mist, cloud, and varied colours of the season, is entitled to our admiration and praise. It speaks a language to be understood by all persons of every nation and every situation in life; because the scenery of nature is unfolded to all eyes, and "he who runs may read."[87]

Both academic discourse and Britton's text associate circumstantial effects with a broad public, extending well beyond the classically educated elite interpellated by history painting. But while academic discourse associates these dazzling visual displays with the sensuous desires of the "vulgar" and the self-interest of artists who pander to them, Britton describes the same effects as an international "language" for representing a subject matter – "the scenery of nature" – that all people can understand and appreciate. The artists engaged in this project are not to be reviled,

Britton argues, but highly esteemed. This defense of a "democratic" form of landscape painting was undoubtedly based partly on Britton's political convictions, which tended toward radicalism.[88] But economic motives would have reinforced this appeal to the literate classes deprived of a liberal education: as a publisher involved in the reproduction of landscape paintings as prints, he wanted to obtain as wide a market as possible for his wares.

One did not have to be a radical to embrace a form of landscape painting whose truth claims are bound up with the representation of naturalistic effects based upon direct observation of domestic scenery. Recently a number of scholars, including John Barrell, John Murdoch, and Ann Bermingham, have argued that the turn from a universalist aesthetic in history and landscape painting was effected by reworking the discourse of nature to inflect the customary and the local rather than the ideal and the transnational.[89] This new aesthetic discourse of common and local nature was ideologically charged insofar as it was related to a conservative (and specifically counter-revolutionary) rejection of a political ideology grounded in universal human nature which, by the 1790s, formed the basis for radical republicanism in both France and England (most notably in the works of Thomas Paine).

In counter-revolutionary political discourse "nature" represented the customary order of culture and society as it had been in the past, and would be in the present if not contaminated by new and artificial principles. "Customary" in this context referred to those accidental, particular, and local features that a society had acquired throughout its history and that rendered it distinct from others.[90] This association of custom with nature and the natural was a signal feature of Burke's *Reflections on the Revolution in France* (1790) which turned on a comparison between the monstrous artificiality of abstract systems of democratic rule in France and the naturalness of the British constitution, which was based upon customary rights of property and the traditional authority of kings, clergy, and aristocracy.[91]

As David Simpson has shown, in the aftermath of the French Revolution, this association of nature with traditional authority reaffirmed a long-standing distinction between a self-declaredly "British" empiricism, derived from the natural philosophy of Locke and Bacon, and "French" theory.[92] Even Payne Knight, who had been attacked in the 1790s by anti-Jacobins for seeming to embrace revolutionary principles in *The Landscape*, adopts this form of counter-revolutionary rhetoric in his attack on the artistic judgment of James Barry in 1810. Barry, whose attachment to democratic politics was widely known, is chastised by Knight for accepting the "wild dreams of French system builders" regarding the structure of the walls of Babylon, rather than attending to the results of a physical analysis performed by a British bishop on a similar structure in England.[93] Within the intertwining discourses of science, art, and politics, scientific empirical observation becomes linked to traditional systems of social and political organization that had developed slowly, as the result of "custom" and "experience." At the heart of this ideologically charged semiotic system is the term "nature" operating as a floating signifier which, by subtle shifts in meaning and inflection, knitted together these diverse discourses, and in doing so gave profound new significance to representations of the domestic landscape.

It is not necessary to document the numerous ways in which the drive for scientific "objectivity" affected the actual practices of representing "customary" or "common" nature in landscape painting in the early 1800s. John Gage admirably analyzes the prominence of *plein air* painting, the use of the oil sketch, and the fascination with scientific instruments like the graphic telescope in his important catalogue essay for *A Decade of English Naturalism*.[94] In so doing, he organizes under the rubric of "naturalism" domestic views of English countryside, produced between 1810 and 1820, which manifest a concern with both locale and local effects of atmosphere via a broad and sketch-like manner. While Gage does not explore the social and ideological implications of the "naturalist" landscape, Andrew Hemingway does, chiefly through examining its philosophical underpinnings and its reception by urban bourgeois intellectuals writing in the metropolitan press. Although Hemingway comments in passing on the nationalist implications of the English subject matter of these works, neither he nor Gage notes that the epistemological grounding of naturalism in empiricism was similarly coded as English (or British).[95] This encoding goes some way toward explaining why English genius could be inscribed in pictures of foreign landscapes (such as Turner's Swiss watercolors, exhibited at Walter Fawkes's town house in 1819), and why descriptions of *all* forms of landscape painting (historical and poetic landscapes as well as domestic and foreign views) tended to focus on the representation of these selfsame naturalistic effects of light and color, rather than on the quality of the drawing or design.[96]

The increasing authority of scientific discourse was bound up with an even broader phenomenon than rampant nationalism in the counter-revolutionary decades: the more general turn toward science and away from religion as the ultimate ground of truth during the eighteenth century "Enlightenment." However, in the early 1800s, landscape painting was not the site of a war between science and religion, but a locus for their mutual reinforcement: the "truths" of nature, discerned by empirical science, and represented in landscape painting, exposed the greater "Truth" of God's power and benevolence. Such a connection between God and the landscape had been commonly made throughout the eighteenth century.[97] What was significant about its manifestation in the early nineteenth century, in widely read treatises such as William Paley's *Natural Theology* (1802), was the appeal to scientific observation and denotation as the guarantee that God's Nature was being truthfully represented.[98]

Despite the popularity of natural theology, however, aesthetic treatises and art criticism rarely made allusions to piety or the "Divine Creator" in discussions of landscape painting. Not surprisingly, it was principally in writings on art by Anglican clergymen such as William Gilpin (and Archibald Alison, whose treatise on aesthetics will be discussed in the next chapter) that the landscape, as viewed and painted, was celebrated as the visual expression of God's power and benevolence. The lack of religious allusions in art reviews may indicate the degree to which the discourse of criticism itself was self-consciously secularized. I suspect that such secularization was part of the drive for professional recognition by bourgeois laymen seeking to distinguish their form of intellectual practice from that of the Anglican clergy, who, through sermons, treatises, and essays, as well as their control of the curriculum at the two major universities, were the traditional purveyors of social and cultural criticism.

Within this increasingly secularized aesthetic discourse, the close observation and rendering of naturalistic effects were not only coded as English and scientifically "truthful"; *in certain cases* they were associated with artistic imagination and originality. The qualification is important, for it is necessary to distinguish works which could be seen to "produce" a particular vision of England through their truthful attentiveness to the changing face of English nature, from those which were seen to embody English genius rooted in ideals of imagination and independent-mindedness.[99] In order to understand the aesthetic and ideological implications of such critical distinctions we must examine a highly popular aesthetic theory that in various guises pervaded the discourse and practices of landscape painting. As formulated by two important intellectuals writing between 1790 and 1811, this aesthetic, which derived its authority from a self-declared "scientific" theory, associated the most ephemeral aspects of the landscape (both painted and observed) with the imaginative power of the human mind.

Chapter 4

The Imaginative Genius,
the "Poverty of Landscape,"
and Associated Pleasures

it [Gainsborough's *The Cottage Door*] possesses all the rich colouring of Rubens; the thinness, yet force and brilliancy of Vandyck; the silvery tone of Teniers; the depth and simplicity of Ruysdael; and the apparent finishing of Wynants.[1]

Mr. Coppin
Fine Arts of the English School, 1812

In contemplating the picture of "Pope's Villa," the mind is alternately soothed and distressed, delighted and provoked. The most pleasurable sensations are awakened by the taste and skill of the painter; and we view the residence of the Twickenham Bard with revived emotions of that delight, which the first perusal of his immortal strains excited . . .[2]

John Britton
Fine Arts of the English School, 1812

BY THE TIME JOHN BRITTON's *Fine Arts of the English School* was published in 1812, the above description of Gainsborough's *Cottage Door*, which the publisher included in his section on the painter, would have seemed distinctly old-fashioned or at best the sort of remark that would be made only by someone whose investment (aesthetic and/or economic) in the old master tradition inhibited his or her ability to think about English painting in any other terms.[3] Indeed many, if not most extended descriptions of contemporary English landscape paintings tended to adopt the critical vocabulary employed by Britton himself in his paean to Turner's landscape, *Pope's Villa at Twickenham*. Instead of reciting a litany of old master techniques, Britton describes the type of feelings, memories, and emotions that would be experienced by people viewing Turner's picture of the recently razed home of one of Britain's greatest poets. Although Britton does not identify patriotic feeling with the emotional response produced by *Pope's Villa*, this association is implicit given both the picture's highly charged national subject matter and the context in which the engraving of it and Britton's discussion appear: a book that is self-

30 Turner. Detail of Figure 33.

declaredly nationalistic in its promotion of native artists. While, as noted in Chapter 3, Britton identifies Gainsborough as a "genuine English artist," no such move is necessary with Turner.[4] The latter's Englishness is assured by the private, yet commonly shared emotions and memories that a national community was expected to experience on viewing works such as *Pope's Villa.*

We have considered how transformations in the practice and discourse of landscape painting around 1800 were affected by socio-political factors such as nationalist sentiment arising from the English counter-revolution and the French wars, the persistence of private rather than public patronage of the arts, and the increasing popularity of leisure pursuits such as domestic tourism and amateur drawing and painting. However, the shift in critical rhetoric so strikingly evident in the two quotes that begin this chapter can only be understood fully by considering developments in the interrelated fields of philosophy, psychology, and aesthetics. These changes offered artists, critics, and viewers a new framework for conceptualizing the relationship between the individual and the domestic landscape and for rethinking their own identity as members of a national community.

The conceptualization of the domestic painter as an imaginative genius was profoundly affected by a body of writing on aesthetics grounded in associationist psychology. This theory of the mind was developed in the writings of John Locke and elaborated by Scottish intellectuals David Hume, David Hartley, Lord Kames, and Thomas Reid. Following Locke, the Scottish philosophers countered the theory that the mind contains "innate ideas" by arguing that impressions perceived by the sense organs and registered in the brain provide the basis of knowledge. The process of association, whereby certain sense impressions become linked with specific feelings or ideas, was understood to serve as the primary organizing mechanism of the mind.[5]

Scholars have for some time recognized the importance of associationism in the practice and discourse of early nineteenth-century landscape painting. Helène Roberts has traced the use of associationist language in the art criticism of the period (and beyond).[6] Without engaging in extended theoretical discussions of associationism, both Kathleen Nicholson and Eric Shanes have devoted close attention to the way Turner sought to elevate his landscape practice through the poetic associations that he introduced, both in the form of glosses that accompany the paintings and in the form of visual puns and symbols within the images themselves.[7]

Most recently Andrew Hemingway has argued that associationist aesthetics provided both a critique of the universalist ideals of academic discourse and a defense of the local and the particular, and thus could be of some use to painters of domestic scenery and their backers.[8] While my account agrees substantially with his, I have chosen to examine certain aspects of contemporary writings on associationism (specifically Archibald Alison's *Essays on the Nature and Principles of Taste* and Francis Jeffrey's review of this work) that Hemingway, pursuing different objectives, did not. In particular I shall take up Alison's discussion of the landscape painter, his frequent allusions to natural scenery, and Jeffrey's insistence on the social nature of aesthetic responses – all of which impinge upon the production of the native genius.

Alison's *Essays on the Nature and Principles of Taste* was first published in Edinburgh and London in 1790, appeared in a second edition in 1811, and by 1817 had been through three more editions. It was arguably the most highly regarded and influential piece of aesthetic writing published between 1790 and the appearance of Ruskin's *Modern Painters* in the 1840s; indeed, it seems likely that the popularity of Payne Knight's *Analytical Inquiry* was severely eclipsed as a result of the re-publication of Alison's *Essays* in 1811.[9]

Whereas academic discourse was predicated upon the existence of an external, fixed ideal of beauty from which standards of taste and a hierarchy of artistic production could be determined, associationist aesthetics propounded just the opposite: external objects were conceived not as repositories of beauty, sublimity, and so forth, but rather as stimuli, capable of triggering trains of associated ideas and feelings in the mind of the viewer. Alison declares that when viewing a scene in nature the spectator is conscious of a variety of images that spring to mind that are very different from the objects of the gaze: "Trains of pleasing or of solemn thoughts arise spontaneously within our minds; our hearts well with emotions, of which the objects before us seem to afford no adequate cause."[10] Such trains of thought are seen to be linked by circumstantial associations rather than the logic of a narrative system. It is the quality, intensity, and sheer number of these associations, not the original object, which are the actual sources of aesthetic pleasure.

Within this scheme the imagination is the primary mental faculty, conceived of as a vast storehouse of memories; when any one memory is stimulated, it is capable of triggering a chain reaction of other thoughts and feelings that are related to the first one. The nature and intensity of the emotional response to an external object is governed by a range of circumstances particular to the viewing subject. Alison observes that young people seem to possess more fertile imaginations and thus stronger feelings than their elders; individual personality and national character also condition the nature of the associations generated in a specific situation.[11] While this connection between national character and the nature of associations that a particular object or image may generate would have immense importance for domestic landscape painters, Alison's primary concern is with those specific circumstances that must prevail for the feelings generated by these associations to be the "emotions of taste," as he terms aesthetic pleasure.

Unlike earlier accounts of taste that employ theories of association, Alison's treatise underscores the importance of natural scenery as a site capable of producing the highest form of aesthetic pleasure. Although he does deal with the associative aspects of the human figure, it is the landscape – actual, painted, or described in poetry – that is adduced as the principal object of aesthetic discourse.[12] For example, he observes that "the majesty of the Alps themselves is increased by the remembrance of Hannibal's march over them."[13] The study of the ancients, which had once helped secure the elevated status of history painting, was now being placed in the service of an aestheticized viewing of the landscape.

Alison draws upon arguments from Thomas Whately's *Observations on Modern Gardening* (1770) to support his claim for the landscape's "natural" capacity to arouse associations leading to aesthetic pleasure. After speaking of the associations triggered by the sight of ruins, Alison quotes Whately:

Even without the assistance of buildings or other adventitious circumstances, nature alone furnishes materials for scenes which may be adapted to almost every kind of expression. Their operation is general, and their consequences infinite: the mind is elevated, depressed, or composed, as gaiety, gloom, or tranquillity prevail in the scene, and we soon lose sight of the mean by which the character is formed.[14]

The aesthetic power of natural scenery lies partly in its universality – its ability to stimulate emotions in all of humankind; and partly in its versatility – its capacity to activate an infinite array of sentiments in such a surreptitious manner that the viewer becomes unable to determine the original source of the emotion. Alison argues that because the power of the emotion resides in the imagination of the viewer rather than in the object, all types of natural scenery are capable of stimulating this at once general and varied aesthetic response. This is a fortuitous situation for if certain "elements in the scenery of nature alone were beautiful, then all men to whom these appearances were unknown must be deprived of all the enjoyment which the scenery of external nature could give."[15]

Such universal access to some form of enjoyment of nature's beauties is an essential component of Alison's aesthetics, because ultimately the Anglican clergyman goes on to link the beauty and sublimity of nature with the power, wisdom, and beneficence of nature's Divine Creator. According to this schema, greater aesthetic appreciation of the natural landscape will lead the viewer to a deeper reverence for God and an enhanced sense of the "moral discipline" that governs the universe.[16] It is noteworthy, however, that Alison does not emphasize the presence of the divine in nature throughout his text – aesthetic pleasure in nature and in landscape painting is consistently presented as an end in itself. Only at the conclusion of his treatise does he argue for a connection between aesthetic pleasure and Christian morality.

While nature can stimulate some form of aesthetic (and potentially moral) response in everyone, the nature of that response will vary widely. For Alison, the associative powers of the imagination provide differential, not equal, access to the pleasures of nature. This differential access is a function of the age, occupation, and education, and by implication the gender and class of the viewer. The associations Alison most prizes are those related to poetry (ancient and modern) and classical history, available only to those privileged to have access to such literature.[17] He acknowledges this distinction between the learned and unlearned viewer when he observes that "even the familiar circumstances of general nature, which pass unheeded by a common eye, the cottage, the sheep-fold, the curfew, all have expressions to them" for those possessing a knowledge of pastoral poetry.[18] That Alison, a classically educated Whig clergyman, establishes in a viewer-based, relativistic theory of taste a hierarchy of associations validating the social and intellectual supremacy of the landed gentry and professional classes is not surprising. Like Payne Knight, the Scottish clergyman was interested in promoting, not undermining, those hierarchies that empower the liberally educated reader and viewer. But Alison, unlike Knight, also credited the landscape painter with a heightened capacity for the aesthetic appreciation of natural scenery:

The beauty of any scene in nature is seldom so striking to others, as it is to a landscape-painter, or to those who profess the beautiful art of laying out grounds. The difficulties both of invention and execution which from their professions are familiar to them, render the profusion with which nature often scatters the most picturesque beauties, little less than miraculous. Every little circumstance of form and perspective, and light and shade, which are unnoticed by a common eye, are important in theirs, and, mingling in their minds the ideas of difficulty, and facility in overcoming it, produce altogether an emotion of delight, incomparably more animated than any that the generality of mankind usually derive from it.[19]

It is the artistic eye which is deemed capable here of extracting the greatest aesthetic pleasure from a natural scene. In the social and epistemological hierarchies adopted by Alison, it is doubtful that the "animated delight" experienced by the artist would be judged superior to the aesthetic response of the liberally educated gentleman. Nonetheless, the positive tone and openness of Alison's text differ sharply from Knight's various pronouncements on artistic prowess, which seem to emphasize the gulf that separates the erudite viewer from the technically gifted artistic producer.

Although Alison treats the artist as an extraordinarily perceptive and sensitive viewing subject, his primary concern is with the artist as a creator whose powerful imagination stores perceptions and then organizes them on canvas around a single "expression." He argues that the landscape painter has the capacity to produce a more aesthetically powerful work than the landscape gardener, because the former has more control over what he selects:

In a landscape . . . the whole range of scenery is before the eye of the painter. He may select from a thousand scenes, the circumstances which are to characterize a single composition, and may unite into one expression, the scattered features with which Nature has feebly marked a thousand situations. The momentary effects of light or shade, the fortunate incidents which chance some times throws in, to improve the expression of real scenery, and which can never again be recalled, he has it in his power to perpetuate upon his canvas.[20]

The stress here is not only upon choice, but upon the formation of a unified composition. Unity is also a prominent regulatory term in academic theory, where it authorizes the hierarchical ordering of forms within a composition, and hence the relationships among the figures and objects depicted.[21] Such an ordering is an ideological process, for it privileges certain individuals, experiences, and relationships at the expense of others. Associationist discourse does not abandon systems of hierarchical ordering, but alters the epistemological framework in which that ordering takes place. Whereas the discourse of history painting relies upon representations of the generic and permanent to enforce unity, Alison identifies the particular, the transient, and even "fortunate incidents of chance" as the affective constituents of an aesthetically unified landscape painting. He insists that such unity requires not only selection of transient and particular effects, but rejection of all that does not contribute to the single expression that the work seeks to convey.[22]

An artist capable of producing a work of great expressive power via such distillation and simplification provides knowing viewers – those privileged to have formed their sensibilities through a classical education, especially poetry – with a profound and satisfying understanding of landscape painting as well as of natural scenery itself. Armed with such knowledge, the viewing subject rejects topographical accuracy in favor of expression:

> The crowd of incidents which used to dazzle our earlier Taste, as expressive both of the skill and of the invention of the artist, begin to appear to us as inconsistence or confusion. When our hearts are affected, we seek only for objects congenial to our emotion: and the Simplicity, which we used to call the Poverty of landscape, begins now to be welcome to us, as permitting us to indulge, without interruption, those interesting trains of thought which the character of the scene is fitted to inspire.[23]

We can recognize in this passage the formulation of the Romantic notion of landscape in which the "character" of external nature resonates with the emotional state of the viewer. Alison describes this process in terms of plenitude and impoverishment: it is by removing those incidents in the landscape that are potentially confusing or inconsistent that the artist is able to stimulate a rich train of associated ideas in the mind and heart of the viewer. This way of producing and viewing the landscape is, of course, profoundly ideological: eliminating those elements of the domestic landscape that could breed contradictory ideas was, at this historical moment, tantamount to denying at the crucial level of representation the existence of those dislocations and conflicts that marked a countryside undergoing unprecedented socio-economic transformation. This change was nowhere more evident than in Alison's native Scotland, where the capital-intensive raising of sheep demanded that former agricultural land, used in subsistence farming, be "cleared" of its human tenants.[24]

Picturesque viewing and sketching also involved removing signs of modernization and social conflict from the domestic terrain in the interests of aestheticization. Alison's argument for the "poverty of landscape" rested instead on an appeal to authenticity. Only by draining the landscape of confusing incident could its "true" character be transmitted to the sensitive beholder.

We have seen how this seemingly magical transformation was effected by Girtin in works like *Kirkstall Abbey*. A gentle melancholy would appear to be the "unifying expression" of the scene, achieved through the use of broad horizontal brushstrokes of somber color.[25] The gloomy sky and the highlighted form of the ruined abbey would be expected to generate a train of associations concerning the decline and fall of a once powerful religious authority. According to the ideas set out by Alison, it is the very simplicity of an image such as this, with its emphasis on tonal and formal unity and circumstantial effect, that provokes the highest form of aesthetic pleasure.

Whereas Payne Knight celebrates the technical virtuosity of the artist over and above his powers of intellect, imagination, or sensibility, Alison is much more willing to accord the artist, in particular the landscape painter, superior powers of imagination and feeling. His most succinct and authoritative statement about the elevated status of the artistic subject occurs in a discussion of the relative merits of imitative versus imaginative landscape painting. In the passage which directly precedes the previously quoted discussion of the "poverty" of landscape he declares:

> It is not for imitation we look, but for character. It is not the art, but the genius of the Painter, which now gives value to his compositions: and the language he employs is found not only to speak to the eye, but to affect the imagination and the heart. It is not now a simple copy which we see, nor is our Emotion limited to the cold pleasure which arises from the perception of accurate Imitation. It is a creation of Fancy with which the artist presents us, in which only the greater expressions of Nature are retained, and where more interesting emotions are awakened than those which we experience from the useful tameness of common scenery.[26]

The writer's call for an art of expression rather than "accurate Imitation" is hardly original; Fuseli's rejection of "map-work" was predicated upon the same distinction, as were most contemporary texts dealing with landscape painting. What *is* noteworthy in this passage is the prominence given to the artistic subject – a prominence which arises out of the instability and vagueness of the word "character" at the end of the first sentence. We are told to look for character in art, a character that seems to be related to the "greater expressions of Nature" referred to towards the end of the passage. And yet the sentence which immediately follows the first leads not to nature, but to the genius of the painter – which is the source of "value" in such paintings. "Character," then, is placed in close syntactical relation to "genius," leaving open the possibility that it is the character of the artist as well as "nature" which is presented on the canvas.

This slippage between character, artistic genius, and nature suggests that the identity of the artist and the character of the landscape are intimately related in ways unlike either of the artistic subject positions we considered earlier. If academic discourse regarded the liberally minded history painter as "transparent," suppressing his private character in order to represent public virtue in ideal forms, and the commercially driven painter was deemed "opaque," representing on canvas only his private interests by the use of mannered effects which efface nature, then, within the parameters of Alison's associationist aesthetic, the imaginative genius was "translucent." That is, specific aspects of nature were understood to be revealed by his powers of observation and specialized knowledge of art, combined with his unique creativity and sensibility. What becomes visible when such "genius" is at work is a mind capable of concentrating and intensifying the emotions generated by a natural scene without distorting the objects or the feelings.[27] The artistic genius is, then, a superior form of cultural transmitter: acutely sensitive to the underlying character and emotion "inherent" in nature, he possesses the unique power to make that feeling accessible to less sensitive viewers via the materiality of paint and canvas.

Although the subject of Alison's *Essays* is the "emotion of taste" he is primarily interested in determining how this emotion is produced, rather than making a sustained and detailed analysis of its effects.[28] The nature and effects of aesthetic pleasure were taken up, however, by Francis Jeffrey in the most important and extensive review of the second edition of the *Essays*, published in the *Edinburgh*

Review in 1811.[29] This review is as much an elaboration of the social nature of aesthetic pleasure as it is an evaluation of Alison's aesthetics. Fully accepting the associationist principle that aesthetic feelings are produced in the mind and are merely stimulated by external objects, Jeffrey goes on to argue that

> except in the plain and palpable case of bodily pain or pleasure, we can never be interested in any thing but the fortunes of sentient beings; – and that every thing partaking of the nature of mental emotion, must have for its object the feelings, past, present or possible, of sensation . . . [therefore] the emotions of beauty and sublimity must have for their objects the sufferings or enjoyments of sentient beings.[30]

A consequence of this intrinsic characteristic of humans to be interested only in other sentient beings is that aesthetic experience is ultimately a social experience. Jeffrey considers literature rather than painting, but, like Alison, his examples are drawn principally from visual perceptions and poetic descriptions of natural scenery rather than human actions. He observes that roaring water brings to mind associations of lamentation or violence; autumn recalls the end of life or the decline of empires; and the sun connotes glory and ambition.[31] While Alison cites similar examples to demonstrate the process by which objects generate feelings, Jeffrey emphasizes the social nature of human responses to inanimate nature.

Jeffrey's insistence on the importance of empathy (or as it was then termed, "sympathy") is consistent with his commitment to the moral philosophy of fellow Scotsmen Francis Hutcheson, David Hume, Adam Smith, and the Professor of Moral Philosophy with whom he studied, Dugald Stewart (to whom Alison dedicated his *Essays*).[32] These writers asserted that moral evaluations are not a function of the reasoning faculty, as many other philosophers had contended. Rather, as Stewart explains, "the words Right and Wrong express certain agreeable and disagreeable qualities in actions which it is not the province of reason, but of feeling to perceive."[33] Smith designates these feelings as moral sympathy or "fellow feeling" and in his *Theory of Moral Sentiments* (1759) writes that "nothing pleases us more than to observe in other men a fellow-feeling with all the emotions of our own breast."[34]

Social empathy so defined is not only the ground of ethical behavior, but also a powerful social force that binds together self-interested individuals in commercial society.[35] The happiness of the individual is the link that permits social empathy, based upon pleasure, to operate as an ethical imperative and to underwrite social cohesiveness. Such happiness, Stewart declares, overrides the need for freedom of political action: "*Happiness* is in truth the only object of legislative *intrinsic* value; and what is called *Political Liberty* is only one means of obtaining this end."[36] This appeal to individual happiness over civic freedom is the fundamental precept of a liberal ideology which promotes the adoption of an economic rather than a political model of commercial society.[37] By this account, the reconfiguration of the civic sphere does not involve a loss of virtue (as civic humanists argued) but its reinscription within the realm of private feeling.

In this liberal paradigm private feelings are far from inconsequential as a means of forging political assent. It is by redirecting (rather than repressing) the feelings associated with self-esteem and self-interest that individuals become subjects of the state. In a review defending the "natural" rights of the propertied to hold political office, published four months before his review of Alison's *Essays*, Jeffrey observes that

> nothing can conduce so surely to the stability and excellence of a political constitution, as to make it rest upon the general principles that regulate the conduct of the better part of the individuals who live under it, and to attach them to their government by the same feelings which ensure their affection or submission in their private capacity.[38]

Posited here is something like Raymond Williams's "structure of feeling," which comprises those fleeting, inchoate experiences and emotions that dominate so much of human consciousness and activity.[39] Jeffrey suggests that those "feelings" and "general principles" governing personal interactions provide the means of interpellating the private individual as a loyal subject. Within such a liberal paradigm, then, the constitution of communal (English) identity is contingent on the prior existence of a private, or interiorized self. These two subjectivities, based on seemingly antithetical notions of community and atomization, were mutually reinforcing at this historical moment when English national identity was strongly bound up with the ideal of individual distinction and independent-mindedness. Jeffrey's writings on aesthetics interlink with such a theory of the individual insofar as he insists on the social nature of aesthetic pleasure, arising from associated ideas, thoughts, and feelings.

Like Alison, Jeffrey believes that social feelings and aesthetic pleasures are circumstantial, and therefore that age, education, and local custom lead to the formation of distinctive tastes among individuals and nations.[40] But the reviewer also takes pains to formulate these distinctions in taste in terms of the "social emotions" produced by different types of external object, which he classifies into three orders of signification.

Despite his insistence that external objects possess no essential qualities of beauty or sublimity, Jeffrey argues that some of these objects operate as "natural signs" – signifiers which invariably and naturally are connected with specific emotions through the laws of nature. Thunder, for example, is always connected with sublime feelings of danger and power. These natural signs are distinguished from a secondary order of signs, which are the arbitrary or accidental indicators of social emotions, and also from a tertiary order, those signs bearing only a fanciful resemblance to the signified emotions.[41] Although the writer maintains that natural signs are important because of their power to engage the social emotions of all people, it is the capacity to bring into play all three orders of sign, and especially the latter two, that is the mark of a highly developed taste. For it is accidental, analogical, and fanciful associations that generate "an endless variety in the trains of thoughts," and consequently produce the most intense and elevated forms of aesthetic pleasure.[42]

Two points emerge from Jeffrey's account of associationist aesthetics: the social nature of aesthetic pleasure, and the contingency of that pleasure on the imaginative power to manipulate and to read a complex interplay of natural, accidental, and fanciful signs. The ideal viewer is not a disinterested subject, but one whose personal and social circumstances allow him/her to be deeply engaged by trains of personal associations generated by the viewing of a landscape. This interest, however, does not remain self-focused, for the emotions which are generated are inescapably empathetic feelings, uniting the subject to others in the social sphere.

Although Jeffrey did not discuss landscape painting in his review of Alison's *Essays*, some of his contemporaries, who were also profoundly affected by associationist discourse, did address the question of how artistic subjectivity might be constituted via the process of viewing and painting the national landscape. Perhaps nowhere in the early 1800s was the genius of a domestic landscape painter more insistently proclaimed and thoroughly explicated than in *Views in Sussex, Consisting of the Most Interesting Landscape and Marine Scenery in the Rape of Hastings.* This volume, published in 1820, comprises five copperplate engravings based on watercolors by Turner, a historical introduction, and a commentary on the individual plates by landscape painter Richard Ramsay Reinagle.[43] Taken together the engravings and text represent an ambitious effort to define the character of the landscape artist in terms of specialized modes of knowing, seeing, and feeling. The project was initiated in 1810 by Tory MP John Fuller, a prominent landowner and Jamaica slave-owner, who commissioned Turner to produce a series of topographical watercolors of his native Sussex. Eric Shanes recounts that Fuller intended to present colored aquatints of some of these drawings to friends, relatives, and the neighboring gentry; and indeed, most of the watercolors represent property of prosperous landowners living in the area around Hastings.[44] Several years after the completion of this initial project W. B. Cooke secured Fuller's financing to engrave and publish five plates based on Turner's Sussex watercolors, along with the explanatory text by Reinagle.

Reinagle's commentary is unprecedented, as far as I have been able to determine, in its fixation on the artistic merit of the images, rather than on the terrain and buildings which are depicted in them. Usually such texts present information about the geographical, historical, and commercial importance of the sites represented, and only occasionally comment on the beauty or masterliness of the images.[45] This emphasis on subject matter is found not only in those text-oriented county histories that include illustrative material, but also in volumes of engraved views such as this one, in which the text serves primarily as a gloss on the prints. Although Reinagle's text does present site-specific information, it is largely a promotion of the genius of the artist, evidenced by his sensibility and command of "science." The professional authority of the enterprise is underscored by the fact that a landscape painter was engaged to write the commentary, as well as by the title of that text: "Scientific and Explanatory Notes." As the complement of image/text makes clear, it is a specific type of science – devoted to the empirical study of the human mind and natural phenomena – which secures both the artist's and the commentator's professional authority.

Whereas most domestic topographies and tour guides stress the natural beauty of the sites depicted, *Views in Sussex* presents the landscape around Hastings as visually unremarkable.[46] The hills and woodlands displayed in these panoramas possess little of the visual variety so prized by Gilpin and Price, and represented so insistently in a print of the environs of Hastings, based on a drawing by William Havell, that was

31   William B. Cooke after William Havell, *View of Hastings*. Copperplate engraving in *Picturesque Views of the Southern Coast of England . . .* , vol. 1, London, 1826. Brown University Library, Providence, RI (photo: Brooke Hammerle).

engraved by W. B. Cooke and first issued in 1816 as part of his *Picturesque Views of the Southern Coast of England* (Figure 31). Indeed the softly undulating hills that are so prominent in Turner's views of Heathfield (Figure 32) and Ashburnham (Figure 33) have a regularity which calls to mind Gilpin's exemplar of the "unpicturesque," a schematic drawing of three smooth mountains (Figure 34), which he counterpoises to a picturesque sketch of mountains with suitably rough and irregular outlines. While both Gilpin and Turner seek to distinguish their productions from topographical drawings, the artistic strategies they employ in aestheticizing (and thereby "elevating") their subjects differ significantly.[47] The picturesque representations of irregular terrain which populate the pages of Gilpin's *Tours* show no trace of the process of aesthetic reconfiguration: without directly comparing one of his views to the site in question, one cannot determine from the internal evidence of the drawing alone precisely how much and in what way he has artfully modified the contours of mountains, changed the location of trees, altered the course of rivers, and so forth. Turner also effects internally undetectable topographical modifications in his Sussex views, as in *The Vale of Ashburnham*, where he highlights the country seat of the Ashburnham family while discreetly "hiding" the primary industrial source of the family fortune, an iron smelter, behind the trees on the right.[48] That said, the artist also pointedly emphasizes, through the use of broad panoramic viewpoints, the visually undramatic contours of recognizable landforms around Hastings in order to make all the more visible the aesthetic "magic" he

32 J.M.W. Turner, *The Vale of Heathfield*, *c.*1815. Watercolor, 14.9 × 22.5 in. British Museum, London.

works upon them. These magical transformations center on the production of varied atmospheric and climatic effects, intensified by W.B. Cooke in translating the watercolors into copper plate engravings, to create a unified feeling or "mood," consistent with the "essential" character of the site.

In his commentary on *The Vale of Heathfield* Reinagle stresses the unexceptional nature of the topography, noting that

> the learned eye in the choice of nature, for the purposes of art, would rather travel on, until some sharpened and angular forms bespeak grandeur, or the distant beauty of mountain scenery, satisfies its anxious search; than rest among forms and features of indecisive character. Is it not a most convincing proof of the genius of the eminent artist we are following, when he surprises, astonishes, or pleases us to a degree of ecstasy, with scenes that the rule of art might condemn? He finds an easy path, which to every other than a genius like his own, would prove a wilderness, and occasion a certain failure.[49]

That viewers can experience sublimity – ecstatic transport and astonishment – in relation to an unremarkable view is presented as evidence of artistic genius. The aesthetic experience of sublimity is not produced here through the representation of a specific set of objects and phenomena – mountains, storms, darkness, and the

33   J. M. W. Turner. *The Vale of Ashburnham*, 1816. Watercolor, 14.9 × 22.2 in. British Museum, London.

like; it is a mental response to the revelation of the sublimity produced by the interaction of common nature and artistic genius. It is noteworthy that whereas for the Reverend Alison feelings of sublimity ultimately lead the individual to an enhanced appreciation of God's power, Reinagle, pursuing other ends, associates such feelings with the appreciation of artistic genius, and, as suggested in the discussion to follow, with love of country. Religious feeling is not precluded in Reinagle's text, it is simply ignored − a move that marks the distinction between the cultural commentary of the British clergy, and the secular criticism of artists and other lay intellectuals.

While this transformation of the mundane into the sublime may appear magical, Reinagle takes pains to insist repeatedly throughout the text that it is "science" and genius which are responsible for the expressive power of the scene:

> There is great science in the contrivance of the sky, and particularly over the house [the seat of Lord Heathfield]; that is the spot to be preferred in the picture as the chief object, though distant; and our admiration is drawn to that point as by a magic spell. Science alone, aided by genius, can do this. These are the high qualities that can enslave and enchant the eye.[50]

The emphasis on the empirically accurate delineation of the cloudy, rainswept sky

34   After William Gilpin, *Non-Picturesque Mountain Landscape*. Aquatint in *Three Essays on Picturesque Beauty*, London, 1792. British Museum, London.

suggests that the artist has marshalled his knowledge of meteorology in order to produce a scene that magically enslaves and enchants the viewer. That this "magic" should not be confused with the affectations of manner and glittering effects which were so strongly associated with artists like Westall and Ibbetson is suggested in a passage describing *The Vale of Ashburnham*: "there is neither affectation in light and shade, nor any seductive attraction created that way: the scene alone recommends this view in a most impressive manner."[51] The view's spectacular light effects represent the natural as mediated through the knowledge and genius of the artist.

In the views of both Ashburnham and Heathfield, Reinagle declares that the "spot to be preferred" is that occupied by the house of a landed proprietor. Although the compositions do not feature these stately edifices at close range, or set them off with picturesque framing devices, their importance within the panorama is unmistakable. The accidental effects that highlight their presence render their dominance of the landscape as natural as the sunlight and the clouds playing over its surface. Traditional social hierarchies are here naturalized and sustained by an aesthetic of the circumstantial, based upon self-proclaimedly "scientific" principles.

Although Reinagle at no point provides readers with an explicit definition of the term "science," his pictorial analyses leave little doubt about the epistemological authority that underwrites both the images and the commentary. In explaining the placement of a rainstorm on the left of the view of *Brightling Observatory as Seen from Rosehill Park* (Figure 35), the writer states that the view affords little extension into vast distances to engage the imagination of the viewer. Consequently, the artist expressed a shower proceeding from the left corner, by which we forget the absence of distance, as that affects the mind two ways. In the first place, it is a natural barrier to the feeling and search in that direction, nor can we avoid proceeding onward as the storm or shower leads. Secondly, the mind, by its own operation, assents, from common experience, that rain generally obscures whatever it passes over. It is thus we are bound to the spot, and feel more interest in what is before us, than if the effect had induced the mind to wander out of the limits of the picture.[52]

This attempt at psychologizing the viewing process is an open, if clumsy, endorsement of associationist principles as the epistemological ground for making aesthetic judgments of the images.

Both the image and text evidence a concern with boundaries – with preventing the gaze of the viewer from wandering off into distances which may promise more interesting vistas. Limiting the gaze by means of a natural and "accidental" phenomenon (a rain shower) limits the potential for the viewer to engage in an unregulated flow of associations and feelings. As a result, the viewer is encouraged to experience an intensity of feeling, and hence an enhanced appreciation of the

35   William B. Cooke after J. M. W. Turner, *Brightling Observatory as Seen from Rosehill Park.* Engraving and etching in *Views in Sussex*, London, 1820. Yale Center for British Art, Paul Mellon Collection, New Haven.

36   William B. Cooke after J. M. W. Turner, *View of Battle Abbey – the Spot Where Harold Fell*. Engraving and etching in *Views in Sussex*, London, 1820. Yale Center for British Art, Paul Mellon Collection, New Haven.

power of artistic genius, while contemplating this unremarkable stretch of Sussex scenery.[53] Reinagle's emphasis upon the visual techniques used to limit and enhance images of natural scenery testifies to the regulatory power invested in the landscape genius. The appeal to the imagination of the viewer is not made by inviting an unrestricted play of imaginative associations, but by a controlled and selective display of features and circumstantial effects that reinforce and enhance a limited set of social feelings associated with the scene represented.

Turner's representation of the historic battleground at Hastings, *View of Battle Abbey – the Spot where Harold Fell* (Figure 36) presents a virtuoso demonstration of the associative possibilities that can be developed from a seemingly uninteresting array of natural objects and features by the selection and enhancement of circumstantial phenomena.[54] Once again Reinagle stresses the visual insipidity of the site (a "plain foreground with some scattered weeds . . . a meagre distance, of no importance in a picturesque point of view, a couple of half withered firs") before explaining how the associative aspects of circumstantial effects transform the viewer's experience of the historic battlefield:

A violent storm is just passing away, having burst its fury at no great distance; this we gather not so much from the mere effect of light and shade, as by an accurate attention to the formation of clouds. Thus a commotion or contention and strife of the elements help to give a feeling necessary to the purpose of this design. . . . The direction of the lines of the clouds in their convolutions calls attention to the spot the Artist has to depict; the decline of the day, expressed by a low light, and long sloping shadows, together with the beautiful circumstance of a fallen tree, add an unexpected strength to the conception. The decay of the few straggling yet standing firs, united with the above circumstances, gives a powerful impression of melancholy and sadness to the scene. To add to all this admirable feeling and exquisite sensibility of combination, both in form and effect, Mr Turner has given us an episode, a hare, just on the point of being run down by a greyhound, which fills the mind of the observer with only one sentiment, that of death, as no other living objects interpose to divert the mind from it.[55]

All of the effects noted in the passage are "accidental": an animal chase, a passing storm, lengthening shadows, and decayed trees. And yet when selected and combined by imaginative genius, such transient effects have the power to operate as "natural signs," to use Jeffrey's term, of sadness and strife, and thus to evoke the historic character of the scene. Character, then, is not a quality represented in the general and permanent forms underlying material nature, as formulated by academic theory. What signifies character are the ephemeral and arbitrary occurrences of selected episodes of human activity that are associated with a specific site. These episodes are then imaginatively constituted through the representation of transient, but "universally" significant effects of atmosphere and weather.

The displacement of specific feelings associated with social conflict and other human actions onto representations of natural scenery involves a repression of human agency in favor of natural law. Existing social relations and historical events are not represented as objects of moral or intellectual scrutiny, but function as sources of aesthetic pleasure derived from the feelings they arouse. When transposed onto natural scenery, these social feelings appear to be in harmony with natural law and therefore immune to question. Since it is seemingly "natural" to feel sadness at the sight of decaying trees and the onset of evening, viewers of *Battle Abbey* are invited to conclude that it is equally "natural" to feel sadness at the defeat of the Saxons in a conflict further naturalized by its representation in the fury of the passing rainstorm and the violence of the animal chase.

In the context of this historical moment, however, to feel sadness at the violent defeat of the Saxons could be a highly politicized sentiment, and one not shared by all British subjects. Some factions among the political opposition to the ruling oligarchy at this time had incorporated a harsh condemnation of the Norman Conquest into their construction of British history.[56] On the other hand it was at this same time that Sir Walter Scott, a Tory supportive of the oligarchy, produced his own defense of the Normans in the novel *Ivanhoe*, published in 1820 (the same year that the Sussex prints were published). The associative processes that underwrite this kind of landscape painting, then, serve to deny such conflicts and are predicated instead upon a community of viewers united in their local interests and in a shared body of political, as well as literary and historical associations.

To acknowledge such local interests was not to abandon one's social identity in favor of the private self, but rather to define the social in terms of customary difference rather than universality. In the dedication of the *Views in Sussex* John Fuller is duly praised by the publisher W.B. Cooke: "The love of the Fine Arts blending itself with your Local Affections . . . induced you to obtain one of the first Artists the present age has produced, to exercise his powerful pencil on its selected Scenery."[57] Although this is a conventional tribute to the beneficent patronage of a landlord, such a concern with the local was particularly acute at this time. Both country Tories and politically liberal reformists were growing increasingly critical of absentee landlords who preferred the high life of the metropolis to the duties of the rural proprietor.[58] Fuller's private interests as an absentee landlord and slave-owner in the West Indies had prompted his vigorous defense of slave labor in the House of Commons in 1810 (at the very moment when he commissioned the Hastings watercolors from Turner). This action made him an unpopular figure in his local constituency – so unpopular, in fact, that he was dropped by the Tories at the next election, in 1812.[59] For Fuller, then, the private circulation and later publication of these views by Turner served to bolster his reputation locally, as a promoter of the historic sites and landed properties of Hastings, as well as nationally, through his patronage of the leading genius of English landscape painting.

Those national characteristics that both distinguish and unite a community of viewers are directly invoked in *The Vale of Ashburnham*. The wide panorama takes in the sweep of Pevensey Bay; dotting its shoreline are the barely discernible forms of Martello towers, recently built defenses against French invasion.[60] Only a viewer who was already aware of the existence of these small circular forts on the south coast would be able to identify them as the tiny dots which are barely distinguishable through the haze that the artist throws over the distant shoreline. Turner's inclusion of these recent structures locates the view in time and space, and could be seen as intended to call up patriotic sentiments. Ashburnham Place, the country seat of the Ashburnham family, John Fuller's neighbors, occupies the center of the composition. It is bathed in a bright patch of sunlight that sets it off from the surrounding wooded hillsides. Unlike the account of *Battle Abbey*, the commentary here emphasizes the richness of the "splendid English view" – a luxuriance derived partly from the wooded hills (the source of fuel for Ashburnham Forge, which, as mentioned above, was screened by the trees on the right), hop-grounds and corn-fields, and partly from the light which dapples the hillsides. After the "delighted eye" roves with pleasure over the scene it alights finally on the house itself:

> English magnificence is then in full view . . . the splendour of English wealth and taste is more displayed in our grand palaces and parks throughout the country than by our metropolitan residences. England is very peculiar in this respect; nor do we think more happy proof can be given of the truth of it than in the scene before us.[61]

The sight gives Reinagle the opportunity to link the feelings of luxury stimulated by the view with those characteristics of Englishness that were promoted by a landed elite over and above the interests of their counterparts in France and an increasingly powerful and aggressive English bourgeoisie.[62]

By the second decade of the nineteenth century the need for the landed interest to reassert its authority to rule in the interests of national harmony took on a new urgency. Both the growing economic power of bourgeois industrialists, especially in the north of England, and the increasing disaffection of the working class were becoming more visible and less easy to ignore or to explain away as temporary aberrations. Before the Napoleonic wars had ended there were two major demonstrations of middle- and working-class opposition to the oppressive power of rival interests: the provincial manufacturers' campaign to revoke the Orders in Council (in effect 1806–12) and Luddite attacks by labourers in 1811–12 in response to the introduction of power looms and shearing-frames into the cotton and woolen industries in the North.[63]

The successful attempt by the manufacturing interests to revoke the trade embargo established by the Orders in Council was a demonstration of the growing economic power of the industrial middle class. This translated into a vocal political presence that placed itself in active opposition to the commercial interests of corporations such as the East India Company (which profited from the Orders in Council) and to landed interests. At the same time the power of the manufacturers was being less successfully challenged by laborers. Luddite activity was, as E.P. Thompson puts it, "the nearest thing to a 'peasants' revolt' of industrial workers" yet experienced in England.[64] Incidents of machine-breaking, combined with an organized campaign to petition Parliament to provide monetary compensation to laborers, ultimately failed to assuage the effects of mechanization and to prevent the repeal of legislation protecting the interests of workers.[65] Nonetheless, the year-long agitation of thousands of workers disturbed the government to the extent that, fearing a fully-fledged insurrection, it sent 12,000 troops to the North – more men than were then fighting Napoleon in the Iberian Peninsula.[66] Despite government success in quashing these actions, it is highly likely that former Luddites played a primary role in organizing the widespread agitation for parliamentary reform which marked the immediate post-war period.

This period, the years between 1815 and 1820, saw a resurgence of inter-class hostility. The post-war trade depression, evident by 1816, combined with bad harvests in 1817 and 1818, provided the context for intense radical and liberal-reformist opposition to oligarchical power – an opposition which, some historians have argued, catalyzed the development of both middle- and working-class consciousness.[67] One opponent of working-class agitation acknowledges the development of inter-class hostility during this period when he declares in 1820:

> Never in any age or country was there more firm an alliance betwixt the higher and lower orders as there existed in Great Britain, until it was fatally disturbed of late years by . . . the spirit of turbulence and faction; . . . the cord has been snapped by the revolt of the labouring classes from their natural protectors and best friends.[68]

This account suggests that a momentous and irreversible change had occurred; current hostilities were more than just a temporary breakdown in the allegedly amicable relations that traditionally existed between rich and poor: the "cord has been snapped," never to be repaired.

Reinforcing this notion of a deep and irrevocable class antagonism were the writings of the leading political economist of the period, David Ricardo.[69] A primary figure under attack in Ricardo's writings is the landlord who, in seeking to maintain an artificially high price for grain by restricting foreign grain imports, caused the wages of laborers to rise and industrial profits to fall. These concerns were specifically relevant to the debates surrounding the passage in 1814 of the Corn Laws, which imposed just such a duty as a means of bolstering the post-war agricultural economy. A committed free trader, Ricardo emphasized in his *Principles of Political Economy and Taxation* (1817) the conflict of interests inherent in land-owners, manufacturers, and consumers in a capitalist economy.[70] His policies elicited vocal opposition from the most widely read quarterly of the day, *Blackwood's Edinburgh Magazine*, which maintained a staunchly Tory defense of the landed interest. In 1818 a writer in that journal took to task both Ricardo and his supporters on the editorial staff of the *Edinburgh Review* for asserting that "the interest of the landlords is always opposed to that of every other class of the community."[71] A year later *Blackwood's* published another essay attacking Ricardo's dictum that rising wages cause falling profits as "a theory which teaches that by the nature of human society, there is a constant and irremediable contrariety of interest between its members, and that a general amelioration, in which all should participate alike, is impossible."[72]

It is in the context of post-war social and political dissension and the concomitant emergence of an economic discourse emphasizing the endemic nature of class conflict to capitalist enterprise that the continued promotion and cultural articulation of the ideal of native genius should be located. Such events provided a strong incentive for the landed elite in England to reformulate their own class identity in a way that stressed their attachment to other classes within the nation, rather than their similarities to continental elites.

In 1820, at the same time as it was repeatedly attacking Ricardo's economic theory, *Blackwood's* published an essay, "On the Analogy between the Growth of Individual and National Genius," which vaunted the power of national character in binding together a people. By making an analogy between a nation and an individual the writer effaces social conflict as a defining feature of a given national community: "For the spirit of a people, as that of a single being, entering upon the world of life it is to possess, finds allotted to itself its own peculiar and individual condition of existence, distinguishing it from all others." Difference is understood here to operate only between national groups: the "spirit of a people" enters into the social body upon its "birth" and enforces coherence on a nation's history and character.[73]

This national character, the writer claims, is strengthened and sustained by the same process of introspection that is the hallmark of the individual artistic genius:

> It is an essential quality of genius in the individual mind, perhaps its distinctive and most constituent quality, that it draws its powers from sources within itself – that its faculties are but the organs, as it were, of a deeper spirit, residing in, and blended with its deepest nature. The man himself . . . with all his sensibilities, recollections, loves . . . is the deep and exhaustless source from which his

genius draws the materials of its conception – the elements of its ceaseless creations. It is the expression of his own individual being, the colouring of life derived through his own sense of his work, that makes the impress of genius on the productions of his art.[74]

Although published accounts of associationist psychology and aesthetics were largely ignored by *Blackwood's*, it is apparent here how compatible a theory of the imaginative genius based upon associative memories is with such a construction of both individual and national genius.[75] Such a native subject is not only *introspective*, but profoundly *retrospective*. Hence, the creative impulse derives its power not primarily from innovation, but from a continuous meditation on its own "deepest nature" as revealed through memory, feeling, and local attachment.

The politically reactionary nature of such a formulation of native consciousness is made clear in the author's discussion of the dual impulses that determine the progress of a nation – subjection to the past and freedom to change. He concludes that "among ourselves the tendency of deviation [from a balance of these two impulses] seems to be towards too great relaxation of the subjection of our minds to the great generations from which we spring." We should, therefore, "understand how much of our welfare . . . depends on our adherence to the spirit and life of our forefathers."[76] Throughout the essay such customary restraints are promoted in connection both with the individual and the national community. Within the terms of such an analogy, the need to regulate through custom and history an excessive desire for political change is addressed on the level of the individual as the necessity to control the creative intellect:

> The human intellect, searching life, nature, and itself, and re-moulding what it has seen into forms of its own, is not an unfettered intelligence, ranging through absolute existence, and creating ideal form. It is the power of a being who in all parts of his nature, is subjected to conditions of life, who, in his sensibilities, his knowledge, his productions, is under restraint of his nature, and of his place among mankind.[77]

Such a formulation of the self-reflecting national subject critiques notions of the subject as an unconstrained universalizing intelligence creating ideal forms. The writer proposes instead a subject deeply bound by the conditions of his/her present life. One of these formative conditions is the geographical locale which that subject occupies. In describing what constitutes the character of a people after the "spirit" has entered into their collective being, the writer declares that

> the life they are to lead dawns on them as they set foot on its [their country's] soil. The earth itself, and the sky, to which their existence from that hour is committed, are the groundwork of that arising life. Mountains, and waters, and woods, and soil, and the climate, which overhangs them all give the first deter-mination to their existence, allotting many of their avocations, and holding in themselves the numberless influences which are to be showered continually from the countenance and the hand of nature on their progressive existence.[78]

The landscape and climate, then, not only form and unify the initial character of a people, but continue to exert a profound influence on their collective development.

The constitutive nature of the landscape on the character of the people who inhabit it was an idea that had considerable currency throughout Europe in the late eighteenth and early nineteenth centuries. It has recently been shown that J. G. Herder's writings on *Klima* (climate) as a formative influence on national characteristics were important for German landscape painters such as Caspar David Friedrich.[79] But in England it was the claim of Johann Winckelmann and others that the cold, damp English climate prevented native artists from producing a successful school of history painting that would arouse the attention, or rather the ire, of domestic artists and cultural commentators.[80] Ironically at the same time that many domestic artists and writers were disavowing the link between climate and national culture, others involved in the promotion of English landscape painting found it in their interests to emphasize the artistic potential and distinctiveness of English climate and topography. For example, William Gilpin compares the "obscurity which is often thrown over distance" in England with the atmospheric clarity of Italian skies, where "very remote objects are seen with great distinction," and concludes that "our grosser atmosphere . . . exhibits various modes; some of which are in themselves more beautiful, than the most distinct vision."[81] Writing at about the same time, Joseph Pott suggests that a truly English school of landscape painting could be produced if domestic painters would refrain from imitating the views of continental masters and concentrate instead on the verdure and mists that characterize English nature.[82] While these accounts do not claim that climate affects national character, their praise of native topography and atmosphere exemplifies the crucial move away from a universalist notion of ideal (Italianate) nature that was necessary in order for the assertion of communal identity via a specific locale to gain prominence in landscape painting in the decades after the French Revolution.

Using different means and media, the *Blackwood's* essay on genius and *Views in Sussex* make similar claims regarding the key role of the domestic landscape in forming and embodying national genius. Turner's images of landed property and historic sites inscribe a notion of the national that naturalized the continued dominance of landowners such as Turner's reactionary patron, Jack Fuller. Appearing the year after the bloody "Peterloo" massacre of parliamentary reformists at Manchester and in the same year as the *Blackwood's* essay on native genius, the prints appeal to a retrospective impulse that naturalizes the unequal distribution of wealth and property and banishes social conflict into battles from a distant Saxon past that is subsumed into the realm of the natural.

The prints can be interpreted as visible manifestations of the constraints that the *Blackwood's* writer places upon genius. The landscape genius is not involved in the creation of ideal forms, but is "subjected" to the conditions of his own (considerable) knowledge, sensibility, and position in the social order. The productions of such an artistic subject in turn invite a viewing experience that is similarly circumscribed. Turner and Reinagle mobilize associationist precepts in a way that attempts to inhibit the free and random flow of ideas; *Views in Sussex* privileges trains of mental images and ideas customarily associated with specific histories and social forms. The notion that social hierarchy induces social harmony is represented visually in the image of the country house situated upon a hilly prominence, at one with the surrounding landscape and yet commanding attention through the brilliance of "natural" highlighting.[83] The formal unity of these sweeping panoramas underscores the notion that there is only one social feeling appropriate to the "inherent" character of the site depicted. What remains invisible (such as political hostility toward Fuller in his own county) is rendered unthinkable within the parameters of an associationist aesthetic and an empiricist science that privileges vision over the other senses in acquiring knowledge and experience.[84]

The images and texts of the *Views in Sussex* suggest that the artistic genius has the unique capacity to reveal national character as it inheres in the locus of the domestic landscape. Furthermore he can identify *with* this native character embodied in the landscape through his own sensibility. "Mr. Turner feels every subject as he ought," Reinagle writes in connection with the view of Brightling Observatory; and, again, in his remarks on *The Vale of Ashburnham*: "Mr. Turner has the essential knowledge and felicity to preserve the real character of all he paints or draws, and by feeling it himself makes his beholders feel it."[85] This process of representation is antithetical to those modern conceptions of Romanticism in which the artistic genius, fleeing the evils of human society, projects his feelings of alienation onto the natural landscape. Rather, feeling and expressing a scene's "true" character involves the sensitive and knowing artist in representing visually the shared body of customary associations that lends social significance to the scene.

As Reinagle's text suggests, the artist's own character is not effaced in this process; his individual sensibility and, equally importantly, his knowledge, is what permits him to identify and communicate these social feelings to less sensitive and knowledgeable viewers. This accords with Alison's account of the superiority of the landscape painter and Jeffrey's emphasis on the superior sensibility and knowledge of the poet in his review of Alison's *Essays*.[86] Whereas the history painter as constituted by academic discourse aspires to the status of the liberally educated viewer, the formulation of the landscape genius reverses this ordering. It is the viewer now who seeks to achieve the sensibility of the artist, stimulated by the associations aroused in the aesthetic contemplation of his works.

The artistic genius's superior power to stimulate the feelings and imagination of viewers is celebrated without reservation in Reinagle's commentary and Alison's *Essays*. Nonetheless constraints are placed on the artist and/or viewer that seem designed to insure that this creative power does not go out of control. Reinagle identifies the powerful emotions generated by the Sussex landscapes as socially binding feelings such as patriotic grief (in the view of Battle Abbey) or national pride (in the view of Heathfield), hence the possibility of genius manifesting and arousing disturbing emotions is foreclosed. The regulation of the viewer's gaze is presented in *Views in Sussex* as a sign of Turner's virtuosity, since this control is required to enhance the expressive intensity of the viewing experience. As noted in Reinagle's remarks about *The Vale of Heathfield*, artistic virtuosity is demonstrated by a work's capacity to "enslave and enchant the eye," and to surprise, astonish, or "please [the viewer] to a degree of ecstasy."

This "aesthetics of enchantment," as we might call it, is also vaunted by Alison when he describes the process of viewing the landscapes of Claude, hearing the music of Handel, or reading the poetry of Milton:

> It is then, only, we feel the sublimity or beauty of their productions, when our imaginations are kindled by their power, when we lose ourselves amid the number of images that pass before our minds, and when we waken at last from this play of fancy, as from the charm of a romantic dream.[87]

In this passage the fantasies kindled in the viewer's imagination by the productions of the artistic genius do not assume a disturbing aspect. Alison emphasizes the link between strong aesthetic feelings and the socialization and passivity of the viewer. Only viewers who are liberally educated and whose minds are unoccupied by private grief or business can have an intense experience of sublimity or beauty.[88] So constrained socially and mentally, such viewers would presumably be incapable or undesirous of dangerous imaginings as the result of their fantastic visions.

In contradistinction to Alison and Reinagle, the writer for *Blackwood's* overtly acknowledges the threat posed by genius in rejecting the notion of "unfettered" intellect. Recall the passage cited earlier which insists that

> the human intellect . . . is not an unfettered intelligence, ranging through absolute existence, and creating ideal form. It is the power of a being who in all parts of his nature, is subjected to conditions of life, who, in his sensibilities, his knowledge, his productions, is under restraint of his nature, and of his place among mankind.

Such an emphasis upon the retrospective rather than the innovative aspect of native genius signals a fundamental concern with the power of the creative individual to stimulate through his productions new and dangerous modes of thinking, feeling, and imagining. Whereas the genius's endorsement of the existing social hierarchy was tacitly assumed by Alison, and visibly demonstrated by Turner in his Sussex views (and textually reinforced by Reinagle's commentary), the writer for *Blackwood's* was less confident about the power of genius to subject itself to a retrospective vision of its own interiority and power at a time of intense social upheaval. He was not alone in harboring such misgivings. As we shall see in examining the critical response to landscape painting in the next chapter, the superior power of the artistic genius to provoke the imaginations of viewers was seldom questioned. What was very much in question, however, was whether the effects of that power on individual viewers and the national community were beneficial or dangerous.

Chapter 5

Genius as Alibi

IN MAY 1814 THE CRITIC FOR THE *London Chronicle* begins his review of the Royal Academy exhibition by noting the lack of "epic" paintings, a situation that is assuaged by the presence of some pleasing landscapes "which while they record no particular event, excite historical recollections by the happy mixture of general costume and figures, with the magnificence of national edifices, and the charms of rural scenery." He goes on to remark that "the eye is dazzled on entering the large room by the glowing freshness and brilliant colouring which distinguish both portraits and landscapes, in this highly decorated chamber. The intermixture and contrast renders the first *coup d'oeil* highly gratifying."[1] While history painting languishes in what literary historian Jon Klancher refers to as this "postrhetorical, postrevolutionary world," "historical recollections" are represented in landscape paintings.[2] Narrativity is forsaken (these works record "no particular event") in favor of associative chains of memories excited by an array of costumes, figures, architecture, and natural scenery. This refraction of history through landscape contributes to the general brilliance of the exhibition space, where the eye is dazzled and gratified by the combination of portraits (of "female loveliness," we are told later in the passage) and colorful landscapes.[3] Such an enthusiastic response to the exhibition's plethora of color, mixture of genres, and mixed genres was an open acknowledgment of the futility of academic practices and principles that attempted to define and differentiate the production of "public" and "private" forms of painting in England. The critic's remarks indicate that certain landscape painters were able to capitalize on this failure by producing works which could hold their own visually within the fashionable spaces of the exhibition and engage the interests of a national public in ways that traditional history painting did not. Such paintings invited individuals to "experience" their common English heritage and identity via the private recollections excited by natural scenery, national monuments, and anonymously costumed figures.

These new types of landscape painting stimulated a re-evaluation of the persona of the native landscape painter that can be traced in critical pronouncements published in the contemporary periodical press. We have seen that within the domain of pictorial representation this reworking of the identity of the landscape painter was perceived by contemporary commentators to center upon painterly displays of surface effects, the production of highly simplified and unified compositions, and the selection of what were deemed exceedingly unremarkable views as subject matter. Clearly the visual impact of these techniques shared some common ground with the eye-catching effects utilized by painters like Westall and Ibbetson. And as in the case of these older artists, the relationship between the young "native geniuses" and the market loomed large in the critical writings about them and their art. At issue was whether their landscapes were perceived to be natural or artificial, and whether they were judged to display the hand of the artist (seeking to promote himself in the marketplace) or his mind (the "natural" effect of native genius).

An examination of art criticism devoted to landscape painting in the periodical press from 1800 to 1820 will give some indication of how newer approaches to painterly landscape techniques were assessed and how they were distinguished from older practices, although the difficulties in analyzing such criticism are formidable.[4] Exhibition reviews of paintings, especially landscapes, tended to be brief and formulaic. Nonetheless, some general patterns and tendencies can be usefully traced. First, consistent with the concerns raised in the 1790s, some landscapes produced from 1800 to 1820 continued to be faulted for their slapdash effects and tawdry color. However, unlike the earlier period, in which few critical voices were raised in a fully elaborated defense of such works, distinctions were now made between the types of effects produced. Strong defenses were raised of certain works and artists, although consensus about particular artists or works was rare.

If a critical consensus did exist it was on the superiority of native artists over foreigners who had formerly achieved popular success in England. This phenomenon was not restricted to landscape painting, as is evidenced in the critical reaction to the British Institution's exhibition in 1814 of works by Hogarth, Wilson, Gainsborough, and Johann Zoffany. The last of these artists, a native of Germany, had enjoyed considerable popularity in England in the second half of the eighteenth century as a painter of conversation pieces and theatrical subjects, yet he was virtually ignored in reviews of the exhibition by writers who focused their attention on the three "founding fathers" of the British school.[5]

Such nationalistic fervor also affected the public reception of landscapes by the Alsace-born Philippe de Loutherbourg, who since coming to England in 1771 had pursued an active career as both a painter and a scene designer.[6] Although his paintings encompassed a range of subjects and genres, in the last two decades of his life (he died in 1812) he was best known at the Royal Academy exhibitions for his scenes of contemporary naval battles and for landscapes depicting sublime phenomena such as storms, shipwrecks, and avalanches. While the artist had always had his detractors, his works of the 1790s and early 1800s had generally been well received. For example, his *Coalbrookdale by Night* (RA, 1801) and *Avalanche or Icefall in the Alps* (Figure 37, RA, 1804) were widely praised for their brilliant color and bold effects.[7] *Avalanche* was the last work that was to garner such general acclaim, however. Increasingly reviews stressed criticisms of his work by earlier writers, such as Joseph Pott in an 1782 essay on landscape painting and Anthony Pasquin in reviews from the mid-1790s. Both men criticized his palette; Pott further characterized his style as affecting a "French pomposity."[8]

In the early 1800s this criticism was taken up by periodicals as ideologically diverse as Rudolph Ackermann's conservative, pro-ministerial *Repository of Arts* and Leigh Hunt's reformist, anti-ministerial *Reflector*. The review of the Royal Academy

37 Philippe Jacques de Loutherbourg, *An Avalanche or Ice-Fall in the Alps*, RA 1804. Oil on canvas, 42.9 × 62.4 in. Tate Gallery, London.

exhibition of 1809 in the *Repository of Arts* includes a brief comment on Loutherbourg's art production generally, before going on to praise works by Turner and Callcott:

> His pictures always bring the painter too much to our mind; and instead of dwelling on the majesty of the scene and partaking of the sentiment intended to be conveyed by the composition, we can think of nothing but the dexterous touch and fine execution of the artist.[9]

This criticism was directed at works such as Loutherbourg's *Landstorm with Overturned Wagon*, which was displayed in that year's exhibition. The painting in the Mead Art Museum now entitled *Landscape with Overturned Wagon in a Storm* (Figure 38) is probably the work in question.[10] It is a typical Loutherbourg scene, depicting a certifiably "sublime" incident, a road accident in the mountains caused by horses taking fright at the fury of a thunderstorm. Anthony Pasquin, whose earlier dissatisfaction with the artist was unabated in 1809, complained in a review for the *Morning Herald* that this picture lacked not only sentiment, but veracity: "this is not English nature. . . . The figures are not of any nation, but a species of Gallo-Britons, sturdy and muscular, with French lineaments."[11]

Leigh Hunt elaborated on this point by suggesting that Loutherbourg was incapable of representing English nature because he lacked an English sensibility. At least that is the implication of the following comment by Hunt in an analysis of English art published in the *Reflector* in 1812:

38 Philippe Jacques de Loutherbourg, *Landscape with Overturned Wagon in a Storm*, RA 1809.
Oil on canvas, 41.5 × 28.4 in. Mead Art Museum, Amherst College, Amherst, MA.

> Loutherbourg, a foreigner, wants the English cast of judgment; he is highly picturesque, and occasionally sublime, particularly in his Alpine scenery; but his luxuriance is apt to become mere flutter and tawdriness, and he works his colours up to such a glow that his landscapes sometimes appear lit up with a conflagration.[12]

It is not apparent from this passage whether or not Hunt believes that the natural landscape has a formative effect on national character. Effectively he comes close to endorsing this sort of "environmental determinism" by suggesting that the painter lacked the (inborn?) judgment needed to represent the English landscape and was most successful when painting the region where he was born and raised.[13] For Hunt (and Pasquin), Loutherbourg's ability to produce highly picturesque compositions does not insulate his work from criticism. On the contrary, the overtly contrived nature of his picturesque scenes, his use of intense colors and spectacular effects, *and* his identification as a French artist (by training if not by birth) renders his work liable to charges of Gallic affectation, with all that this phrase implies.

The power of nationalist sentiment in artistic discourse during the final years of the Napoleonic wars is suggested by its invocation in journals as politically opposed as the conservative *Repository* and Leigh Hunt's reformist *Reflector*. In articles on national character written in 1812, both periodicals stress the intellectual vigor and independent-mindedness of the English – qualities which Hunt associates especially with the middle classes and the anonymous writer for the *Repository* finds through-out the social hierarchy.[14] The latter journal marshals this notion of Englishness in defense of the political status quo. Adopting a militantly anti-French stance, the writer declares the corruption in the English system of political patronage to be insignificant compared to the military despotism of Napoleonic France.[15] Hunt, on the other hand, stresses that it is domestic political corruption – specifically engen-dered by the government of William Pitt and "his unphilosophical school" – which is threatening to undermine the tradition of English independence and independent thinking.[16] Given this consensus about what constituted the ideal of Englishness (if not the best method of maintaining it) and the concomitant strength of nationalist sentiment at this moment, it is questionable whether anyone but a native British artist could have been regarded as capable of depicting the "true character" of a domestic landscape.

If foreign artists were disqualified from representing English nature, the reverse was not necessarily the case: an English cast of mind may have been shaped by local circumstances, but the qualities of "mind" and sensibility gained through such conditioning often were seen to enable English artists and writers to represent the "true nature" of another country.[17] In 1819, for example, Turner was heralded for his bold and original portrayals of that same Alpine region which figured so promi-nently in Loutherbourg's *oeuvre*. Turner's Swiss views garnered the lion's share of the publicity surrounding the British watercolors displayed in 1819 at Walter Fawkes's private gallery in Grosvenor Square. Included in this exhibition were his views of Mont Blanc, the Lake of Thun, the Valley of Chamouni, and the upper falls of the Reichenbach River. The last work (Figure 39) presents a spectacular display of the artist's technical mastery of the watercolor medium. The surface of the painting is covered with small brushstrokes so deftly worked that one delicately modulated hue appears imperceptibly to merge into another.[18] In the center of the composition the mist thrown up by the fall is created entirely by Turner's scraping the surface of the paper. Exceeding the academic requirements for "breadth" or compositional unity, the end result is an Alpine vision in which mountains, mists, sky, and rainbow appear consubstantial. This is "poverty of landscape" with a vengeance – a *tour de force* of a genius whose knowledge and imagination enables him to transform base matter into shimmering presences of light and color.

A picture such as *The Upper Falls of the Reichenbach: Rainbow* employs artistic conventions that are arguably every bit as contrived as Loutherbourg's Alpine scenes. However, most critics who commented on Turner's watercolors saw his sensibility and creativity as enhancing rather than distorting the "true" character of the site depicted. For example, the critic for the *Champion* reviewing the Fawkes exhibition praises Turner for his "strength of conception, depth of feeling" and originality, and goes on to extol the "life" he breathes into his productions ("his foliage moves . . . in the breeze . . . his water invites one to bathe"). He concludes by quoting some doggerel by the eighteenth-century critic known as Peter Pindar, in order to draw a pointed contrast between Turner's work and Loutherbourg's:

There is nothing about his [Turner's] pictures, to remind the beholder of the verses of the satirist –

> And Loutherbourg, when heaven so wills
> To make brass skies and golden hills
> With marble oxen in glass meadows grazing,
> Your pictures really will be most amazing![19]

The critic for the *London Chronicle* endorses such a view of Turner's work, but casts it in a larger national framework. "Turner," he declares,

> is perhaps the first artist in the world in this powerful and brilliant style, no man has ever thrown such masses of colour upon paper. . . . The art itself [watercolor] is *par excellence* English, no continental pencil can come near the force, freedom, and nature of our professor, and as such independently of the general promoting of fine taste, there is patriotic spirit displayed in its patronage.[20]

English genius ("*par excellence*"!), is characterized by a power and bravura which ensure that "effects" and intense color – so frequently identified with a feminized, Gallicized practice – could instantiate a masculine Englishness if presented with "force" (colors are "thrown," rather than applied) and "freedom," the essential characteristic that distinguishes English artists and English subjects from their continental counterparts. Secured by such a manly, independent, English identity, the artistic subject can "show himself" in the most fashionable sphere of society and emerge as a genius, not a sycophant.

It is in this sense that genius operates as an alibi, functioning in places regarded by proponents of traditional history painting as inimical to the high-minded appreciation of serious art. Graced by genius, the spaces of fashionable leisure and of high culture merge, transforming the people who inhabit them – at least that is what the *Repository of Arts* claims for Fawkes's Gallery, which was inundated by visitors from the *haut ton*: "When a picture-gallery becomes a fashionable lounge, the art itself steals insensibly on the imagination, and captivates the mind by the richness and variety of its moral energies."[21] The language used here, with its allusions to the enthrallment of the imagination by rich and varied images, conjures up the discourse of associationism, revised and reformulated for a fashionable setting. Whereas Alison insisted that it was the viewer at rest, undisturbed by business or personal cares, who was capable of producing imaginative associations upon viewing landscape paintings or natural scenery, the *Repository* writer suggests that the imaginative viewer, actively engaged in the pursuit of metropolitan leisure, can be surreptitiously captivated by works radiating "moral richness and energy" – a phrase which is resonant both with the plenitude of images and the social feeling called up by the power of associative imaginings.[22]

Like virtually every other review of this exhibition, the *London Chronicle* and *Repository* lavish praise on the owner of the aforementioned "fashionable lounge," Walter Fawkes, for his patronage of domestic artists.[23] The exhibition was acclaimed as a true expression of patriotic spirit on the part of a wealthy landowner who not only collected exclusively British art, but made it available (if only fleetingly) to "the English public," which in this instance meant those privileged mem-

39 J.M.W. Turner, *The Upper Falls of the Reichenbach: Rainbow*, 1810? Watercolor, 11 ×
15.5 in. Yale Center for British Art, Paul Mellon Collection, New Haven.

bers of society who possessed the leisure, manners, fine clothing, and sense of
cultural entitlement necessary to gain entrance to such a fashionable event. In
reviewing the exhibition the critic for the pro-ministerial, conservative *London
Chronicle* begins by praising Fawkes's town house as the abode of "an opulent and
manly-minded English landowner." It is "furnished with great elegance, not with
French elegance, but something that we like much better, the solid and pure taste
of England."[24] Once again French anti-types are mobilized in order to present
Fawkes as the paragon of the "manly" public-spirited private citizen whose taste in
art is a manifestation of his own English independent-mindedness and sensibility.
Fawkes's exhibition took place at the low point of the post-war depression, a time
of extreme political unrest. As noted in the previous chapter, the landed elite was
subject to renewed and increasingly vociferous attacks on its public and private
morals, and ultimately on its capacity to govern. Hence, cultural events such as
Fawkes's exhibition became an occasion for the spokesmen for the landed elite to
reiterate their claim to patriotic virtue and public authority. In these circumstances
it was still deemed advisable to define the English ruling class in opposition to their
French counterparts, despite the fact that four years had elapsed since Napoleon's
defeat and a Bourbon king again occupied the French throne.

The *Repository* critic also praises Fawkes for his support of that most "English" of art forms, watercolor: "The patronage given to the arts by Mr. Fawkes is truly English: his collection consists entirely of water-colour drawings – a department of art which has been peculiarly studied and perfected in this country."[25] The review concludes with the optimistic prediction that the time is fast approaching "when like the days of Athens, it will be impossible for a man to be great and at the same time obscure." It will no longer be the case that "the noble enthusiasm of a mind like Barry's shall work its own ruin by brooding over neglect and disappointment."[26] One can only imagine how Barry (who died in 1806), with his dedication to large-scale history paintings designed for public display in government buildings or churches, would have felt about having his professional and personal failure invoked in celebrating this form of "English patronage" – namely, wealthy collectors displaying for a limited time, in their private town houses, cabinet-sized landscape watercolors that were usually sequestered in portfolios.[27]

Given *Repository of Arts* publisher Rudolph Ackermann's financial interest in promoting fashion and fashionable accomplishments like watercolor painting, it would appear far from coincidental that his magazine sought to dissolve the traditional antipathy between high, moral public art and the world of commerce and fashion by vigorously promoting the English geniuses of the new school of landscape painting. The *Repository* repeatedly touted the heightened imagination and sensibility possessed by artists in comparison with the rest of humankind – a distinction allegedly evident in the painter's enhanced capacity to respond to scenes of common nature. This point was underscored in an article published in 1817 entitled "On the Superiority of the Painter's Feelings." It describes the landscape painter as an enthusiast who responds more deeply to views of common nature than the ordinary person and cites Gainsborough as an example of an artist who drew purely for personal pleasure scenes in the environs of his native village in Suffolk. The ability to respond deeply to common nature is taken by the writer as a sign of moral purity; "votaries of dissipation" also seek out nature, but fail to derive true value and meaning from the experience.[28]

The writer amalgamates commonly opposed discourses on commerce and the countryside in order to extol the pleasures of viewing the natural landscape:

> to indulge in the contemplation of the purest scenes of pastoral nature, to pore over the near and distant landscape, and to watch the gradations of light and shade on the surrounding scenery, have ever been the highest enjoyment of those on whom Providence has lavished the luxury of intellect.[29]

The moral purity of nature is here invoked through an appeal to the luxury, indulgence, and pleasure that had traditionally been associated with the negative aspects of commercial life in the metropolis.[30] Morally pure, yet clearly sensual pleasure is aroused in the viewer via the action of spontaneous processes of nature: subtle changes in light and shade catalyze a plentitude of pleasurable (and pure) thoughts and feelings. Note that nature is here posited chiefly in terms of ephemeral effects of light and shade, as it is in a later passage where the writer asserts that morally elevating feelings are produced at that moment when the "sun tinges the horizon or recedes from the eye, until the whole outline is melted into vapour."[31]

The artistically knowledgeable reader would recognize that such a description of "nature" also serves to describe the paintings of Girtin, Turner, Callcott, and others who dissolve the forms of nature into veils of brilliant, carefully modulated color.

While promoting the immense powers of genius on the one hand, the purveyors of commerce and fashion construct the viewer as a consumer of "morally rich" imagery. This spectator is either an admiring female (as described in *Ackermann's New Drawing Book of Light and Shadow*), who supports native genius by her patronage and amateur interest in drawing landscapes, or a passive male enthralled by the charms of painting, which is personified as a seductress who preserves both her modesty and the essential character of nature. "On the Superiority of the Painter's Feelings" also invokes divine Providence in explaining "man's" love of nature, but, as its title attests, the article is primarily concerned with celebrating the creative power and heightened sensibility of the landscape painter. While for a clergyman like Archibald Alison the ultimate goal of the spectator's aesthetic encounter with nature is to increase his/her love and reverence for God, the professionalization and concurrent secularization of cultural criticism served effectively to redirect awe before God to awe before the powers of artistic genius. We have already seen such a reconfiguration of the sublime in Reinagle's text for *Views in Sussex*; likewise an unnamed (and still untraced) review of the 1819 Fawkes exhibition supports the idea that the sublime effect of landscape painting is to establish the superiority of an artistic genius like Turner: "By the magic of his pencil, we are brought to the regions of such rare and awful grandeur that criticism is baffled; and while we are absorbed in admiration, we reel conscious of our incompetence to offer any detailed remarks of the use made by this artist of the materials which come within the contemplation of few and within the employment of still fewer."[32]

For paintings to "steal insensibly on the imagination" in the crowded spaces of public exhibitions and private galleries, they not only had to appear natural and unselfconscious, but needed to compete visually with the highly colored works and richly dressed visitors that filled both public and private exhibition spaces.[33] The dilemma this presented some artists is clear from the comments of a critic reviewing the Royal Academy exhibition of 1806 for the *British Press*.[34] He faults Loutherbourg's *Evening* for its artificially fiery sun, while criticizing William Daniell's *New Bridge, Durham* for being painted "too tenderly for an exhibition room." In 1810 the critic for the *Monthly Magazine* evidences awareness of both of these criteria. He begins his Royal Academy review by warning British artists that if domestic painting runs "riot after effect and manner" it might "sink below the level of the Dutch and Flemish schools of fac-similists and face-painters."[35] But in the next month's issue the critic declares that "the uncommon brilliancy of this charming picture [Turner's *Petworth, Sussex, the Seat of the Earl of Egremont: Dewy Morning*, Figure 40] produces the same effect on the neighbouring pieces, as hanging them against the pier of a window through which the sun is shining."[36] Turner's painting is seen here to kill the works around it, but the brilliance of its orange-gold sky and water does not raise the charges of affectation and self-display that so often dogged Loutherbourg. Other criticisms that the painting received suggest the reason for such a distinction: they all focus on the degree to which Turner is successful in representing the vaporous atmosphere and the water. These

40 J.M.W. Turner, *Petworth, Sussex, the Seat of the Earl of Egremont: Dewy Morning*, RA 1810. Oil on canvas, 36 × 47.5 in. Tate Gallery and the National Trust (Lord Egremont Collection), Petworth House, West Sussex.

judgments range from the censure of *La Belle Assemblée*, which sees the work as descending into confusion because it lacks sufficient tonal contrast, to the *Public Ledger*'s praise for the light scumbling and glazing that "happily expressed" the water and dewy air.[37] Despite such differences of opinion, these and other critics tacitly indicate that the artist's concern is the accurate representation of natural effects, and not self-representation.

This distinction is crucial, if subtle, and marks the difference between the native genius and the crass producer of landscapes as a cultural commodity. Robert Hunt describes the complex relationship that exists between genius and nature at the conclusion of his review of the British Institution exhibition of 1814. He complains that most of the artists in the exhibition lack originality and then goes on to define that term (very much as Reinagle does in *Views in Sussex*) as "the power that makes us, while looking on their works, forget the workmen, and pay due homage to Genius and Science, by thinking only of the aspects and operations of Nature."[38]

In order to understand how the artistic subject is being constructed within the terms of this definition it is useful to consider the distinction Peter de Bolla makes with regard to subjectivity in the context of oratory. He differentiates between a subject's being a product of discourse and being an effect of discourse. The distinction is a subtle, but very important one. In the first instance, "the account of subjectivity as *product* is based on a notion of self-projection, as if the internal subject strives to give as good an impression as possible to the others who constitute society. It suggests that one might make oneself in discourse."[39] The situation is analogous to the critical construction of Loutherbourg as an artist who tries "too hard," who shows himself too strongly in his works, so that we "forget nature and think only of the workman," to reverse Hunt's terms. The second form of subjectivity as an *effect* is described by de Bolla as

> something which just happens to appear in certain discursive forms and operations; it is less a property of the individual than a function of specific discursive situations. In this case one should not appear to be trying: in order to present oneself in the best possible light to others one should be not seen to be making any perceptible effort.[40]

Hunt's formulation of genius and originality possesses some of this public impersonality, since viewers are to pay homage to "Genius and Science," the capitalization suggesting that it is the abstract properties of these entities viewers honor when confronted with an original work.

Nonetheless, the ideal of the genius differs from the kind of public man de Bolla is describing, since it connotes singularity as well as creative power, and therefore could only be recognized as a manifestation of an individual artistic personality. Critics throughout the period frequently characterized artists by the expressive quality of their work. For example, in 1813 W. H. Pyne, writing in the *Repository of Arts*, characterizes the works of Turner and Girtin in terms designed to distinguish their individual creative temperaments: "Turner's works were the most admired for sentiment, and Girtin's for boldness and spirit; yet each adhered so cleverly to nature, and possesses such original merit, that it became difficult to decide which was the greater genius."[41]

Making stylistic differentiations between individual personalities was a common feature of art criticism, but in the case of landscape painting at this particular moment, these expressive distinctions took on a special force, sustained by the powerful authority of nationalist discourse. For it was through the landscapes of artists with such distinctive sensibilities that less sensitive and imaginative viewers gained access to the essential character of the natural world, registered through transitory effects playing over its surface.

This focus on individual sensibilities was, however, gender specific. My examination of exhibition reviews in the periodical press between 1795 and 1820 suggests that distinctions in personal style were seldom if ever made among women artists; their gender is presented as the major determinant of their manner of painting. For example, Leigh Hunt, in his *Reflector* essay on art in Britain, condemns Angelica Kauffman's forays into the male preserve of history painting as "feeble" and "fluttering."[42] Robert Hunt shared his brother's preconceptions and opinions on this issue, as is obvious from his obituary of Kauffman in 1808: "The grandeur of epic painting has never been conceived by female genius"; he goes on to assert that women are only capable of displaying the "gentle feelings of the human heart."[43] On the other hand both brothers professed a fondness for the rustic genre scenes of Harriet Gouldsmith. When she exhibited *The Fisherman's Cottage* at the Royal Academy in 1810, Robert Hunt praised it for its delicacy, elegance, lack of affectation, and simplicity – terms that could be taken to apply equally to the character of the image and to a widely disseminated contemporary feminine ideal that artist could be seen to embody.[44] Although simplicity in landscape painting could signify the transformative powers of a masculine imagination, its appearance here in close association with the terms "elegance" and "delicacy" undercuts any notion of magical power or intellectual boldness. Furthermore, Gouldsmith's chosen genre of rustic life subjects was seen to require imitative skill rather than imaginative power, thus was deemed fitting for a woman artist. As noted previously, landscape painting lent itself to copying by women amateurs, but the kinds of expressive landscape that gained publicity both in print and on display in public and private collections, were clearly regarded as the province of male professionals.

Among the expressive effects that two of the most successful male professionals, Callcott and Turner, were employing in the second decade of the century were those obtained by saturating the canvas with broad expanses of graduated warm-toned pigments, especially red ochre, yellow, and orange. This use of a closely modulated palette of advancing, high-key color produces works capable of functioning in an exhibition space quite effectively – witness Turner's *Petworth*, which "killed" the paintings around it. It is not only the intensity of colors, but their extension across the surface of relatively large-scale canvases that enables such works to capture viewers' attention.

This point is made by the reviewer for the *London Chronicle* in 1812. Commenting upon Callcott's *Littlehampton Pier* (Figure 41), he writes that it is a "delightful performance, with daylight finely expressed; it does not owe its beauty to strong oppositions, and although placed in the midst of red coats and strong-coloured pictures, keeps its ground on account of its unaffected simplicity."[45] "Unaffected" is the key word, for what distinguishes the "translucent" artistic subject – the man of genius and sensibility – from the "opaque" man of the market, is that he seeks the representation of nature, not himself.

Consensus was a rare commodity among art critics. In the case of Callcott, most agreed that his works were highly simplified and atmospheric, but there was less agreement on how natural and unaffected they were. His reputation was made on the basis of predominantly English scenes – panoramic marine, forest, and coastal scenes like *Littlehampton Pier*, which were frequently compared with the works of the seventeenth-century Dutch masters, as well as with his friend and colleague, Turner.[46] A few figures or ships provide the only sources of incident in compositions marked by broad expanses of water and sky and painted in subtly modulated tones. A case in point is his *Cowboys* (Figure 42), exhibited at the Royal Academy in 1807. Emulating seventeenth-century Dutch models, especially Cuyp, the foreground figures of the boys and dog dominate a landscape reduced to a few trees and hills rendered indistinct by the hazy atmosphere. A full two-thirds of the canvas is encompassed by an uninterrupted expanse of sky that, excepting the patch of blue in the upper right, is rendered in closely modulated brown to golden tones. While

41 Augustus Wall Callcott, *Littlehampton Pier*, RA 1812. Oil on canvas, 55.3 × 41.8 in. Tate Gallery, London.

the picture includes standard picturesque features – trees, rustic figures, and farm buildings – the work is aggressively anti-picturesque in its disposition of these elements. All but the boys and their dog are relegated to the distant horizon, with the picturesque grouping of these figures undercut by the simplification of the composition and the overarching dominance of the sky and the hazy atmosphere that conveys the heat and humidity of an overcast summer day.

Cowboys clearly was designed to call to mind Cuyp's highly simplified, light-suffused pastoral scenes, and yet the reviewer for the *Star* disavowed this connection in order to praise the artist's attention to English nature: "This is one of Mr. Callcott's best pictures, because in it he has trusted more to his own observance of English Nature than to Foreign Works of Art."[47] Most commentators did acknowledge the correspondence between Callcott's work and those Dutch masters so highly regarded by English collectors, especially Cuyp. For example, the artist Thomas Uwins wrote in a letter to a friend that "Callcott has fairly outboated himself; his picture of the entrance to the port of London is quite as fine as anything Cuyp ever painted, or anything that has ever been done in this way, in

42 Augustus Wall Callcott, *Cowboys*, RA 1807. Oil on canvas, 49.2 × 40.2 in. Herbert Art
Gallery, Coventry.

43   Aelbert Cuyp, *Herdsmen with Cows*, *c.*1660. Oil on canvas, 39.5 × 56.8 in. By Permission of the Trustees of Dulwich Picture Gallery, London.

any age or country."[48] Uwins was referring to Callcott's highly acclaimed *The Pool of London* (Figure 44), which was one of the most successful pictures exhibited at the Royal Academy in 1816. Concerned that the artist might be seen only as an imitator, the *Repository of Art*'s review of the painting awkwardly attempts to negotiate the apparent contradiction between the artist's invocation of the Dutch master and fidelity to English nature by making a series of negative assertions:

> To say, as has been said, that it is more like Cuyp than nature, is not true, and to say it is not like both would be so likewise; but to say, that even the Marquis of Stafford's Cuyp, which it most resembles, is equal to it, would be unjust also. Of this species of style we think this the very best picture we ever saw, in point of colour, composition, drawing, and brilliancy of daylight; in those it has no equal.[49]

The most straightforward way to understand such muddled prose and the painting that it describes is to see them as attempts to meet two different standards for assessing domestic landscape: one still based on old master models and another based on an increasingly authoritative appeal to the empirical observation of "common" English nature.[50]

More to the point, however, I would propose that Callcott's taking up of Cuyp was particularly successful because the Dutch artist had a reputation in England for addressing the same set of representational demands as contemporary English artists. John Landseer, for example, praises Cuyp's ability to create "admirable" paintings out of very simple materials ("a few cattle and a setting sun"). This reference

44 Augustus Wall Callcott, *The Pool of London*, RA 1816. Oil on canvas, 60.3 × 87 in. Trustees of the Bowood Settlement, Calne, Wiltshire.

appeared in a review of Turner's *Forest of Bere* (Figure 45, exhibited Turner Gallery, 1808) which, he declares, "is nothing as a subject, [but] . . . everything as a picture." Landseer concludes by claiming that "the pride of Cuyp . . . would be humbled, we conceive, by a too near approach to this picture of Turner."[51]

Eight years later, a reviewer for the *Annals of the Fine Arts* praises one of Cuyp's "landscape with cattle" subjects (see, for example, Figure 43, *Herdsmen with Cows*) in much the same terms as the *London Chronicle* used to describe Callcott's *Littlehampton Pier*.[52] According to this critic, the Cuyp, which was on display at the newly opened Dulwich Gallery, is "full of that truth of nature just bordering on the artificial, that characterizes this master's best works, and is a proof of the superiority of the true natural tone of colouring over the gaudy exhibition style of some of its more assuming neighbours" – its neighbors being works by Francis Bourgeois and the eighteenth-century French landscape and marine painter Claude-Joseph Vernet.[53] Cuyp, then, was a sanctioned old master model for the kind of artistic subject who, in his treatment of atmospheric effects, treaded more or less successfully the fine line between nature and affectation. This borderline defines the narrow limits within which the genius (the "translucent" subject who neither shows himself ostentatiously nor disappears altogether) can operate without becoming a mechanical imitator or a mannerist.

While critical discourse generally endorsed the efforts of contemporary artists to compete with and adapt the techniques of masters like Cuyp, other northern masters proved to be less acceptable.[54] The reviewer for the *Star* who praised Callcott's *Cowboys* for its rejection of foreign models, was in fact alluding here to his own negative assessment of Callcott's *Market Day* (Figure 46), also exhibited in 1807, which he complained was overly indebted to the Dutch artist Waterloo, and therefore displayed "no breadth of light or shade, or combination of parts."[55] The latter work featured a rutted and serpentine road, a foreground marked by a decayed log with twisted limbs, and a background screen of irregularly massed foliage. Callcott utilizes stark contrasts of light and shade to indicate the sun's breaking through the storm-darkened sky, yet the general tone of the work is exceedingly somber, in keeping with Dutch landscape tradition of Ruysdael and Hobbema. In its fixation on picturesque irregularity of form and patchy distribution of light and shade, Callcott's picture appeared old-fashioned and pointedly un-English in comparison with his *Cowboys*; it is not surprising that his later compositions became dominated by broad atmospheric effects.

Rubens, while prized by English collectors, also provided a risky model for contemporary painters of domestic landscapes. James Ward's rustic animal scenes and landscapes frequently invoked the manner of the Flemish master and suffered critical and academic condemnation as a result. His *Bulls Fighting, with a View of St.*

45   J. M. W. Turner, *The Forest of Bere*, TG 1808. Oil on canvas, 35 × 47 in. Tate Gallery and the National Trust (Lord Egremont Collection), Petworth House, West Sussex.

46   Augustus Wall Callcott, *Market Day*, RA 1807. Oil on canvas, 58 × 100.8 in. Tabley Collection, University of Manchester, Manchester (photo: Courtauld Institute of Art).

Donatt's Castle, Glamorganshire (Figure 47) was rejected from the Royal Academy exhibition of 1804 for being too closely patterned after Rubens's *A View of the Château de Steen, Autumn* (Figure 48), which had entered George Beaumont's collection earlier that year.[56] Ward's work follows Rubens's in depicting an extensive panorama, richly varied both in the picturesque objects shown – cottages, castle, rustic figures, sheep, and meandering road – and in the patchwork of warm-toned colors, punctuated in Ward's work by the red and white bulls in the foreground. Like Rubens, Ward adopts a rope-like, twisted line, which lends a further complexity and energy to the composition.

Some sense of the critical discomfort with Ward's taking up of Rubens can be traced in the comments of the critic for the *Repository of Arts* who, in 1809, complains that Ward's pictures generally are "obscured by affectation. . . . He seems to think it of more importance to paint like Rubens than to paint like nature." Robert Hunt in the *Examiner* in 1817 likewise observes that Ward's *Bulls Fighting* is a close imitation of the "trailing pencil, profuse touch and gay colouring of RUBENS's landscapes" and then goes on to ask: why "does Mr. W. copy RUBENS rather than Nature?"[57] Compared to Cuyp's vaporous golden hazes, Rubens's brilliant color and tortuous, decorative line were eye-catching, but not deemed natural enough to be suited to contemporary landscapes.

Turner says as much in his final perspective lecture, first delivered to students at the Royal Academy in 1811.[58] He notes that while the Flemish master had acquired mechanical excellence in coloring, he "disdained to hide, but threw around his tints like a bunch of flowers."[59] Unlike Cuyp, Rubens flaunted his handicraft, debasing both the artist and the work. Declaring that Rubens "could not be happy with the bare simplicity of pastoral scenery or the immutable laws of nature's light and shade," Turner observes that the figures in his *Landscape with Waggon* are lit in various directions. "These trifles about light," he writes, "are so perhaps in Historical compositions, but in Landscape they are inadmissible and become absurdities

47　James Ward, *Bulls Fighting, with a View of St. Donatt's Castle, Glamorganshire, c.*1803. Oil on panel, 51.5 × 89 in. Victoria and Albert Museum, London.

48　Peter Paul Rubens, *A View of the Château de Steen, Autumn*, 1636? Oil on panel, 53.4 × 81.3 in. Courtesy of the Trustees of the National Gallery, London.

destroying the simplicity, the truth, the beauty of pastoral nature in whose pursuit he always appears lavish of his powers."[60] Beyond aiming a barb at history paintings that treat light effects as mere trifles, Turner repeats the need to maintain an aura of simplicity, as well as "truth" when representing natural scenery.

The writings of Alison, Reinagle's commentary on Turner's Sussex views, and the criticism of works by Callcott, Turner, and Cuyp discussed above all indicate that the notion of "simplicity" in landscape at this time had a dual signification. It called up not only an image of modesty and naturalness antithetical to Rubenesque (or picturesque) affectation and artificiality, but also a vision of the artist who effects magical transformations of common and unremarkable materials. Robert Hunt makes the point quite explicitly in 1808 when he praises the execution of Callcott's *A Mill, near Llangollen*: "The magic of this artist's pencil has here converted a few of the simplest materials of rural nature into a most interesting picture."[61]

Other critics and commentators, however, were less enthusiastic. Bafflement and concern mark the response of the critic for the *Monthly Mirror* in assessing two of Callcott's earliest exhibited landscapes. Commenting on the artist's *Banks of a River* (RA, 1802) he notes that "this is an accurate representation of the partial colouring of nature, but is of so abstract a kind as rather to appear a part of a picture than an entire composition."[62] The critic declares that the other landscape "appears more the indulgence of a peculiar disposition, than an adherence to real objects." Unlike Alison, the critic does not celebrate this projection of individual artistic character onto the natural objects of representation; rather he sees it as an unsuccessful attempt to develop a personal style. "Nothing," he continues, "is more difficult than to form a style of distinct singularity, and nothing more dangerous; yet there is always merit in the ambition."[63] Such a statement testifies to the ambivalence and anxiety that suffused attempts to define and regulate artistic subjectivity. An artist who self-consciously attempts to "produce himself" (to use de Bolla's term) through a singular style of painting is not simply condemned by this writer, as he would have been by Reynolds or by Dayes. Instead he is both criticized and commended for his effort, and warned that such a project of self-representation is difficult and dangerous.

Similar criticisms, it should be recalled, were leveled against artists such as Westall, Bourgeois, and Loutherbourg who appeared to be promoting themselves rather than representing nature through the use of brilliant color and light effects. Not surprisingly, some critics directed these same criticisms at Turner, Callcott, and Girtin. For example, Girtin's effects were declared to be "spotty" by the *St. James Chronicle* (2–8 May 1800); the *Morning Post* (18 June 1812) assailed Callcott's *Hampton Court Bridge* (RA, 1812) for being extremely mannered and artificial; and Turner was harshly attacked by the *Champion*'s critic on 12 May 1816 for producing artificial, gaudily colored works that were "intended to become a striking point of attraction on the walls of the Exhibition." A more general critique along these lines was launched by the *New Monthly Magazine*'s critic in a review of the Royal Academy exhibition of 1820. The writer begins by noting that like the portraitist competing for attention in the exhibition, the painter of local views "is also compelled to paint, in bright and exaggerated colours, that his piece may have some chance of attracting notice among the gaudy mass of the portraits." Like

Fuseli, the writer bemoans the proliferation of imitative landscapes and the corresponding lack of imaginative landscapes. He goes on to observe that critics have directed public attention to mechanical skill, and this combined with the public's tendency to seek pleasure in imitation leads to the popular success of works such as a hypothetical "view of Broad-St.-Giles, executed in a dashing style, a red and yellow, brown and blue, properly distributed in the foreground, and carried off *secundum artem* with the truth of linear perspective and proper allowance of air."[64] But unlike these critiques, the *Mirror* reviewer's assessment of Callcott's work as "an accurate representation of the partial colouring of nature . . . of so abstract a kind as rather to appear a part of a picture than an entire composition" suggests sources of concern that were not previously voiced by critics. While earlier works were seen to dazzle the spectator with their scattered lights and brilliant surface displays, the newer works were more often faulted for their excessive simplicity and indistinctness.

The critic for the *Repository of Arts* alludes to this type of criticism of Callcott's work in his Academy review of 1809 when he writes: "The observation usually made on his pictures is that they are barren in subject, that the interest of the picture is not in proportion to the quantity of canvas occupied."[65] Some viewers apparently were disconcerted rather than enthralled by the sight of large areas of canvas devoted so largely to the representation of sky and water.[66] Callcott was not the only artist to garner such criticism. In the late teens Copley Fielding had been exhibiting marine and coastal views such as *Sunset off Hastings* (Figure 49, 1819), which depicts an expanse of beach, sea, and sky, dramatically lit by the rays of the setting sun. In 1819 the critic for the *Champion*, reviewing the annual exhibition of the Society of Painters in Oil and Water-Colours, praises the effects represented in Fielding's sea and coast scenes, but then issues a warning: "We wish our artists, however, may not become too fond of making *pictures of nothing*. Expanses of skies and seas and sands, and the mere phenomenon of the elements are fit *accompaniments* – but they are hardly *subjects* for pictures."[67]

The phrase "pictures of nothing" most likely derives from Hazlitt, who used it with regard to Turner on at least two occasions in 1815–16. In February 1815 Hazlitt launched a similar criticism in favorably comparing two other works by Fielding, *Morning* and *View from Rydal Woods*, to the Scottish views exhibited by Thomas Hofland in the British Institution. Fielding's latter work, Hazlitt writes,

is a fine, woody, and romantic scene, which in some degree calls off our admiration from the merit of the artist to the beauties of nature. This is a sacrifice of self-love which many of our artists do not seem willing to make. They too often chuse their subjects, not to exhibit the charms of nature, but to display their own skill in making something of the most barren subjects.

We think this objection applies to Mr. Hofland's landscapes in general. The scene he selects is represented with great truth and felicity of pencil, but it is, generally speaking, one we should neither wish to look at, nor to be in. In his *Loch Lomand* and *Stirling Castle*, the effect of the atmosphere is finely given; but this is all. We wish to enter our protest against this principle of separating *the imitation* from *the thing imitated*, particularly as it is countenanced by the authority

49   Copley Fielding, *Sunset off Hastings*, 1819. Watercolor, 15.4 × 20.7 in. Victoria and Albert Museum, London.

of the ablest landscape painter of the present day, of whose landscapes some one said, that "they were pictures of nothing, and very like!"[68]

Hofland's *Stirling Castle* (Figure 50), may be the canvas to which Hazlitt refers. Compared to Ward's view of St. Donatt's Castle, with its rich abundance of color and objects, *Stirling Castle* offers the viewer only a pair of mountain sheep in a foreground otherwise undistinguished, a middle ground of tonally undifferentiated trees and scrub brush, and a shimmering distance of hazy mountains and grazing lands. Even the castle, shown as a rectilinear form silhouetted against an overcast sky, offers little picturesque interest. Hazlitt's criticism, like that of the *Champion* critic in 1819, is not a charge of artificiality, of transforming nature into a gaudy seductress. Nor is the issue, as Hazlitt implies, simply that Hofland has separated "the imitation from the thing imitated," for he states that the artist has truthfully rendered the site selected.[69] Rather, Hofland is judged to have abandoned significant subject matter altogether. Viewers are invited to admire the brilliant execu-

50   Thomas Christopher Hofland, *Stirling Castle*, *c.*1815. Oil on canvas, 51.5 × 71.8 in. Tate
Gallery, London.

tion of natural effects that signify individual artistic imagination and professional
prowess, rather than being drawn into a landscape imbued with native feeling and
historical recollections.

Seven months prior to these remarks Hazlitt had published an essay on
Gainsborough, discussed earlier, in which he extolled the virtues of artistic professionalism and the exercise of a bold, masculine intellect in opposition to the mental
lassitude of the effete, aristocratic amateur.[70] However, he regarded such creative
energy and professional skill as misdirected if taken to excess. He reiterated this
point in the context of an essay, "On Imitation," published in the *Examiner* in
1816, where the practice of imitating objects in nature is defended on the grounds
that "imitation renders an object, displeasing in itself, a source of pleasure, not by
repetition of the same idea, but by suggesting new ideas, by detecting new properties, and endless shades of difference."[71] The production of this expanding knowledge of the object is a source of pleasure in and of itself; "knowledge is pleasure as
well as power," as Hazlitt puts it. Turning then to the sphere of artistic practice, he
considers the pleasure derived from the production and contemplation of art
"which none but artists feel," due to their superior knowledge, powers of imagination, and sensibility. While this specialized power of seeing and representing
objects brings pleasure to the artist, it also threatens to isolate him. "True genius,"
he declares, "though it has new sources of pleasure opened to it, does not lose its
sympathy with humanity."[72] He then warns that "some artists among ourselves

have carried the same principles [of technical obscurantism] to a singular excess." In a footnote to this remark he launches an attack on Turner,

> the ablest landscape painter now living, whose pictures are, however, too much abstractions of aerial perspective, and representations, not properly of the objects of nature as of the medium through which they are seen. They are the triumph of the knowledge of the artist, and of the power of the pencil over the barrenness of the subject.

After making an analogy between Turner's works and the world in its chaotic state before creation, he repeats the phrase that these are "pictures of nothing and very like."[73] Following this attack on the landscape painter, Hazlitt declares the connoisseur and dilettante to be even more prone to this kind of pedantry, since they possess less sensibility than artists, and are "proud of their knowledge in proportion as it is secret."[74]

I have quoted from this section of the essay at some length in order to demonstrate the difference that exists between Hazlitt's attack on artists (and connoisseurs) who are overly enthralled with technical knowledge and execution and academic attacks on imitation that reduce the artist to the status of an artisan. The danger here resides not in the banality of mechanical reproduction, but in the love of specialized knowledge. The result is an aesthetic elitism that has the same isolating effect as the most esoteric form of history painting. Ironically, those practices that modern scholars recognize as constituting "naturalism" in early nineteenth-century landscape – selecting of "common" views as subject matter, bold use of color, and attention to natural light effects – were seen by Hazlitt and other contemporaries as threatening to devolve into a form of obscurantism which alienates rather than attracts. For within the terms of such a critique, the artistic subject is not degraded by pandering to the vulgar multitudes via works which appeal only to their senses. Instead such displays of professional skill are seen artificially to elevate the artist, whose productions baffle the understanding of viewers, reducing them to a state of wonder which bespeaks passive admiration of a knowledge they do not possess. Although Hazlitt had no interest in promoting art as a democratized form of public edification (despite his radical politics), it is clear that he had misgivings about the power and status that "secret" (specialized) knowledge could confer upon individuals bound up with their own pleasure and self-interest.[75]

Among the various techniques that made visible the disjuncture (both physical and epistemological) between the subject position of the viewer and that of the landscape artist, none was more contentious than the indistinct rendering of forms – especially foreground forms.[76] Peter de Bolla has argued that it was the need to enforce a coherence between the position of the spectator and the artist via the system of one-point perspective that accounts for the publication in the eighteenth century of at least seventeen perspective treatises, all reiterating the same Albertian system of rules. This system fixes a single "point of sight" for the picture that in effect becomes a transparent window on the "real" (even if what is regarded as real is defined by a theory of ideal forms). In the process, de Bolla notes, the viewing subject becomes identified with the position of the creative subject – the artist. This identification allows the spectator to experience subjectivity in the true Point of Sight. What is "seen" from here is not a representation but the self mastering the real as the veil of representation is torn apart. . . . The viewing subject is no longer subjected to representation but becomes the master of it, master of subjection, master of itself.[77]

Such mastery implies that nothing is hidden from the spectator by the artist. Distant objects can be depicted indistinctly without doing violence to this principle, since the artist is presumed to lack the visual access to such objects from the point of sight. But a general obscurity, or indistinct rendering of foreground forms signifies knowledge withheld, retrievable only through the power of the imagination.

It was this quality of "unknowability" that prompted Burke to consider indistinctness a source of sublimity. The experience of the sublime occurs when the mind is stimulated to exert its powers of imagination to the limit in order to comprehend that which is obscure and indistinct. This link between indistinctness and the power of the imagination was confirmed by other eighteenth-century writers such as Alexander Gerard and remained a popularly received notion well into the nineteenth century.[78] William Gilpin, who, we recall, identified as singularly English the obscurity caused by the vaporous atmosphere of the domestic landscape, linked the creative imagination to the indistinctly rendered forms of the landscape sketch. In the hands of a master,

when the enthusiasm of his art is upon him, he often produces from the glow of his imagination, with a few bold strokes, such wonderful effusions of genius, as the most sober, and correct productions of his pencil cannot equal.

It will always be understood, that such sketches must be *examined* also by an eye *learned in the art* and accustomed to picturesque ideas – an eye, that can take up the half-formed images, as the master leaves them; give them a new creation; and make up all that is not expressed from its own store-house.[79]

The landscape sketch remains a strictly private representation, for its indistinct "half-formed images" require a viewer with a highly cultivated imagination in order to assure the completion of the composition in a way that is congruent with the artist's intent.[80] In other words, only minds sufficiently schooled in how to imagine correctly can be trusted to examine works that call for an active exercise of the creative imagination as part of the viewing process. Such a legislation of the imagination also ensures that the subject positions of viewer and artist remain congruent in pictures that may not contain a clearly fixed "point of sight."

Reynolds also connected the free exercise of the imagination with the sketch and then went on explicitly to reject indeterminacy in painting:

We cannot on this occasion, nor indeed on any other, recommend an undeterminate manner, or vague ideas of any kind, in a complete and finished picture. This notion, therefore, of leaving any thing to the imagination, opposes a very fixed and indispensable rule in our art, – that every thing shall be carefully and distinctly expressed, as if the painter knew, with correctness and precision, the exact form and character of whatever is introduced into the picture. This is what with us is called Science, and Learning; which must not be sacrificed and given up for an uncertain and doubtful beauty, which . . . will probably be sought for without success.[81]

The transparency of the artistic subject requires the appearance of a complete and publicly revealed knowledge of the object of representation. For Reynolds, indistinctness signifies not simply imagination, but a specifically private imagining incompatible with the public nature of the highest forms of painting.

The kind of indeterminacy that was acceptable in a private sketch was only acceptable in a finished painting placed on public display if the critic was, in the first place, willing to accept the incongruence between the viewing positions of artist and viewer, and secondly, willing to trust that viewers imaginatively would complete such "partial" images in a manner that was socially benign. In fact, few writers endorsed indistinctness with the enthusiasm accorded the other artistic techniques and devices discussed above. As Hazlitt's attack of 1816 suggests, it was Turner who was most noted (or notorious) for obscurity.[82] While he was repeatedly criticized because his foregrounds and figures were not clearly "made out," Callcott's pictures were seldom if ever criticized on the grounds of obscurity. Indeed his works were sometimes favorably compared to Turner's because their figures and foregrounds were more particularized.[83]

John Landseer, the engraver and publisher of the short-lived *Review of Publications of Art*, was one of the very few writers consistently to identify indistinctness as a sign of professional mastery, both in Turner's art and in his own practice of engraving. In a review of the *Landscape Scenery of Scotland*, which contains engravings Landseer made from pictures by William Scrope, Landseer puffs his own ability to render the indistinctness of the atmosphere through the process of engraving. In writing about his engraving of Dunstaffnage Castle he asserts that the hazy obscurity marks "the superior knowledge of the engraver in the theory, as much as its successful exhibition, proclaims his power in the practice, of his profession."[84]

In the same publication Landseer repeatedly identifies Turner's ability to conceal his hand and reveal only the "presiding mind" in his capacity to throw a hazy obscurity over the sea-pieces, forest scenes, and city views exhibited in his gallery in 1808.[85] Although he emphasizes that such artistic feats reveal an imagination far superior to that of the average viewer, the spectator is not reduced to a state of complete bafflement, as other critics had insisted. Rather the viewer's imagination is stimulated by such productions, much as Alison and Jeffrey had described in their discussion of associationism. Hence the "indistinct distance of mingled groves and edifices" of Turner's *Richmond Hill and Bridge* (Figure 51) leaves the imagination to "wander over Richmond, and finish the picture from the suggestions of the painter."[86] Comparing Turner's indistinctness with the poetical "indication, or suggestion," of Virgil, Landseer declares that "by eloquently addressing the fancy and the passions, [he] excels those painters who are exhausting their subjects, and their means of art, and annihilating the pleasures of the spectator's imagination."[87] The writer sees no danger emerging from the fancies unleashed by such undefined representations, presumably because he assumes that viewers would be guided (and thus restrained) by the "suggestions of the painter" introduced in such works.

In this respect Landseer's formulation of the public for painting differs from that of Alison and Jeffrey. As a printmaker and publisher Landseer addresses himself to

51   J. M. W. Turner, *View of Richmond Hill and Bridge*, TG 1808. Oil on canvas, 36 × 48 in. Tate Gallery, London.

the needs and pleasures of a broad, literate, but not necessarily erudite public – a public which, he remarks in 1808, would be more deeply moved by a scene of hop-pickers in a garden than an epic painting of classical gods or heroes.[88] On the other hand Alison and Jeffrey, like Gilpin in his remarks on private sketches, are concerned with the play of the imagination in relation to highly cultivated viewers – specifically, an intelligentsia drawn from the gentry and upper middle class. Despite the commitment of Jeffrey to specialized modes of knowledge such as modern political and economic theory, he and Alison assume that their readers have a grounding in both ancient and contemporary history and literature. It is this liberal education which provides the storehouse of ideas and images to be stimulated by views and representations of natural scenery.[89]

Other writers were not so sanguine about the control of viewers' fancies when presented with indistinct imagery. Foremost among them was Richard Payne Knight, who railed against the evils of obscurity in his political and aesthetic writings. His initial attack came in *The Progress of Civil Society* (1796).[90] Making direct reference to Britain in a Whiggish paean to its balanced constitution, Knight insists that socio-political reforms must not threaten or call into question the legitimacy of this order:

> Let Britain's laws abuses still correct.
> And from corruption's fangs her state protect;

> But let not wild reforms or systems vain,
> The legal influence of command restrain . . .
> Let patronage and splendour guard the throne,
> And all its dignity and influence, own;
> For wealth where well secured, o'er all will reign,
> And its possessor's power, supreme, maintain.[91]

The references to "wild reforms" and "systems vain" situate this text within counter-revolutionary discourse, at its height in 1796, which sought to discredit Painites
and other English radicals advocating systemic political change in accord with
American and French republican models.

Mindful of the political context of Knight's poetic enterprise, we turn to his
remarks on indistinctness in the poem's preface, wherein he disparages the production of poetical images that are obscure and indistinct "from an excess of what
painters call breadth." Although Knight was writing here about poetry rather than
painting, his remarks are couched in visual metaphors suggestive of his overarching
concerns about the need to police the limits within which the imagination of the
artistic producer and consumer (viewer/reader) may operate. He warns that the
young and ignorant are apt to be dazzled by that which they cannot comprehend,

> but which, being darkly shown through the mysterious glimmer of lofty and
> sonorous expressions, seems great in proportion as it is incomprehensible;
> whence their imaginations, being excited and not limited, form phantoms of
> their own, and conclude them to be the meaning of what they are reading.[92]

The claim here is that indistinct imagery has the power to misrepresent the "true"
intentions of the artist/poet. In their place are the private visions of the those (the
"young and ignorant") whose minds are not formed and regulated by the strictures
of high culture. Knight's readers would have been aware of the political valence
accorded to this image of phantoms conjured up by the powers of an unlimited
imagination, for this kind of language was commonly used to describe those "wild
reforms and systems vain" which led to the events of 1789 and the killing of the
king and queen only three years before this poem appeared.[93] Hence, a type of
cultural "anarchy" is registered in this passage in terms that invite comparisons with
an anarchic disregard for existing socio-political structures.

Obscurity is also abjured as a source of the sublime in Knight's aesthetic treatise,
An Analytical Inquiry into the Principles of Taste (1805). Although Knight advocated
"massing" as a way for artists to represent visually those sense impressions conveyed
to the eye by foliage, rock forms, and other natural phenomena seen at a distance,
such suppression of detail must not be taken to excess. Forms and objects must
preserve their identity in order to stimulate the mind's production of trains of
associated ideas and feelings. As Knight puts it, "obscurity is privation," and therefore does not stimulate expansive thinking.[94] Since Knight's concern in this treatise
is with the development of cultivated taste based upon a study of past art as well
as the ancient classics, at no point does he concern himself with the possibility of
private "phantoms" arising in the mind of viewers.[95] Obscurity in this instance

obstructs the stimulation of the cultivated imagination. In both texts of 1796 and 1805, then, indistinctness is attacked for impeding the production of a socialized imagination – either by promoting the private fantasies of the uneducated or by failing to nourish the culturally regulated imaginations of the educated.

Allied with Knight's concerns about the artistic regulation of the viewer's imagination is his repeated effort to control artistic genius by submitting it to the authority of the market and the slow processes of artistic study (but not academic training). In the second decade of the century, when Knight was a Director of the British Institution, he authored two, possibly three, of the prefaces for catalogues which the Institution published in connection with special exhibitions. The first of the catalogues was published in 1813 for an exhibition of paintings by Joshua Reynolds. In the preface Knight praises Reynolds for not being "one of those aspiring geniuses – those self-selected favourites of nature, who imagine that professional eminence is a spontaneous gift of heaven." Instead we are told that the painter

> toiled patiently for many years through all the initiatory drudgery of the art, gained practice by undertaking whatever was offered, at the lowest price by which he could subsist; and by the gradual and spontaneous impression made by his *gradual* progress to excellence . . . *gradually* raised himself in public estimation.[96]

Earlier we examined statements by writers who promoted a free market as an appropriate forum for the circulation of works by independent-minded English artists. Knight himself endorses this position in *The Progress of Civil Society*, where he declares that public patronage of the arts is unnecessary, for "by the public favour or neglect/Alone is genius raised, or dullness check'd."[97] In the Reynolds catalogue, on the other hand, Knight's emphasis is upon the artist's subjection to the low prices dictated by the market and to the drudgery of acquiring artistic training – a training that implicitly involves a suppression of individual "genius" to the dictates of the old master tradition which the British Institution so strongly promoted.

In the 1796 poem and the 1813 catalogue, then, two different characterizations of the relationship between the artistic subject and the market are presented. I would argue that these differences do not represent a shift in Knight's thinking, but show how the notion of artistic genius was flexible enough to accommodate such varied deployments, even by a single individual or interest group, depending upon the particular objective. In Knight's case, his concern that artists should not receive *carte blanche* in the form of support from the public coffers in no way contradicts his concern that native genius be constrained by the rigors of mechanical training.[98] In the first instance, promoting artistic autonomy becomes a means of impugning the need for public support, while in the second the tactic is to promote the economic and ideological subjection of genius.

The year after the Reynolds exhibition the British Institution mounted its show of works by Hogarth, Wilson, Gainsborough, and Zoffany. While the preface to the 1814 British Institution catalogue for the exhibition remains unattributed, it seems highly likely that Knight was also its author. Not only did he write the prefaces for the years preceding and following it, but the text is consonant with his views on painting practices, evidenced by the comments on Wilson's landscapes:

> Wilson will be contemplated with delight – few artists have excelled him in the tint of air, perhaps the most difficult point of attainment for the Landscape Painter; every object in his pictures keeps its place, because each is seen through its proper medium. This excellence alone gives a charm to his pencil; and with judicious application may be turned to the advantage of the British Artist.[99]

To suggest that this concern for atmospheric clarity – that each object in a land-scape "keep its place" – was intimately related to the wider project of keeping native genius in *its* place, might appear to be making a facile and ill-considered analogy between two unrelated undertakings. However, a general survey of Knight's political and aesthetic writings testifies to his overarching desire to police the individual imagination at the points of production and reception.

Such reservations about the power of the artistic imagination were not confined to connoisseurs bent upon asserting their cultural authority over that of artists. Edward Dayes's posthumous essays on painting also contained strictures against unregulated imagination, as did his "Professional Sketches of Modern Artists," with its condemnation of Girtin's passionate character.[100] Lacking moral discipline, Girtin's imagination was judged by Dayes to be incapable of producing a serious or substantial body of work. It is worth recalling the latter's warning in his essays on painting that judgment is required to prevent the imagination from "riot[ing] at the expense of reason," and his observation that "we often confound genius with an active imagination, not recollecting that excess is not its character."[101] These pas-sages from the "Essays" and the biographical sketch were very likely inspired by the resentment of an older artist whose student had surpassed him. But what is of primary interest here is not Dayes's motivation, but the way in which a particular style of painting served to connote a strong imagination, and how that mental faculty was elided with moral dissolution, and in Girtin's case, even premature death.

Despite their concern about the moral or social consequences of imagination taken to excess, neither Dayes nor Knight sought to integrate an overt political critique of revolutionary reform with an aesthetic critique of the imagination and the reductive, undefined imagery with which it was associated. However, the same year that Dayes's *Works* and Knight's *Analytical Inquiry* were published (1805), an essay appeared which addressed the politics of the "romantic" imagination directly. "On the Application of the Epithet Romantic" was written by the Baptist minister John Foster and published as part of his *Essays in a Series of Letters to a Friend*, which went through three editions in seven months. Foster had been associated with revolutionary republicans in Ireland in the mid-1790s, but by the early 1800s had moderated his political stance considerably, as the *Essays* demonstrate. Although he remained disdainful of the trappings of royal power, he maintained strong support for the traditional institutions, social hierarchies, and hegemonic system ordering British society.[102] In his essay Foster defines the term "romantic" as the "ascendancy of imagination over judgment."[103] This was a state of mind that he accepted in youth as necessary in stimulating religious faith and supplying the energy needed for embarking on the affairs of life. Upon reaching maturity, however, imagination must be held in check by reason and judgment.[104] Much of the essay dwells on the evils that arise from the excesses of the imagination, which Foster describes in highly visual terms:

> Imagination may be indulged till it usurp an entire ascendancy over the mind . . . imagination will throw its colours where the intellectual faculty ought to draw its lines; imagination will accumulate metaphors where reason ought to deduce arguments; images will take the place of thoughts, and scenes of disquisitions. The whole mind may become at length something like a hemisphere of cloud-scenery, filled with an evermoving train of changing melting forms, of every colour, mingled with rainbows, meteors, and an occasional gleam of pure sunlight, all vanishing away, the mental like this natural imagery, when its hour is up, without leaving any thing behind but the wish to recover the vision.[105]

This passage demonstrates (once again) just how closely the landscape effects we have been analyzing – veils of color, brilliant effects of sunlight, and the indistinct, shifting forms of clouds – were connected to the associative powers of the imagination. Foster employed these ephemeral atmospheric effects as a metaphor for the mind itself, a mind which eschews logical argument for associative imagery – "trains of changing melting forms." Unlike apologists for associationism, Foster did not identify these effects with the essential character of a site or an object. Rather they were seen as irrational conjurings which, beyond producing fantasies, carry over into thoughts about "the vulgar materials that constitute the actual economy of the world." Imaginative habits of mind distort conceptions of the "true" nature of these materials, rendering the mind incapable of making sound judgments about them.[106]

The precise nature of Foster's concern becomes apparent when he details the consequences of such an imagination taken to excess. First he suggests that such an imagination can so enthrall individuals of either sex that they presume they are destined for some extraordinary fate, and therefore reject social norms ("they will perhaps disdain regular hours, usual dress, and common forms of transacting business").[107] Such visions, then, not only fueled the interests of the private over the socialized self, but actively promoted the outright rejection of those systems and practices which seek to position private individuals in the social sphere.

The dangers of such imaginative visions goes beyond the production of eccentric individuals. Foster also insists that the unregulated imagination gives birth to utopian visions at variance with human nature, which he conceived to be "social, self-interested, inclined to the wrong [and] slow to improve."[108] Utopian visions of a society in which there is an equality of property division and modes of living are the result of imagination overpowering sober reason – that pragmatic and rational power which recognizes the "truly" greedy, indolent, and ignorant character of humankind.[109]

Although Foster's consideration of the effects of unconstrained imagination is set in a different context from Knight's, both the former radical and the Foxite Whig identify these mental powers as a threat to the hegemonic process that positions individuals within the social order. If unregulated by reason or undisciplined by traditional education, the imagination could feed upon the private fantasies of the individual, weakening or subverting the bonds which tie her/him to society. Although William Hazlitt opposed Foster and Knight in defending artistic genius and political (not cultural) democracy, we saw that the radical essayist also was disturbed by the prospect of genius "losing its sympathy with humanity." For him, we recall, this state of affairs ensued when the artistic subject indulged only in displays of its own secret knowledge, exemplified by landscape painters' abandonment of subject matter in favor of painterly effects and indistinct, chaotic forms. His concerns coupled with those of Knight, Dayes, and Foster, as well as those voiced by the anonymous art critics we examined earlier, suggest the degree to which the production of the fully autonomous artistic subject via the practice of landscape painting was regarded as powerfully compelling and (thus) in need of regulation.

As indicated in Chapters 3 and 4, the imaginative landscape artist as a category of the individual drew a large degree of its power and appeal from its ability to circulate throughout a range of discourses and social formations. It could accommodate a nationalist rhetoric of manly, independent-mindedness, while meeting the demands of a modern commercial society for modes of seeing and knowing that could not be supplied by a classical education. Heralded for possessing the sensibility and imagination that distinguished them from mechanical imitators, the landscape painters who were seen to occupy this category of the genius were deemed capable of producing works that were both expressive and eye-catching.

What is striking about these political, economic, epistemological, and cultural demands is that they all call forth an increasingly atomized, privatized concept of the individual. Such a subject, however, does not conduct commercial and domestic affairs behind a veil of privacy, but performs his/her interiority in public. In his study of the broad transformations occurring in civil society throughout this period Jürgen Habermas emphasizes this performative aspect of the interiorized subject: "Subjectivity, as the innermost core of the private, was always already oriented to an audience."[110] The power, and for some, the danger, of the formulation of the artistic subject as a genius derives in part from its ambiguous relationship to its public.

That ambiguity rests in the fact that genius both stands for and stands above an expanding public no longer confined to the erudite sector of the landed elite. We can discern this ambiguity in the promotion of professional landscape watercolorists in Ackermann's various publications (such as the *Repository* and *New Drawing Book of Light and Shadow*) that celebrate the quintessentially English character of landscape watercolors by artists such as Turner and Girtin, and yet stress the magical power of such producers to dazzle a domestic public composed of men and women from the commercial and landed classes. In a somewhat similar fashion Leigh Hunt lauds the English quality of manly and active independent-mindedness that marks the works of artists such as Turner, while offering as evidence Turner's ability to produce works which baffle the connoisseurs.[111] We also noted the imaginative artist's ability to signify creative productivity while enforcing an informed, but nonetheless passive pleasure on Alison's liberally educated viewers.

Attempting to mitigate the disjunction between active productivity and passive consumption are those who stress that through the productions of artistic genius, viewers can acquire a deeper understanding and feeling for the true character of the English landscape, and thus for the true nature of the customary values that define Englishness itself.[112] Yet in these various accounts there is no suggestion that viewers can gain for themselves the superior knowledge and enhanced sensibility possessed by the imaginative artist, since that knowledge is the special province of the professional and such a heightened sensibility is deemed an inherent trait of genius. Viewing subjects thus are alienated from their own capacity to imagine and experience directly and completely (without the aid of genius) their national identity as it is inscribed upon the face of the English landscape.

Contemporary writers from across the ideological spectrum endorsed the need for the mediation of the landscape genius, and frequently described the experience of viewing a work of genius as a pacifying one. A writer in the *Repository of Arts* in 1814 enthusiastically praises John Varley's watercolors, *A Plot of Rising Ground* and *Thomson's Grave,* declaring that they "would administer repose to a mind maddened by fury itself. The contemplation of such subjects produces a calm highly stimulative to the feelings of humanity."[113] Robert Hunt echoed these sentiments that same year, when he quoted John Landseer who assured viewers living "in a world of trouble and inquietude" that the "sum of human happiness would be greatly increased" if everyone possessed the perceptions and tastes required to enjoy landscape painting.[114] Thus while the artistic genius as constituted in landscape painting was regarded as active, bold, masculine, the viewer was correspondingly pacified. Even though his/her imagination is stimulated, that stimulation leads to thoughts of social harmony, not to bold innovations or new syntheses of ideas and feelings.

It is perhaps the wide acceptance of the role of the genius to pacify and socialize that made Turner's tendency toward indistinctness so troubling. For such a practice subverts the process of mediation, and presents instead the prospect of an artistic subject which is so autonomous that it has no longer the need or capacity for social engagement. Faced with that prospect, the viewer can either turn away in baffled admiration or anger, or accept the challenge tacitly offered to engage in private imaginings unregulated by a "superior" knowledge and sensibility. In the war decades immediately following the French Revolution, but before the rise of a fully formed mass culture industry, it was still possible to believe that dire social consequences might accompany the actions of such a private, unregulated imagination.

Conclusion

THIS STUDY HAS EXAMINED THE ATTENUATION of one form of the artistic producer and the rise to prominence of another in England during and immediately after the Napoleonic wars. Arguably, history painting furnished few English artists, even in the eighteenth century, with the professional status accorded them in academic discourse. But by the early nineteenth century, attacks on the Academy, on public patronage of the arts, and on the ideal public for such painting – the leisured, liberal-minded man of property – made the history painter even less viable as a professional model and a national ideal of the creative individual. Many, if not most of these attacks on academic history painting came from an intelligentsia of political reformists and economic liberals allied with the educated sectors of the middle class and gentry. Their criticism of the elite culture culminated in demands not for a radical redistribution of property and power, but for a reformulation of the terms in which the cultural, social, and economic authority of the propertied and monied classes was to be sustained.

The landscape genius was one (and only one) outcome of this reformulation. Part of the appeal of this conceptualization of the artist was its versatility; it was capable of supporting, and in turn was supported by, a broad range of social interests. In examining the essay "On the Analogy between the Growth of Individual and National Genius" we saw that a writer allied with country Tory interests could forward a notion of national genius that directly invoked the power of the land to shape the character, traditions, and history of a people. Such a retrospective construction of native genius accorded well with the principles of associationism, particularly as propounded by Alison, which explained the aesthetic pleasure gained in contemplating representations of natural scenery through just such retrospective imagining. Taken in these terms, genius is regarded as the power to produce intense and pleasurable feelings for what is already known, rather than the capacity to represent what previously had been unimaginable. In considering the writings that appeared in *Blackwood's* and the productions of Turner for Tory landowner John Fuller, I have examined how such a formulation of native genius reinforced notions of national cohesion and traditional social relations during a period of inter-class conflict in the second decade of the century.

On the other hand, the radical Hazlitt's contempt for what he regarded as a debased aristocracy and their corrupt cultural and political institutions fueled his support of a notion of artistic genius that was defined by its disregard for institutional

52 Turner. Detail of Figure 39.

rules and its opposition to the indolence and self-indulgence of the leisured amateur. Not only was his notion of the professional genius qualified by industry,
masculine energy, and sensibility, but, above all, it was marked by an originality and
creativity that was inherent, not learned.

Hazlitt's notion of genius conforms closely to the idea of the Romantic genius
(especially the poet) promoted by many modern scholars. Equally isolated from
(and superior to) the corrupt ruling elite and the unlettered masses, the genius who
turns his attention to the contemplation of nature is regarded by such scholars as the
beleaguered victim of the dehumanization of social relations that increasingly
marked commercial life in early nineteenth-century England.[1] However, in the case
of the landscape painter, we have seen that the socially alienated genius could
become a counterproductive force for a radical like Hazlitt. His endorsement of
Turner's creativity was tempered by the concern that in demonstrating his command over a highly specialized artistic practice, the artist had alienated himself from
all but the elite few who also possessed this specialized and secret knowledge.

While Hazlitt expressed the concern that the genius must in some way remain
tied to his public, he certainly did not advocate that those ties be commercial ones.
However, the notion of genius, even of the isolated genius, was not antithetical to
those interests that actively promoted a capitalized market economy and the political forms which sustained it. The compatibility of genius with commercial interests is evident in a previously discussed review from the *London Chronicle* in 1819,
which offers lavish praise for Turner's watercolors: "The art itself is *par excellence*
English, no continental pencil can come near the force, freedom, and nature of our
professor."[2] The writer follows these remarks with this observation on the isolation
and moral purity of the artist:

> The men whose minds are busied over the picture or the statue, must be so
> many men rescued and raised from the ignorance and insubordination of lower
> life; their enthusiasm is kindled like the vestal's urn from a source above the
> crimes and clouds of the world. Biography represents the great multitude of
> those solitary and rapt spirits, as comparatively unstained; unfitted for the vulgar
> intercourses of less gifted society, and living even in the midst of cities in a kind
> of holy and hermit contemplation.[3]

This account of the artist as a "solitary and rapt spirit" or a hermit, "rescued" from
the "vulgar intercourses" of quotidian life, might seem to function as a critique of
commercial society comparable to that offered by Hazlitt, Leigh and Robert Hunt,
and other reform-minded social critics. However, by stating that "biography" has
shown the artist to be placed in a relationship with society that is fixed and
unchanging throughout the ages, the writer implies that the present state of those
relations in commercial society appears to be no different – and more importantly,
no worse – than it ever was.

It is noteworthy that biography has replaced history here as the authoritative
source of judgments about the status of the artist in society.[4] Such a turn to
biography is consistent with the production of a form of domestic landscape painting that relies upon the singular sensibility and intellect of the artistic individual as
the means of revealing to a national public its own essential nature.[5]

The key to the native landscape genius's ability to function at one and the same time as an autonomous subject, insulated from the vitiation of a market-oriented society, and also as a social subject who represents the ideals of that society, is contingent upon the way in which individual autonomy is socially regulated. The elision of the artist's character – his singular capacity to feel, to recognize, and to represent the essence of the landscape – with the symbolic character of the domestic landscape as the locus of individual and national freedom, fixes the individuality of the native genius firmly within the domain of social. That is, personal autonomy is *the* signal feature that identifies the landscape genius as a member of the social body. Yet accounts in the mainstream press, such as the above-cited passage from the *London Chronicle*, and in fashionable magazines, such as Ackermann's *Repository of Arts*, stress the fact that while the landscape genius embodies the essence of the national spirit, he is not subjected to the depredations of the social body. We recall the strong emphasis placed by these critics and other writers (such as Alison and Reinagle) upon the magical and transformative powers of the landscape genius in fashioning profoundly affecting images of color and light from the basest and simplest materials. Such a transformation of common nature into native character served to lift such representations and their makers out of the realm of material production (and the domain of amateur practice).

In the course of this quasi-alchemical process the ultimate magic trick is performed upon the body of the native genius himself: in a spectacular disappearing and reappearing act, he enters the spaces of exhibition and display within the urban marketplace and succeeds in annihilating the competition with his bravura effects; but upon closer inspection, it is discovered that he seems never to have been in the marketplace after all. For he has an alibi which places him within the locus of external nature in its customary (rather than its ideal) guise. The encounter which takes place there does not produce social disaffection, or a heightened awareness of nature as Other. On the contrary, the native genius's embrace of the natural leads him back to an experience of his own social identity within a community marked by social empathy not economic self-interest; for it is that community of feeling alone which gives meaning to external nature. In this way the genius stages his reappearance as a social actor in the purified domain of the natural. His alibi secure, he remains uncontaminated by the market, yet victorious over it.

It might appear that such an alibi would wear thin over the course of nearly two centuries. However, the landscape genius, embodied above all in the public persona of Turner, continues to be promoted as the purified essence of Englishness while at the same time serving the financial interests of diverse sectors of the Western economy. At a time when the detritus of commercial societies threatens the landscape on a world scale, it remains to be seen if it is possible to reconfigure the artistic and viewing subject in a way which will facilitate a reappraisal of what has for so long been a vexed and mystified relationship between land, human society, and personal freedom.

Notes

Introduction

1. "Notices of the Pictures in the Forty-Second Exhibition of the Royal Academy, Somerset-House," *Repository of Arts* 7 (June 1812), p. 341.

2. [W. H. Pyne?], "Observations on the Rise and Progress of Water Colours," *Repository of Arts*, February 1813, pp. 92–3. I concur with Ann Pullan that Pyne was very likely the author of this and other articles in this series, which extended over several issues of the *Repository*. Pyne frequently wrote for this magazine on the subject of watercolor, and these articles echo in substance and language those he was known to have authored for his own later publication, *The Somerset House Gazette*. See Ann Pullan, "Fashioning a Public for Art: Ideology, Gender and the Fine Arts in the English Periodical *c*.1800– 25" (Ph.D. diss., University of Cambridge), 1992, p. 282.

3. As Andrew Wilton and others have noted, the titular hero of the picture, Hannibal, is not obviously visible in this portrayal of the rear of the Carthaginian army, which has been ambushed by a detachment of Swiss mountain fighters. See Wilton, *Turner and the Sublime* (Art Gallery of Ontario and the Yale Center for British Art exhib. cat., Chicago: University of Chicago Press, 1982), p. 74.

4. Edward Dayes. *The Works of the Late Edward Dayes* (London: E. W. Brayley, 1805), p. 258.

5. "Royal Academy – Exhibition 1798," *London Packet*, 4–7 May 1798. Based upon his landscape reviews for this year, the critic's ire seem to have been directed at landscape painters such as Julius Caesar Ibbetson, whose *Miners Setting out to Encounter the French* was described as "a work of haste, painted for sale" (9–11 May). Turner's subdued, almost monochromatic *Dunstanburgh Castle* [National Gallery of Victoria, Melbourne], on the other hand, was judged by the critic to be both natural and sublime (7–9 May 1798). Contemporary criticism of Ibbetson is considered in Chapter 2.

6. Jon Mee, *Dangerous Enthusiasm: William Blake and the Culture of Radicalism in the 1790s* (Oxford: Clarendon, 1992). Mee discusses various types of religious enthusiasm and popular radicalism and the counter-revolutionary critique they engendered in his opening chapter (pp. 20–74); on the attempts of middle-class radicals associated with publisher John Johnson's circle to dissociate themselves from working-class radicals, see pp. 222–3.

7. V. N. Voloshinov uses the concept of the "multi-accentuality of the sign" to describe a situation in which diverse interest groups, classes, and class fragments adopt the same linguistic signs (or visual imagery), but invest them with different meanings, depending on the groups' particular ideological needs. In such a circumstance such a sign or visual representation can become an arena of ideological contestation [V. N. Voloshinov, *Marxism and the Philosophy of Language* (New York: Academic Press, 1973), pp. 21–3].

8. Subjectivity, of course, is theorized in different ways depending upon the discipline, or discursive framework (psychoanalytic, linguistic and so forth). I employ subjectivity here as a means of understanding the production of social identity, drawing upon what loosely can be termed post-structuralist theories of the individual arising out of Marxism, discourse theory, feminist studies, and semiotics.

9. Issues of subjectivity are central to Foucault's work. I have found particularly helpful "The Subject and Power," afterword to Herbert Dreyfus and Paul Rabinow, *Michel Foucault:*

Beyond Structuralism and Hermeneutics (Brighton: Harvester, 1982), pp. 208–26.

10. John Barrell, *The Dark Side of the Landscape. The Rural Poor in English Painting 1730–1840* (Cambridge: Cambridge University Press, 1980); Ann Bermingham, *Landscape and Ideology: The English Rustic Tradition, 1740–1860* (Berkeley: University of California Press, 1986); Stephen Daniels, *Fields of Vision: Landscape Imagery and National Identity in England and the United States* (Princeton: Princeton University Press, 1993); Andrew Hemingway, *Landscape Imagery and Urban Culture in Early Nineteenth-Century Britain* (Cambridge: Cambridge University Press, 1992); Michael Rosenthal, *Constable: The Painter and his Landscape* (New Haven and London: Yale University Press, 1983). See also the Bibliography for recent essays and articles by these scholars on the subject of landscape painting.

11. Daniels, p. 5. Sam Smiles also addresses the issue of nationalism and visual culture in this time period as it relates to images of the ancient Britons in *The Image of Antiquity: Ancient Britain and the Romantic Imagination* (New Haven and London: Yale University Press, 1994).

12. "Exhibition of Paintings – Royal Academy," *Repository of Arts*, June 1809, p. 490. The works Constable exhibited in the first two decades of the century seldom garnered either positive or negative evaluations of the artist's "mind" or "hand." The only direct reference to his mind in early criticism was made by *Examiner* critic Robert Hunt, who was generally well disposed to the artist. In suggesting that his British Institution exhibits of 1817 were better than previous works Hunt writes: "Mr. CONSTABLE here shews that he can screw up his resolution to conquer in some degree that inertness of mind, which, while an object of importance is aimed at, prevents its full success by the neglect of some valuable requisites of active performances. In plain words, his finishing and drawing are a little better than formerly, though still far below the standard of his colouring and general effect" (*Examiner*, 2 March 1817). This no doubt was intended as encouragement, but to be characterized, even retrospectively, by an "inertness of mind" was to be damned with faint praise at a time when artists like Turner and the late Girtin were being touted for their powers of bold and original thinking.

13. Linda Colley, *Britons: Forging the Nation,*

1707–1837 (London and New Haven: Yale University Press, 1992), p. 6.

14. See, for example, Leigh Hunt's article, "Remarks on the Past and Present State of the Arts in England," *Reflector* 1 (1812), p. 215, in which he lists Barry and Wilson among English painters.

1 The Crisis of the English School and the Question of Genre

1. "Monthly Retrospect of the Fine Arts," *Monthly Magazine*, July 1810, p. 577.

2. The notable exception is Andrew Hemingway who has examined at length the cultural politics of naturalist landscape painting in his book, *Landscape Imagery and Urban Culture in Early Nineteenth-Century Britain* (Cambridge: Cambridge University Press, 1992). But while he thoughtfully considers issues of genre in his discussions of art criticism, aesthetics, and academic discourse, he is not chiefly concerned with landscape as a genre that was involved in the production of a specifically English identity.

3. Morris Eaves, *The Counter-Arts Conspiracy: Art and Industry in the Age of Blake* (Ithaca, NY, and London: Cornell University Press, 1992). See his discussion of "The Problem of the English School," pp. 3–8, for a concise review of the history of this persistent problem.

4. Genre painting offered yet another alternative to the representation of communal (British) identity that would prove highly successful in the nineteenth century. Despite the public acclaim and accolades (including a knighthood) garnered by artists such as David Wilkie, the genre painter was not construed primarily as imaginative, sensitive, and independent-minded – in short as a genius. Sorely needed is a study of early nineteenth-century British genre painting that analyzes its mode of representing a new public for art and examines the construction of the genre painter as a particularly British phenomenon.

5. John Barrell, *The Political Theory of Painting from Reynolds to Hazlitt: The Body of the Public* (New Haven and London: Yale University Press, 1986). For important critiques of Barrell's thesis see reviews of his book by Andrew Hemingway ["The Political Theory of Painting without the Politics," *Art History* 10:3 (September 1987), pp. 381–95] and Pamela Divinsky ["The Visual and Conceptual Category of the Public," *Oxford Art Journal* 10:1 (1987), pp. 92–8].

6. Within the ideological framework of civic humanism, the possession of such mental powers was attributed to men, since woman were seen as incapable of abstract reasoning, and, more narrowly, only to those men whose wealth permitted them the economic independence to rise above private concerns (Barrell, *Political Theory*, pp. 65–8). In her *Strictures on the Modern System of Female Education* (1799) evangelical reformer Hannah More distinguishes the intellectual capacities of men and women through reference to the landscape: "Both in composition and action they [women] excel in details; but they do not so much generalize their ideas as men, nor do their minds seize a great subject with so large a grasp. . . . A woman sees the world, as it were, from a little elevation in her own garden, where she makes an exact survey of home scenes, but takes not in that wider range of distant prospects which he who stands on a loftier eminence commands" [More, quoted in Bridget Hill, *Eighteenth Century Women: An Anthology* (London: Allen and Unwin, 1987), p. 51]. Although More is concerned here with relating qualities of mind to the gendered spaces of the public and private spheres, her reliance on these types of visual metaphor demonstrates the compatibility of a political theory based upon the mental capacity for abstraction with an artistic theory of ideal forms.

7. Helmut von Erffa and Allen Staley, *The Paintings of Benjamin West* (New Haven and London: Yale University Press, 1986). See pp. 87–100 for an overview of West's royal commissions and a discussion of the reasons for his fall from favor; for a description of the scheme to decorate St. Paul's Cathedral, see p. 8.

8. David Solkin, *Painting for Money: The Visual Arts and the Public Sphere in Eighteenth Century England* (London and New Haven: Yale University Press, 1993), for Hogarth see pp. 78–105; Penny, pp. 199–206, and Wright, pp. 214–46.

9. While Solkin astutely analyses the critical commentary spawned by this institutional rivalry in terms of the political crisis of the late 1760s, he does not consider the pragmatic reasons that might drive professional artists to support the Academy rather than the Society (ibid., pp. 247–76). I suspect that in large part the success of the former was due to the professional benefits that artists believed would come from its pedagogical commitment to classical art and literature. A knowledge of the classics was recognized as *the* underlying "qualification" which distinguished the traditional professions (law, the Church, medicine) from other forms of labor. Thus, in addition to providing access to exhibition space, training, and the like, the Academy could claim for its members a professional status which the Society of Artists, eschewing a monolithic aesthetic and encouraging a diversity of art and craft practices, was unable and/or unwilling to meet. Iain Pears has demonstrated that another factor contributing to the "rise" in prominence of the professional artist was the "dramatic fall from grace" of the artisan as a result of the "de-skilling" of trades such as coach painting and sign painting. See Pears, *The Discovery of Painting: The Growth of Interest in the Arts in England 1680–1768* (New Haven and London: Yale University Press, 1988), pp. 113–19.

10. In an essay entitled "Sir Joshua Reynolds and the Englishness of English Art" [in *Nation and Narration*, ed. Homi Bhabha (London: Routledge, 1990), pp. 154–76], Barrell examines the English counter-revolutionary reaction to the French Revolution and its effect on Reynolds's universalist aesthetics as articulated in his unpublished "Ironic Discourse" (1791). However he does not consider more widely the construction of Englishness in art works and writings which were displayed and circulated in the 1790s and beyond.

11. D. G. C. Allan, "The Society of Arts and Government, 1754–1800: Public Encouragement of Arts, Manufactures, and Commerce in Eighteenth-Century England," *Eighteenth-Century Studies* 7:4 (1974), p. 441. For a fuller account of the Society and its membership, which also includes a discussion of Barry's commission for the Great Room, see D. G. C. Allan and John L. Abbott, eds, *The Virtuoso Tribe of Arts and Sciences: Studies in the Eighteenth-Century Work and Membership of the London Society of Arts* (Athens, GA, and London: University of Georgia Press, 1992).

12. The only other large-scale project executed around this time was the decoration of the Royal Chapel at Windsor by Benjamin West, begun in 1779, two years after Barry started work on the Adelphi paintings.

13. "Minutes of the Society of Arts," 27 April 1774, cited in William Pressly, *The Life and Art of James Barry* (New Haven and London: Yale University Press, 1981), p. 86. Earlier, in 1760, the Society had experienced conflicts

with Reynolds and other leading artists associated with the St Martin's Lane Academy over the fees to be charged visitors to an exhibition of contemporary British art held in the Great Room of the Society's former premises in Denmark Court. For a full account of this controversy see Brian Allen, "The Society of Arts and the First Exhibition of Contemporary Art in 1770," *Royal Society of Arts Journal* 139 (March 1991), pp. 265–9.

14. Pressly, *Life . . . of Barry*, pp. 86–7.

15. James Barry, "On Design," in *The Works of James Barry, Esq.*, 2 vols. (London: Cadell and Davies, 1809), 1, pp. 395–6 (emphasis in the original). Barry's sentiments are consistent with eighteenth-century academic discourse. Joshua Reynolds, for example, recommended that history painters select classical and Biblical subjects since these "were familiar and interesting to all Europe, without being degraded by the vulgarism of ordinary life in any country." See Reynolds, *Discourses on Art*, ed. Robert Wark (New Haven and London: Yale University Press, 1959; orig. pub. 1797), Discourse IV, p. 85. Future page references to specific Discourses are from this edition.

16. Barrell, "Sir Joshua Reyolds and the Englishness of English Art," p. 159 (emphasis in the original).

17. Allan, "The Society of Arts," p. 437. Allan cites accounts by an anonymous Frenchman in 1788, Society Secretary Samuel More in 1797, and Arthur Aikin in 1818 which identify the private nature of the association as a feature that distinguishes it from organizations on the continent. In 1860 Gladstone made the point most forcefully when he declared that the Society "had been from the first . . . the spontaneous offspring of private intelligence, and had reflected in its proceedings, as a voluntary institution, all the features of the English character."

18. Barry explains the significance of the fighting animals in his *Account of a Series of Pictures in the Great Room of the Society of Arts, Manufactures, and Commerce at the Adelphi* (1783), in *Works*, 2, pp. 326.

19. For the contemporary response to this image see William Pressly, *James Barry: The Artist as Hero* (Tate Gallery exhib. cat., London, 1983), p. 83.

20. Barry, 2, p. 333.

21. Social commentaries were rife with allusions to luxury as a feminine vice. In Bernard Mandeville's account of luxury in his extended "Remarks" on *The Fable of the Bees*, for example, he finds it necessary to defend luxury from the charge that "it effeminates" the people [Bernard Mandeville, *The Fable of the Bees: Or Private Vices, Publick Benefits*, 2 vols., intro. F.B. Kaye (Oxford, Clarendon, 1957; orig. pub. 1732), 1, p. 115]. J.G.A. Pocock discusses Gibbon's account of the debilitating effects of commerce and civilization on the sexes in *Virtue, Commerce and History* (Cambridge: Cambridge University Press, 1985), pp. 117–18. Remarkably for a male artist/writer of this period, Barry continues his discussion of *Commerce* by protesting that "our females . . . are totally, shamefully, and cruelly neglected, in the appropriation of trades and employments"(2, p. 333). Despite this enlightened remark, by choosing to represent visually the evils of commerce via the display of "sportive" and "wanton" females the artist further reinforces the increasingly vocal demands by bourgeois reformists that female activity should be strictly regulated and confined to the domestic sphere.

22. In addition to West, Angelica Kauffman, Joshua Reynolds, and Paolo Matteis all produced paintings that were directly or indirectly based on this subject.

23. See for example, Reynolds, Discourse IV, pp. 58–9.

24. Pressly, *Life . . . of Barry*, p. 109.

25. Ibid., p. 107.

26. The print is reproduced in Pressly, *Life . . . of Barry* as Plate 33, p. 46.

27. I am grateful to David Solkin for his observations on the status of the *Fall of Satan* and *Venus Rising* within the *Distribution of Premiums*.

28. Barry, 2, p. 307.

29. For Boydell's project see Winifred Friedman, *Boydell's Shakespeare Gallery* (New York: Garland, 1976); and Sven Bruntjen, *John Boydell, 1719–1804: A Study of Art Patronage and Publishing in Georgian London* (New York: Garland, 1985). For Macklin and Bowyer, see T.S.R. Boase, "Macklin and Bowyer," *Journal of the Warburg and Courtauld Institutes* 26 (1963), pp. 148–77. An especially insightful account of these attempts to market history painting via publishing enterprises is contained in Eaves, pp. 33–62.

30. Foreigners Angelica Kauffman and Philippe de Loutherbourg produced paintings for the Gallery, but they had both established themselves as successful and highly respected artists working in Britain in the 1780s and 1790s. Winifred Friedman records that thirty-four

pictures were exhibited in 1789; when the Gallery closed in 1802 that number had increased to about one hundred seventy (Friedman, p. 3).

31. The first number of the large engravings appeared in 1791; the nine-volume text edition was published in 1803, too late to avert the demise of the Gallery (Bruntjen, p. 11).

32. The paintings from Macklin's Poet's Gallery, together with those he commissioned for an illustrated Bible, were sold by lottery in 1797; Boydell's and Bowyer's paintings were sold, also by lottery, in 1805. Fuseli was engaged by publisher John Johnson to produce illustrations for a volume of Milton with annotations by William Cowper, but the venture fell through. Fuseli pursued the idea of a "Gallery of the Miltonic Sublime," which opened in May 1799 but was forced to close permanently in July 1801 [Richard Altick, *The Shows of London* (Cambridge, MA: Harvard University Press, 1978), p. 108].

33. Bruntjen, p. 109.

34. See Barrell, *Political Theory* for a detailed analysis and comparison of the academic writings of Reynolds, Barry, and Fuseli.

35. Barry, 2, p. 307.

36. The literature on Dayes is sparse. The standard account of his activities as a topographer remains J. Dayes, "Edward Dayes," *Old Water-Colour Society's Club* 19 (1964), pp. 45–55. For his activities in copying and reworking amateur drawings see also C. F. Bell, "Fresh Light on Some Water-colour Painters of the Old British School, Derived from the Collections and Papers of James Moore, F. S. A.," *Walpole Society* 5 (1917), pp. 47–83.

37. For a discussion of Dayes's historical drawings see David Blayney Brown, "Edward Dayes: Historical Draughtsman," *Old Water-Colour Society's Club* 62 (1991), pp. 9–21.

38. Nine of his essays were published in the *Philosophical Magazine* between January 1801 and March 1803; they were then collected by Edward Brayley after Dayes's death in May 1804 and published in 1805 as *The Works of the Late Edward Dayes* (London: E. W. Brayley), along with a tenth essay on coloring landscapes, a series of brief biographies of British artists, and a tour of Derbyshire and Yorkshire.

39. Reynolds's *Discourses* are the principal eighteenth-century texts dealing with academic practice to be cited here because Dayes, like many of his contemporaries, considered them the most authoritative. This is not to suggest, however, that Reynolds's no-

tions were original. As Robert Wark points out, they were largely a synthesis and modification of aesthetic theories of seventeenth- and eighteenth-century British and French writers (Wark, "Introduction," *Discourses*, p. xxiii).

40. Richard and Samuel Redgrave, *A Century of British Painters* (Ithaca, NY: Cornell University Press, 1981; orig. pub. 1866), p. 155.

41. Edward Dayes, "Professional Sketches of Modern Artists," *Works*, p. 329.

42. In this passage Dayes may also have been tacitly criticizing Girtin's political radicalism, which also could be viewed as an "excessive" activity consistent with a passionate nature.

43. Martin Hardie, *Water-colour Painting in Britain*, 3 vols. (New York: Barnes and Noble, 1967), 2, p. 2.

44. Dayes's critique of painterly surface effects also would apply to the portraits of Thomas Lawrence and the literary and historical painting of artists like William Hamilton and Richard Westall. As successful as these artists were, however, they were never characterized as imaginative geniuses in the way that Turner and Girtin were.

45. Dayes, *Works*, p. 191. Future page references to this work are included in the body of the text.

46. The idea that the function of painting was to represent public virtue via universal and ideal forms, rather than the external appearances of nature, was promoted by English aestheticians beginning with the Third Earl of Shaftesbury early in the eighteenth century. Reynolds reasserted this association between public virtue and ideal beauty in his *Discourses*. For a discussion of these issues in Shaftesbury's and Reynolds's writings see Barrell, *Political Theory*, pp. 27–33 and 76–99.

47. David Solkin discusses the efforts of these writers to mobilize art as a socializing force in *Painting for Money*; see especially pp. 220–2.

48. Two of the best accounts of the development of amateur drawing practices are Kim Sloan, "Drawing – a 'Polite Recreation' in Eighteenth-Century England," *Studies in Eighteenth Century Culture* 2 (1982), pp. 217–40 and Ann Bermingham, "'An Exquisite Practice': The Institution of Drawing as a Polite Art in Britain," in *Towards a Modern Art World*, ed. Brian Allen (New Haven and London: Yale University Press, 1995), pp. 47–66.

49. For insightful analyses of female subjectivity within artistic discourse and practice see Ann Bermingham's "'An Exquisite Practice'" and

her essay, "The Origins of Painting and the End of Art: Wright of Derby's *Corinthian Maid*," in *Painting and the Politics of Culture: New Essays on British Art 1700–1850*, ed. John Barrell (Oxford and London: Oxford University Press, 1992), pp. 135–64; see also Ann Pullan, "'Conversations on the Arts': Writing a Space for the Female Viewer in the *Repository of Arts* 1809–15," *Oxford Art Journal* 15:2 (1992), pp. 15–26.

50. For an analysis of the status of genius in Reynolds's *Discourses* see Robert Uphaus, "The Ideology of Reynolds' *Discourses on Art*," *Eighteenth Century Studies* 21:1 (Fall 1978), pp. 59–73.

51. In seeking to explain how discrete discourses (on nature, for example) function within a larger discursive nexus Peter de Bolla has determined that adjacent discourses are frequently deployed as a means of legislating (i.e., regulating) a given discourse which threatens to become excessive, such as the discourse on the imagination or the sublime. The success of such a regulatory move is dependent on the authority of the neighboring discourse being unquestioned. Key legislative terms (such as tradition, nature, and reason) are undefined and unexamined, since they remain outside of the discursive analytic [de Bolla, *The Discourse of the Sublime: History, Aesthetics and the Subject* (Oxford: Blackwell, 1989), pp. 11–13 and 54–5].

52. "Royal Academy – 1798," *Monthly Mirror* 6 (July 1798), p. 29.

53. Figure 13, *View of Mynnydd Mawr, North Wales*, reproduces a watercolor in the British Museum that was a sketch for a Welsh view Girtin may have exhibited in 1799.

54. [John Taylor], "Royal Academy," *True Briton*, 10 May 1799, and "Royal Academy," *Sun*, 13 May 1799. Three months before the Royal Academy exhibition opened in May 1799, Joseph Farington recorded in his *Diary* that Edward Lascelles (who had commissioned watercolors from both Turner and Girtin and purchased one of Girtin's exhibited views of *Beth Kellert*) judged Girtin to be superior to Turner, "who they say effects his purpose by industry – the former more [by] genius – Turner finishes too much." *The Diary of Joseph Farington*, ed. Kenneth Garlick, Angus Macintyre, and Kathyrn Cave (New Haven and London: Yale University Press, 1978–84), 9 February 1799.

55. For reviews of *Harlech Castle*, see [John Taylor], "Royal Academy," *True Briton*, 4 May 1799 and *Sun*, 13 May 1799; Taylor's review of *Caernarvon Castle* appeared in the *True Briton* on 10 May and in the *Sun* on 17 May 1799. The latter work is in a private collection. For a color reproduction see Andrew Wilton, *J.M.W. Turner: His Art and Life* (New York: Rizzoli, 1979), Plate 47.

56. Farington, *Diary*, 27 May 1799.

57. Dayes's argument here closely follows Reynolds's discussion of taste and opinion in Discourse VII. However, unlike Dayes, Reynolds adopts a pragmatic position in recommending that artists should to some extent accommodate opinion, for "whilst these opinions and prejudices . . . continue, they operate as truth; and the art, whose office is to please the mind, as well as instruct it, must direct itself according to *opinion*, or it will not attain its end" (p. 122). For a further analysis of opinion and prejudice in Discourse VII see Barrell, *Political Theory*, pp. 141–5.

58. The above-cited passages are only two of several in Dayes's writings in which his anti-commercialism, and aesthetic traditionalism are articulated in a language which derives from the discourse of civic humanism. According to J.G.A. Pocock, civic humanism is an oppositional discourse which advocates certain notions of property ownership, citizenship, and virtue together with a return to the original precepts of the Ancient Constitution [J.G.A. Pocock, *The Machiavellian Moment: Florentine Political Thought and the Atlantic Republican Tradition* (Princeton: Princeton University Press, 1975), pp. 462–505]. Although Dayes does not specifically refer to the Ancient Constitution, his condemnation of William the Conqueror and glorification of the Saxon King Alfred and General Fairfax (a leader in Cromwell's army) in a posthumously published travel account are strong indications of his sympathy with a constitutionalist reading of early English history ("An Excursion through the Principal Parts of Derbyshire and Yorkshire," in *Works*, pp. 158, 161, and 168). Dayes's endorsement of such a reading of history, combined with his appeal to reason, critique of luxury and fashionable life and exhortations to personal and public virtue strongly indicate a reformist politics which was expressed in civic humanist language.

59. These remarks derive from Reynolds's discussion of manner; see especially Discourse VI, pp. 102–3.

60. Britain had been a market for continental painting throughout the eighteenth century,

to the chagrin of domestic artists like Hogarth. In the 1790s and early 1800s, however, this situation was exacerbated by large number of princely and aristocratic collectors on the continent who were selling off their paintings to avoid fines or confiscation at the hands of the invading forces of Napoleon [Gerald Reitlinger, *The Economics of Taste: the Rise and Fall of Picture Prices 1760–1960* (London: Barrie and Rockliff, 1961) pp. 39–40]. As a result the trickle of old masters and old master imitations which made their way across the Channel increased to what seemed like a disastrous flood when viewed from the perspective of alarmed British artists. For a further discussion of old master collecting see Francis Haskell, *Rediscoveries in Art: Some Aspects of Taste, Fashion and Collecting in England and France* (London: Phaidon, 1976); a contemporary account of the art market by a dealer can be found in *William Buchanan and the Nineteenth Century Art Trade: One Hundred Letters to his Agents in London and Italy*, ed. Hugh Brigstocke (London: Paul Mellon Centre, 1982).

61. My use of the concept of "transparency" derives from de Bolla's analysis of eighteenth-century English treatises on oratory. The public orator in these accounts is forbidden to impose his private personality on the texts he speaks. Rather, he must become "transparent," so that the meaning and expression of the texts may pass through his body unaffected by his individuality (de Bolla, p. 151).

62. Reynolds, Discourse VI, p. 103.

63. Following the traditional mode of instruction in drawing, Dayes advises beginners to copy the human figure (p. 281). Kim Sloan has observed that the practice of teaching new students to copy the human figure, even if they were seeking training in another genre such as landscape, was common procedure among private drawing masters, in academies where drawing was taught, and in eighteenth-century drawing books (Sloan, pp. 219 and 236).

64. For the development of stopping out, scraping, and other techniques in this period see Hardie, 1, pp. 33–40. Hardie records that as early as 1800 James Roberts, the author of a practical guide to painting, recommended that students consult the watercolors of Turner and Girtin (ibid., 2, p. 1). See also James Roberts, *Introductory Lessons with Familiar Examples in Landscapes for . . . Painting*

in Water-Colours (London: Bulmer, 1800), p. 9.

65. Dayes's watercolor was published as an engraving in *The Itinerant* in 1796.

66. [W. H. Pyne?], "Observations on the Rise and Progress of Painting in Water Colours," *Repository of Arts*, February 1813, p. 93. Pyne's remarks were made with reference to Girtin. See supra, "Introduction," n. 2, for the attribution of this article to Pyne.

67. Cf. Reynolds, Discourse VI: "Art in its perfection is not ostentatious; it lies hid, and works its effect unseen" (p. 101).

68. Dayes here is paraphrasing John Dryden who wrote in his poem "To Sir Godfrey Kneller" (1694): "Mean time, while just Incouragement you want,/You only Paint to Live not Live to Paint" (quoted in Solkin, p. 289, n. 92).

69. R. W. Lightbown is perhaps not being overly dramatic when he suggests in his Introduction (unpaged) to the Cornmarket reprint (London, 1971) of the artist's *Works* that "Dayes' life, in its aspirations and in its failure, is a version in miniature of the tragedies of Barry and Haydon."

2   Of Old Masters, French Glitter, and English Nature

1. Martin Archer Shee, *Rhymes on Art* (London, 1805), p. x.

2. For Hogarth's "war" with English patrons of old masters, see Ronald Paulson, *Hogarth*, 3 vols. (New Brunswick, NJ: Rutgers University Press, 1992), 2, pp. 229–39.

3. In the body of his poem Shee emphasizes the importance of history painting as a public genre when he writes that "subjects connected with history, which illustrate the actions of the sage, the hero, and the patriot, are those which appear most worthy of the pencil in a free state" (*Rhymes on Art*, note to line 193, p. 258). Shee also charged that monumental public sculpture was unduly neglected by official patronage. For a provocative account of why the national government largely refrained from funding public monuments to British military heroes see Linda Colley, "Whose Nation? Class and National Consciousness in Britain 1750–1830," *Past and Present* 113 (November 1986), pp. 97–117.

4. Morris Eaves, *The Counter-Arts Conspiracy: Art and Industry in the Age of Blake* (Ithaca, NY, and London: Cornell University Press, 1992), p. 84.

5. Shee, *Rhymes on Art*, Preface, p. xxiv; cited in Eaves, pp. 94–5.

6. Shee, p. 40.

7. Gerald Newman, *The Rise of English Nationalism: A Cultural History 1740–1830* (New York: St. Martins, 1987); Linda Colley, *Britons: Forging the Nation 1707–1837* (New Haven and London: Yale University Press, 1992).

8. See Newman, pp. 63–122, where he discusses how middle-class writers and artists, most notably Hogarth, mobilized an anti-French stereotype as a way of critiquing a corrupt English aristocracy steeped in French culture and manners.

9. The notable exception is Peter Funnell, who discusses the art writings of William Hazlitt (especially in 1814–15) and Richard Payne Knight as rebuttals to calls for increased patronage by men like Hoare [Funnell, "William Hazlitt, Prince Hoare, and the Institutionalisation of the British Art World," in *Towards a Modern Art World*, ed. Brian Allen (New Haven and London: Yale University Press, 1995), pp. 145–55].

10. [Robert Hunt], "Royal Academy Exhibition," *Examiner*, 29 April 1810, p. 268.

11. This section of the book also appeared in revised form as "Reflections on the Patronage of the Fine Arts," in the *Champion* (14 May 1815, p. 159), a newspaper edited by Scott. For a brief discussion of English attitudes to French and British art patronage as expressed in the contemporary press, see also Andrew Hemingway, *Landscape Imagery and Urban Culture in Early Nineteenth-Century Britain* (Cambridge: Cambridge University Press, 1992), p. 117.

12. John Scott, *A Visit to Paris in 1814* (London: Longmans, 1815), pp. 5 and 7.

13. Ibid., p. 209.

14. Ibid. See also Scott's piece in the *Champion*, "The Public Exhibition of Paintings," 7 May 1815, pp. 149–50, which makes the same point about the English preference for individual choice and taste in the arts over the need for large public displays.

15. For a discussion of other writers and institutions (such as the newly founded quarterlies) which associate intellect and independent thought with the middle class see Jon Klancher, "Reading the Social Text: Power, Signs and Audience in Nineteenth Century Prose," *Studies in Romanticism* 23 (Summer 1984), pp. 183–204; this argument is more fully elaborated in his *The Making of English Reading Audiences, 1790–1832* (Madison: University of Wisconsin Press, 1987). Andrew Hemingway also discusses this phenomenon in terms of the growth of the urban intelligentsia and their promotion of intellectual autonomy as a necessary condition for artistic and literary production (*Landscape Imagery*, p. 34).

16. "Fine Arts," *Le Beau Monde* 1 (January 1807), p. 163.

17. The *New Monthly Magazine* was established in this year, 1814, by Henry Colburn in overt opposition to the liberal-to-radical *Monthly Magazine*. For an account of the *New Monthly*'s textual strategies in forming an educated middle-class readership see Klancher, *The Making of English Reading Audiences*, especially pp. 62–8.

18. "Claudius," "On the Patronage of the Arts," *New Monthly Magazine*, 1 March 1814, pp. 121–2.

19. Ibid., p. 121.

20. English art hanging on the walls of country houses enjoyed access to a wider public than the friends and family of the owners if the house was open to tourists, or if the works were described in tour guides. Nonetheless, these avenues of display and publicity were generally much more restricted than those available to paintings shown (even temporarily) in the metropolis. See Hemingway, *Landscape Imagery*, pp. 1–7, for an analysis of the commodity status of painting as inscribed in the spaces of the city described by a number of artists and writers in the contemporary periodical press. This present study adopts Hemingway's position on art criticism as a form of writing different from academic and philosophical writing, "determined by particular constraints of context which made it of limited length . . . and which also demanded that it be topical, political, and even fashionable or amusing according to the precise organ in which it appeared" (ibid., p. 105).

21. This is a central theme of Neil McKendrick, John Brewer, and J.H. Plumb, *The Birth of a Consumer Society* (London: Hutchinson, 1983) and Colin Campbell, *The Romantic Ethic and the Spirit of Modern Consumerism* (Oxford: Basil Blackwell, 1987).

22. Neil McKendrick, "The Consumer Revolution of Eighteenth-Century England," in McKendrick et al., p. 10.

23. Considering the large size of the drawings, their bright colors, and the heavy gold frames, Martin Hardie speculates that the works were designed to compete not only

with the pictures hanging beside them, but with oil paintings on exhibition across the city at the Royal Academy. Hardie, *Water-colour Painting in Britain*, 3 vols (New York: Barnes and Noble, 1967), 1, p. 41.

24. John Opie, *The Lectures of John Opie* (orig. pub. 1809), in *Lectures on Painting by the Royal Academicians*, ed. Ralph Wornum (London, 1848), p. 257.

25. "Fine Arts," *Le Beau Monde*, 7 January 1807, pp. 163–4.

26. In the 1770s there was a immense surge in building in urban centers; town house construction in London accelerated after 1774 with the passage of the London Building Act [David Cannadine, *Lords and Landlords: the Aristocracy and the Towns, 1774–1967* (Leicester: Leicester University Press, 1980), p. 31]. A constellation of factors contributed to the financial boom of the Napoleonic war years among the upper and upper middle classes: huge profits made in agriculture, sharp increases in domestic consumption and foreign trade, and vast fortunes made from a National Debt that nearly tripled between 1780 and 1800 [Peter Kriedte, *Peasants, Landlords and Merchant Capitalists. Europe and the World Economy, 1500–1800* (Leamington Spa: Berg, 1980), p. 130ff.].

27. *St. James Chronicle*, 11–14 June 1791, quoted in Christopher Sykes, *Private Palaces. Life in the Great London Houses* (New York: Viking, 1986), p. 223.

28. Sykes, p. 234.

29. Ibid., pp. 234–7.

30. *William Buchanan and the Nineteenth Century Art Trade: One Hundred Letters to his Agents in London and Italy*, ed. Hugh Brigstocke (London: Paul Mellon Centre, 1982), p. 78, Buchanan to Irvine, 3 June 1803. See Peter Funnell, "Richard Payne Knight 1751–1824: Aspects of Aesthetics and Art Criticism in Late Eighteenth and Early Nineteenth Century England" (Ph.D. diss., Oxford University, 1985), pp. 49–54 for a further discussion of the English taste for brightly colored paintings and the "lower" genres.

31. Buchanan, p. 79 for the letter to Irvine, 3 June 1803, in which he advised against buying large portraits of paintings of saints, and any large-sized pictures whatsoever; p. 84 (letter to Irvine, 6 June 1803), and p. 89 (letter to Irvine, 23 July 1803).

32. Ibid., p. 91, letter to Irvine, 23 July 1803.

33. Prince Hoare, *An Inquiry into the Requisite Cultivation and Present State of the Arts of Design in England* (London, 1806), p. 142.

34. The Baring Fete," *True Briton*, 8 May 1806. Due to a merger in 1804 the name of this journal changed from the *True Briton* to the *Daily Advertiser, Oracle and True Briton*. For the sake of simplicity, the former name will be used throughout the period of its publication, from 1801 to 1809.

35. Sydney Checkland, *British Public Policy 1776–1939* (Cambridge: Cambridge University Press, 1983), p. 22.

36. Francis Haskell observes that among aristocratic or mercantile dynasties, only the Baring family, beginning with Francis, evidenced a keen interest in old master collecting that was sustained over several generations [Haskell, *Rediscoveries in Art: Some Aspects of Taste, Fashion and Collecting in England and France* (London: Phaidon, 1976), p. 124].

37. According to Haskell it is difficult to know which Dutch pictures from the Baring collection were obtained by Francis, but he did buy the works of Berchem, Mieris, and Steen at the Grefier Fagel sale in 1801 (Haskell, p. 199, n. 5). William Whitley records that Francis Baring lent a Rembrandt to the first exhibition of the British school held in 1806 (the exhibition is discussed below p. 40) (Whitley, *Art in England 1800–1820* (New York: Macmillan, 1928, p. 111). Although Baring was most noted for his collection of Dutch masters, he purchased English pictures by Opie, Northcote, and Peters at the sale of Boydell's Shakespeare Gallery (Haskell, p. 199, n. 5).

38. For an informative account of the establishment of the British Institution see Peter Fullerton, "Patronage and Pedagogy: The British Institution in the Early Nineteenth Century," *Art History* 5:1 (March 1982), pp. 59–72.

39. See ibid., pp. 64–5, for a discussion of the founding and the immediate success of the British School.

40. Ibid., p. 64; the works on display at the first British School in 1806 are listed in Whitley, p. 111. Eight of the twelve northern works shown were in the collections of the Governors.

41. Shee, *Elements of Art* (London, 1809), p. 28.

42. Ibid., pp. 26–7.

43. *The Diary of Joseph Farington*, 16 vols., ed. Kenneth Garlick, Angus Macintyre, and Kathryn Cave (New Haven and London: Yale University Press, 1978–84), 21 May 1815. In addition to Farington's *Diary*, accounts of the Academicians' resentment of the British Institution's promotion of old

masters are provided in Felicity Owen and David Blayney Brown, *Collector of Genius: A Life of Sir George Beaumont* (New Haven and London: Paul Mellon Centre, 1988), pp. 176–83; and Fullerton, pp. 59–72.

44. Speculation about the authorship of this notorious pamphlet raged at the time of publication and continues to the present. Although the attribution in the British Library Catalogue is to the painter Robert Smirke, there is no hard evidence to support it. David Blayney Brown has noted the similarity between certain passages of this work and a letter which the landscape painter A.W. Callcott wrote in 1808, but as Brown also correctly observed, a number of artists at the time made similar criticisms of the British Institution (Owen and Brown, pp. 183–4).

45. *A Catalogue Raisonnée of the Pictures Now Exhibiting at the British Institution* (London, 1815), quoted in Fullerton, p. 68. In 1810 a stinging attack on old master collecting was made in the fashionable magazine, *La Belle Assemblée*. Asserting that old master paintings are little understood by their wealthy owners, the author goes on to remark that "their fortunate possessors are always calculating their worth, and having them surveyed and appraised as frequently as the timber on their estates" ("Retrospect of the Fine Arts," *La Belle Assemblée*, December 1810, p. 340). The reference to the surveying of timber serves to underscore the fact that profit-making and financial calculation, far from being restricted to a commercial bourgeoisie, were of fundamental concern to landed proprietors. This mercantile consciousness, rather than a liberal taste, the argument ran, is what fueled the contemporary market for old masters.

46. "British Gallery of Pictures," *Morning Post*, 18 June 1813.

47. The desire to promote academic (i.e., "serious") painting was underscored by the fact that the Institution originally banned portrait painting from its annual exhibitions of modern art.

48. Although a discussion of portraiture is outside the scope of this investigation, further examination is needed of the debates on this genre in the decades around 1800. While portraiture continued to be attacked by those critical of the effects of commerce on both the arts and the moral character of individuals, there were also, increasingly, defenses of the genre as representing English sociability. For such a defense, see [John Britton], "Royal Academy," *British Press*, 5 May 1803.

49. *Walks in a Forest* went through at least nine editions in the first fifteen years after its publication. Like his friends and fellow evangelicals William Wilberforce and Hannah More, Gisborne advocated a moral reform of all levels of British society that served to reaffirm existing hierarchies of class and gender. This program is fully elaborated in his widely read *An Enquiry into the Duties of Men*, 2 vols. (London, 1794) and *An Enquiry into the Duties of the Female Sex* (London, 1797).

50. See David Solkin, *Richard Wilson: The Landscape of Reaction* (Tate Gallery exhib. cat., London, 1982), pp. 68–70, for a discussion of the philosophical concept of *concordia discors* in the context of Wilson's landscapes. Four years prior to the publication of *Walks in a Forest* Edmund Burke had utilized this notion in praising the organization of the French Estates-General before the Revolution wrecked its harmony: "In your old states you possessed that variety of parts corresponding with the various descriptions of which your community was happily composed; you had all that combination and all that opposition of interests; you had that act and counteraction which, in the natural and in the political world, from the reciprocal struggle of discordant powers, draws out the harmony of the universe" [Burke, *Reflections on the Revolution in France*, ed. Thomas Mahoney (Indianapolis and New York: Bobbs-Merrill, 1955; orig. pub. 1790), p. 40].

51. Thomas Gisborne, *Walks in a Forest*, 4th edn. (London, 1799; orig. pub. 1794), p. 10.

52. Ibid., pp. 64–5.

53. Regarding this passage, Gisborne states that he is following Reynolds's notes on Charles Dufresnoy's *De Arte graphica* on the proper disposition of light and shade throughout a composition (Gisborne, *Walks in a Forest*, p. 65).

54. Gisborne's own residence, Yoxall, was located in Needwood Forest. A friend of his, Bishop Porteus, writing to Hannah More in 1797, noted that Gisborne "has a very handsome and delightful habitation in the very heart of Needwood Forest, a large tract of ground belonging to the crown, and abounding with all those rude and picturesque scenes which produced his 'Walks in a Forest'" [quoted in Benedict Nicolson, "Thomas Gisborne and Wright of Derby," *Burlington Magazine*, 107 (1965), p. 61].

55. This same year, 1794, also saw the publication of Richard Payne Knight's didactic poem, *The Landscape*, which images society

as a diversified landscape. Unlike Gisborne, Knight used the image of the forest as a metaphor for wild "native liberty," which drew charges of Jacobinism from more conservative Whigs like Horace Walpole, who thought Knight was advocating revolution [Frank Messmann, *Richard Payne Knight: The Twilight of Virtuosity* (The Hague and Paris: Mouton, 1974), pp. 65–84].

56. The works Sandby exhibited that year included a view of Tunbridge, a view of the Eagle Tower of Caernarvon Castle, and two other works entitled *Morning* and *Evening*.

57. "Royal Academy," *Morning Post*, 4 June 1795. Given the similarity between this review and those written by Pasquin at the same time, it is highly likely that Pasquin himself was the author of this anonymous review.

58. In addition to contemporary France, Venice, Holland, and Carthage were offered by artists and cultural critics as historical examples of the negative impact of commerce on the arts. Thus Henry Fuseli, Professor of Painting at the Royal Academy from 1801 to 1805, argued in a lecture before the Academy in 1801 that the commercial activity of Venice's patricians, princely merchants, and artisans ensured that Venetian paintings could be little more than fashionable luxury goods. See *The Life and Writings of Henry Fuseli*, 3 vols., ed. John Knowles (London, 1831), 2, p. 362.

59. For a discussion of early English collectors of Watteau see Robert Raines, "Watteaus and 'Watteaus' in England before 1760," *Gazette des Beaux Arts*, 6th series, 86 (February 1977), pp. 51–64; Selby Whittingham discusses the impact of Watteau on English artists, particularly Turner, in "What You Will; or Some Notes Regarding the Influence of Watteau on Turner and Other British Artists," Parts I and II, *Turner Studies* 5:1 (Summer 1985), pp. 2–24 and 5:2 (Winter 1985), pp. 28–48.

60. John Barrell, "'The Dangerous Goddess': Masculinity, Prestige, and the Aesthetic in Early Eighteenth-Century Britain," *Cultural Critique* 12 (Spring 1989), p. 103.

61. Like the *Post* critic, Fuseli described the "allure" of color in highly sexualized terms, as did John Opie in his Royal Academy lectures of 1807, where color is described as "the Cleopatra of the art" (Fuseli, 2, p. 362; John Opie, *Lectures*, in Wornum, p. 314). For a discussion of the manner in which seventeenth-century French aesthetic discourse constructed analogies between painted canvases and painted women see Jacqueline Lichtenstein, "Making Up Representation: The Risks of Femininity," *Representations* 20 (Fall 1987), pp. 77–87; and Lichtenstein, *The Eloquence of Color: Rhetoric and Painting in the French Classical Age* (Berkeley: University of California Press, 1993; orig. pub. in French 1989).

62. Loutherbourg's work will be examined in Chapter 5. Francis Bourgeois was a student of Loutherbourg who exhibited rustic landscapes ("landscape with cattle" being a favorite theme) at the Academy throughout the 1790s and early 1800s. Dayes harshly criticized his color as "chalky" and his handling of light and shade as "often violent and spotty" [Dayes, "Professional Sketches," in *The Works of the Late Edward Dayes* (London: E. W. Brayley, 1805), p. 322]. Other critics complained simply that his work was mannered and repetitive (see Royal Academy reviews in the *Morning Chronicle*, 4 May 1792 and *British Press*, 14 May 1803). For a fuller account of his career see Giles Waterfield, "'That White-Faced Man': Sir Francis Bourgeois, 1756–1811," *Turner Studies* 9:2 (Winter 1989), pp. 36–48.

63. Ibbetson made a tour of the Isle of Wight, where this scene is located, in 1791. In 1792 he exhibited seven views of the island at the Royal Academy. The artist's biographer, Mary Rotha Clay, suggests that *Sand Quarry at Alum Bay* may have been the work exhibited that year under the title *View of the Beach, Isle of Wight* (no. 449) [Clay, *Julius Caesar Ibbetson 1759–1817* (London: Country Life, 1948), p. 30].

64. The phrase is that of the continually frustrated history painter Benjamin Robert Haydon who had utter disdain for connoisseurs who failed to commission and otherwise support large-scale didactic paintings. In a diary entry from 1808 that clearly refers to the English taste for Dutch landscape and genre paintings, he observed, "wherever I go a string of technical phrases that are for ever on the tongue, without effort or reflection, are perpetually uttered – how that flower is imitated, what a colour that turnip is, how delightful is that cabbage, look at that herring – wonderful" [*The Diary of Benjamin Robert Haydon*, 5 vols., ed. W. B. Pope (Cambridge, MA: Harvard University Press, 1960–3), 1, p. 4].

65. In 1796, Anthony Pasquin (the pseudonym of John Williams) accused Ibbetson of "running to extremes" in painting landscapes with a "brazen hue" (Pasquin, quoted in Clay, p. 8).

The critic for the *Star* praised Ibbetson's landscapes exhibited at the RA in 1804 for their "spirited style," but went on to declare that "he has fallen into a spotty manner, peculiarly his own, which robs his productions of much of the merit which they would otherwise possess" (*Star*, 19 May 1804).

66. "Royal Academy Exhibition, 1798," *London Packet*, 9–11 May 1798; the same critic, commenting on Ibbetson's *Bowder Stone in Borrowdale*, exhibited the following year, declared its "spottiness of manner" to predominate to the point of "slovenly excess" ("Royal Academy Exhibition, 1799," *London Packet*, 29 April–1 May 1799).

67. This work was one of a number of scenes Westall produced in the late 1790s which depicted shepherds, harvesters, and other members of the agrarian working class caught in the midst of a storm, faithfully persevering in their labor, or waiting patiently for the disturbance to pass. Such a theme was no doubt an especially reassuring one for Westall's patron, Payne Knight, and others in the properted classes, at a time when workers in France had instigated a revolution metaphorically cast as a natural cataclysm by Burke and other British commentators. Although Knight's *The Landscape* was attacked by some conservative Tories for its so-called republican sentiments, the Herefordshire landowner was in fact a strong supporter of traditional hierarchies and, by 1796, a savage critic of the French. In that year Knight voiced concern that the repressive measures imposed by the British state in the wake of the Revolution were not strong enough to control the growing power of the mob [Alex Potts, "A Man of Taste's Picturesque" (review of *The Arrogant Connoisseur*, ed. Michael Clarke and Nicholas Penny), in *Oxford Art Journal* 5:1 (1982), pp. 70–6].

68. Only two such references to Gainsborough have come to my attention. One occurred in the *London Packet*, 27–30 April 1798, in which the critic noted that Westall's *Sunset* was reminiscent of the best of Gainsborough. The other appeared in the radical *Monthly Magazine*, which in its "Retrospect of the Fine Arts," April 1801, praised Westall for eschewing Arcadian fantasies, and continuing the tradition established by Gainsborough, of showing English figures set in English scenery. The openness of works of art to contrary readings is well illustrated by such a response, for most published criticism of Westall's work insisted on the *un*-English quality of his figures and his surface effects.

69. For a discussion of Westall's patrons, supporters, and critics see Richard Westall, "The Westall Brothers," *Turner Studies* 4:1 (Summer 1984), p. 24.

70. [Richard Payne Knight], review of *The Life of Sir Joshua Reynolds*, by James Northcote, in *Edinburgh Review* 23 (September 1814), p. 287.

71. Richard Payne Knight, *An Analytical Inquiry into the Principles of Taste* (London, 1805), p. 304. *Storm in Harvest* is invoked in this passage as evidence that "tragedies taken from common life" can be as interesting and affecting as the classical tragedies traditionally associated with history painting.

72. Anthony Pasquin [John Williams], *Critical Guide to the Royal Academy Exhibition of 1796* (London, 1796), p. 21, cited in Shelley Bennett, "Anthony Pasquin and the Function of Art Journalism in Late Eighteenth-Century England," *British Journal for Eighteenth Century Studies* 8:2 (1985), p. 201.

73. For an analysis of the gendering of color in seventeenth-century French aesthetics see Lichtenstein, *The Eloquence of Color*, especially pp. 185–95.

74. "Exhibition of Paintings . . . at the Royal Academy," *St. James Chronicle*, 6–8 May 1800.

75. C. R. Leslie, letter, 14 September 1812, quoted in Westall, p. 25.

76. Pasquin, quoted ibid., p. 24.

77. See, for example, "The Arts – Remarks on the Present Exhibition," *True Briton*, 22 May 1807. In 1814 Richard Westall held a private exhibition of his works (312 in all) in Pall Mall. As Richard J. Westall notes in his article on his forebear, the exhibition nearly bankrupted Westall, but did receive positive reviews in the London press. The *Repository of Arts* heralded Westall as a key figure in the development of watercolor in England and critics for *The Times* and *New Monthly Magazine* praised his works for their splendor and elegance (Westall, pp. 29–31).

78. "Royal Academy," *True Briton*, 3 May 1800.

79. Michael Clarke's catalogue entry for the picture notes that Knight's enthusiasm for Westall's *Flora* was considered "additional proof of his bad taste," by banker and poet, Samuel Rogers, and also "regretted" by Knight's friend, George Beaumont [Michael Clarke and Nicholas Penny, ed., *The Arrogant Connoisseur: Richard Payne Knight, 1751–1824* (Whitworth Art Gallery exhib. cat., Man-

chester: Manchester University Press, 1982), p. 186].

80. "The Arts – Remarks on the Present Exhibition," *True Briton*, 22 May 1807; emphasis in the original.

81. *Political Essays on Popular Subjects, Containing Dissertations on First Principles; Liberty; Democracy and the Party Denominations of Whig and Tory*, 3rd edn. (London, 1801), p. 15.

82. Ibid., pp. 22–3. The term "innovation" took on an almost universally pejorative meaning in the late 1790s and early 1800s, being synonymous with revolutionary political and social change.

83. The debate over color and line has a long and complex history. For a recent account of the *desegno/colore* debate in seventeenth-century France see Lichtenstein, *The Eloquence of Color*, pp. 138–68.

84. For the attack on *The Landscape* see supra, Chapter 2, n. 55.

85. [Richard Payne Knight], review of *The Life of Sir Joshua Reynolds*, p. 285.

86. Peter Funnell, "'Visible Appearances,'" in Clarke and Penny, pp. 82–92. For a more fully developed account of Knight's activities as a connoisseur and aesthetician see Funnell's excellent doctoral dissertation, "Richard Payne Knight, 1751–1824."

87. Funnell, "'Visible Appearances.'" See p. 88 for a discussion of "massing," pp. 88–9 for Knight on the picturesque, and pp. 89–92 for his discussion of Knight's views of the old masters.

88. See Funnell, "'Visible Appearances.'" pp. 86–8 for Knight's discussion of sight and its relationship to his theory of painting. The scientific study which Knight discusses was a famous case from 1728 of a boy born blind who gained his sight at the age of fourteen; William Cheselden, the surgeon who removed his cataracts, carefully observed and recorded the process by which the boy was able to make judgments about the nature of his visual impressions.

89. This accords with Andrew Hemingway's astute observation regarding the general project of "philosophical criticism," that is, the writings of eighteenth-century Scottish philosophers such as Lord Kames, Adam Smith, David Hume, Thomas Reid, and their later English followers such as Payne Knight. Hemingway writes that the "conception of explaining the experience of aesthetic pleasure in terms of principles discovered by the 'science' of human nature, defines the central project of philosophical criticism. It was con-

ceived as an inquiry which would deduce general principles from observed regularities in human behaviour, and subject received authorities to critical scrutiny on that basis" [Hemingway, "The 'Sociology' of Taste in the Scottish Enlightenment," *Oxford Art Journal* 12:2 (1989), p. 5].

90. David Simpson, *Romanticism, Nationalism, and the Revolt against Theory* (Chicago and London: University of Chicago Press, 1993). This pitting of British empiricism against the French "love of system" is a phenomenon which will be discussed more fully in Chapter 3. It should be noted here that Knight repeatedly invokes this ideologically charged rhetoric in attacking the system of rules imposed arbitrarily by professors of the Royal Academy. For a brief discussion of the connection between Knight's "Burkean" distrust of academic rules and his politics, see Hemingway, *Landscape Imagery*, p. 58.

91. [Richard Payne Knight], review of *The Works of James Barry Esq., Historical Painter*, in *Edinburgh Review* 16 (August 1810), p. 320.

92. See Chapter 4 for an extended discussion of associationism in the context of landscape painting. The most thorough account of associationism is M. Kallich's *The Association of Ideas and Critical Theory in Eighteenth-Century England* (The Hague and Paris: Mouton, 1970). For a concise and extremely astute recent analysis of the subject see Andrew Hemingway, "The 'Sociology' of Taste in the Scottish Enlightenment." Hemingway discusses Knight's "take" on associationism in *Landscape Imagery*, pp. 48–61.

93. See, for example, Funnell, "'Visible Appearances,'" pp. 82–6 and Samuel Monk's classic *The Sublime: A Study of Critical Theories in Eighteenth-Century England* (New York, Modern Language Association, 1935), especially pp. 160–3.

94. Knight, *Analytical Inquiry*, pp. 149 and 194.

95. Ibid., pp. 139–40.

96. [Knight], review of *The Works of James Barry*, p. 316.

97. [Knight], review of *Life of . . . Reynolds*, p. 266.

98. [Knight], review of *The Works of James Barry*, p. 298.

99. Ibid., pp. 308–9.

100. Ibid., pp. 299–310, and *Analytical Inquiry*, p. 98.

101. In *The Landscape* (London, 1794) Knight does advise English landscape painters to follow the example of the Dutch, and cultivate the

particular beauties of "our cool and wat'ry skies" (p. 87), but this hardly amounts to an endorsement of a national school of painting based upon an ideal of Englishness.

102. Knight, *Analytical Inquiry*, p. 286.

103. Hemingway, *Landscape Imagery*, p. 60.

3 The Domestic Landscape as Contested Ground: Amateur Dabblers versus Native Geniuses

1. Martin Archer Shee, *Rhymes on Art* (London, 1805), pp. 50–1.

2. Peter Funnell sets out the history of the debate in his dissertation. It began with Knight's questioning Price's use of the term "picturesque" in the second edition of *The Landscape* (1795). Price responded to Knight in his *Dialogue on the Distinct Characters of the Picturesque and Beautiful* (1801) and Knight in turn began his *Analytical Inquiry* as a definitive response to Price, although it ultimately encompassed much broader aesthetic questions [Funnell, "Richard Payne Knight 1751–1824: Aspects of Aesthetics and Art Criticism in Late Eighteenth and Early Nineteenth Century England" (Ph.D. diss., Oxford University, 1985), p. 7].

3. For an extensive discussion of copyists and imitators of Gainsborough see John Hayes, *The Landscape Paintings of Thomas Gainsborough*, 2 vols. (London: Sotheby Publications, 1982), 1, pp. 237–98; Wilson's students, followers, and copyists are similarly discussed in W. G. Constable, *Richard Wilson* (Cambridge, MA: Harvard University Press, 1953), pp. 132–50.

4. Hayes, 1, pp. 237–8.

5. The dealer Vandergucht told Joseph Farington that Wilson was selling better than Gainsborough in 1794, [*The Diary of Joseph Farington*, 16 vols., ed. Kenneth Garlick, Angus Macintyre, and Kathryn Cave (New Haven and London: Yale University Press, 1978–84), 15 July 1794)]; for the sale of the *Niobe* to Francis Baring see Gerald Reitlinger, *The Economics of Taste: The Rise and Fall of Picture Prices 1760–1960* (London: Barrie and Rockliff, 1961), p. 75. W. G. Constable has an extended discussion of the prices and critical reception of Wilson's landscapes in the 1790s and early 1800s, based largely on entries in Farington's Diary (Constable, pp. 125–9).

6. David Solkin, *Richard Wilson: The Landscape of Reaction* (Tate Gallery exhib. cat., London, 1982), p. 20.

7. Edward Edwards, *Anecdotes of Painters Who Have Resided or Been Born in England* (London: Leigh and Sotheby, 1808), p. 86.

8. *Sun*, July 1814, cited in Constable, p. 121.

9. For a thorough analysis of Discourse XIV in the context of press criticism which fueled the competition between Gainsborough and Reynolds, see David Brenneman, "The Critical Response to Gainsborough's Painting" (Ph.D. diss., Brown University, 1994), Chapter 5.

10. Joshua Reynolds, Discourse XIV, *Discourses on Art*, ed. Robert Wark (New Haven and London: Yale University Press, 1959; orig. pub. 1797), p. 253.

11. In a backhanded compliment to Gainsborough, Reynolds here professes his preference for "genius in a lower rank of art, to feebleness and insipidity in the highest" (Reynolds, Discourse XIV, p. 249).

12. Edwards, p. 134.

13. [William Hazlitt], "On Gainsborough's Pictures," *Champion*, 31 July 1814, reprinted in *The Complete Works of William Hazlitt*, 21 vols., ed. P. P. Howe (London and Toronto: J. M. Dent, 1933), 18, p. 35.

14. Peter Funnell, "William Hazlitt, Prince Hoare, and the Institutionalisation of the British Art World," in *Towards a Modern Art World*, ed. Brian Allen (New Haven and London: Yale University Press, 1995), pp. 145–55.

15. Reynolds, Discourse XIV, pp. 250 and 253.

16. Ibid., pp. 257–8.

17. Edwards, p. 139.

18. Sam Smiles, "'Splashers,' 'Scrawlers' and 'Plasterers': British Landscape Painting and the Language of Criticism, 1800–40," *Turner Studies* 10:1 (Summer 1990), pp. 5–11.

19. Ibid., p. 8.

20. [John Hoppner], review of *Anecdotes of Painters*, by Edward Edwards, in *Quarterly Review* 1:1 (February 1809), p. 48. Edward Edwards, on the other hand, concurred with Reynolds's more positive assessment of Gainsborough's late works, which he quotes at great length in his *Anecdotes of Painters* (p. 137).

21. [Hoppner], p. 48.

22. Ann Pullan notes that the prospectus for the *Fine Arts of the English School*, published in the February 1810 issue of the *Repository of Arts*, emphasizes that the work was attempting to rival French and British works promoting old master painting. See Pullan, "Fashioning a Public for Art: Ideology, Gender and the Fine Arts in the English Periodical *c.*1800–

25," (Ph.D. diss., University of Cambridge, 1992), p. 92.

23. John Britton, *Fine Arts of the English School* (London: Longman and Hurst, 1812), p. 24.

24. Ibid.

25. Emilie Buchwald has considered the interrelationship between Gainsborough's landscape settings and picturesque landscape gardening in "Gainsborough's 'Prospect, Animated Prospect,'" in *Studies in Criticism and Aesthetics, 1660–1800: Essays in Honor of Samuel Monk*, ed. Howard Anderson and John Shea (Minneapolis: University of Minnesota Press, 1967), pp. 358–79; while John Hayes has considered Gainsborough's impact on the young Uvedale Price, one of the chief "theoreticians" of the picturesque (Hayes, 1, p. 280).

26. [W.H. Pyne?], "Observations on the Rise and Progress of Painting in Water Colours," *Repository of Arts*, April 1813, p. 219.

27. Edward Dayes's lowly assessment of topographical landscape drawing has already been noted. Topographical views were also associated with panoramas, which though extremely popular in early nineteenth-century Europe, were excluded from the category of high art.

28. Uvedale Price, *Essays on the Picturesque*, 2nd edn, 3 vols. (London, 1810; orig. pub. 1794), 3, p. 275f.

29. As Ann Bermingham has demonstrated, this aestheticization of the rural poor was part of a larger attempt by the propertied elite to contain or negate the socially destabilizing effects of enclosure, rural depopulation, and urban industrialization on the laboring population of the countryside. The ability to convert rural decay and poverty into a cultural 'asset' – an aesthetically pleasing view or picture – was ascribed to the same class of property owners whose capital investments in agricultural land and control of systems of poor relief largely produced the extremes of wealth and poverty which were the sources of rural dislocation and discontent [Bermingham, *Landscape and Ideology: The English Rustic Tradition 1740–1860* (Berkeley: University of California Press, 1986), pp. 73–83].

30. Richard Payne Knight, *An Analytical Inquiry into the Principles of Taste* (London, 1805), pp. 148–9.

31. This insistence on the elevated character of the picturesque was consistent with the shared opinion of Knight and Price that current taste in landscape gardening was in dire need of reform – an issue which affected most directly the landed gentry and those gentlemen of the commercial and financial classes who could afford to purchase enough property to landscape. For two insightful analyses of Price's views on landscape gardening see Stephen Daniels, "The Political Iconography of Woodland in Later Georgian England," in *The Iconography of Landscape*, ed. Denis Cosgrove and Stephen Daniels (Cambridge: Cambridge University Press, 1988), pp. 43–82; and S. Daniels and Charles Watkins, "Picturesque Landscaping and Estate Management: Uvedale Price and Nathaniel Kent at Foxley," in *The Politics of the Picturesque: Literature, Landscape and Aesthetics since 1770*, ed. Stephen Copley and Peter Gartside (Cambridge: Cambridge University Press, 1994), pp. 13–41.

32. This point is made most forcefully by Kim Ian Michasiw in "Nine Theses on the Picturesque," *Representations* 38 (Spring 1992), p. 78.

33. William Gilpin, *Three Essays on Picturesque Beauty; on Picturesque Travel; and on Sketching Landscapes* (London, 1792), p. 87.

34. Gilpin's tours circulated in manuscript form for years before being published in the 1780s and 1790s.

35. Gilpin frequently used an oval format in his sketches, perhaps as a way of referencing the ovoid or circular shape of the Claude glass and similar optical devices popular with domestic tourists.

36. For a discussion of the touristic gaze and the distinctions between visual and economic possession of the landscape see Carole Fabricant, "The Literature of Domestic Tourism and the Public Consumption of Private Property," in *The New Eighteenth Century: Theory, Politics, Literature*, ed. Felicity Nussbaum and Laura Brown (London and New York: Methuen, 1987), pp. 254–75.

37. In his *Three Essays* Gilpin writes that he doubts that "every admirer of picturesque beauty, is an admirer of the *beauty of virtue* . . . *but* . . . we dare not *promise* him more from picturesque travel, than a rational, and agreeable amusement. Yet even this may be of some use in an age teeming with licentious pleasure; and may in this light at least be considered as having a moral tendency" (p. 47; emphasis in the original).

38. Those passages from Gilpin's tours not directly related to picturesque sketching or viewing have been all but neglected by scholars. A welcome exception is Stephen Copley, who has recently analyzed Gilpin's des-

cription of lead mines in Cumberland. See Copley, "William Gilpin and the Black-lead Mine," in Copley and Garside, *The Politics of the Picturesque*, pp. 42–61.

39. William Gilpin, *Observations on the River Wye* (London, 1782), p. 35.

40. Ann Bermingham, "System, Order and Abstraction: The Politics of English Landscape Drawing around 1795," in *Landscape and Power*, ed. W. J. T. Mitchell (Chicago and London: University of Chicago Press, 1994), pp. 87–8.

41. Bermingham notes that one of the harshest attacks on Gilpin appears in a drawing manual published by landscape painter and drawing master William Marshall Craig. Craig attacks Gilpin for substituting a false and arbitrary system of representation for one which seeks to render, transparently and empirically, the individual character of natural objects. Bermingham suggests that Craig's discomfort with Gilpin's generalized and arbitrary system of notation was associated with a wider counter-revolutionary concern that words/ images were becoming divorced from the things they were supposed to represent. This detaching of sign from referent permitted new, and potentially revolutionary, meanings to pervert the traditional ("natural") meanings of concepts such as nature and liberty [Bermingham, "System, Order, Abstraction," pp. 93–8]. Bermingham's analysis supports the overarching argument made here regarding the increasingly problematic status of systems of generalized representation based upon philosophical appeals to idealism (Barry, Wilson) or to a purely painterly visual aesthetic (late Gainsborough, Gilpin, Ibbetson). It should be noted, however, that Gilpin, like Price and Knight, was a fiercely nationalistic Whig, devoted to the maintenance of the status quo (see for example his *Moral Contrasts* of 1798, which is in part a diatribe against foreign travel and foreign manners and morals).

42. The growing number of female amateurs can be largely attributed to the greater importance of drawing, playing musical instruments, singing, and other polite "accomplishments" as a sign of genteel, but increasingly commodified femininity. For a discussion of the distinction between the male connoisseur, who looks, and the accomplished woman who produces herself as a work of art to be looked at, see Ann Bermingham, "The Aesthetics of Ignorance: The Accomplished Woman in the Culture of Connoisseurship," *Oxford Art Journal* 16:2 (1993), pp. 3–20.

43. "Water-colour Exhibitions," *Repository of Arts*, June 1810 (supplement), p. 429. Ann Pullan notes that this attack on landscape painting was unusual for the *Repository*, which usually promoted the genre, along with the medium of watercolor – a positive stance in keeping with the business interests of the publisher, Rudolf Ackermann (Pullan, "Fashioning a Public for Art," pp. 283–4).

44. For an informative but uncritical description of Ackermann's various business enterprises see John Ford, *Ackermann 1783–1983: The Business of Art* (London: Ackermann, 1983). Ann Pullan has analysed in depth the manner in which the *Repository of Arts* constructs a female viewer and consumer of high art in her dissertation, "Fashioning a Public for Art," pp. 267–303, and in an article, "'Conversations on the Arts': Writing a Space for the Female Viewer in the *Repository of Arts* 1809–15," *Oxford Art Journal* 15:2 (1992), pp. 15–26.

45. Thomas Rowlandson produced a large number of colored drawings for projects ranging from the *Microcosm of London* to the *Tour of Dr. Syntax*. Peter Bicknell and Jane Munro note that Ackermann circulated drawings by artists such Girtin and Payne, and suggest that David Cox most likely provided drawings for *Ackermann's New Drawing Book of Light and Shadow* (London: Ackermann's, 1812), discussed below. See Bicknell and Munro, *Gilpin to Ruskin: Drawing Masters and Their Manuals, 1800– 1860* (Fitzwilliam Museum exhib. cat., Cambridge, 1988), pp. 11 and 31.

46. Pullan, "Fashioning a Public for Art," pp. 284–5. My discussion of female amateurs is greatly indebted to Pullan's analysis of periodicals, especially the *Repository* and its female readership.

47. "Exhibition of the British Institution," *Repository of Arts*, 1 March 1819, p. 174.

48. It is worth noting that this situation persists to the present day. In the Royal Academy's 1991 exhibition, "The Great Age of British Watercolors, 1750–1880," not a single work by a woman was shown. Indeed, the contribution of amateurs (of either gender) to the development and promotion of English watercolor has largely been ignored in the vast literature on the subject.

49. Ann Bermingham has analyzed the way in which the picturesque was seen to signify feminine qualities in "The Picturesque and

Ready-to-wear Femininity," in Copley and Garside, *The Politics of the Picturesque*, pp. 81–119; see especially pp. 82–6.

50. James Plumptre, *The Lakers* (London, 1797), p. 20. Such parodies should not be taken as a sign of the decline of the picturesque, as has been asserted by writers like Christopher Hussey, but rather as a mark of its popularity [Hussey, *The Picturesque* (London: Cass, 1967; orig. pub. 1927), p. 126]. The continued vitality of the picturesque is evidenced by the sheer number of picturesque landscape paintings, and drawings produced in the Napoleonic war period (and beyond), which were multiplied by their reproduction as individual prints, in series of picturesque views, and as illustrations in tour guides and local histories.

51. Although oil painters may not have been as deeply affected as watercolorists by the "leveling" effects of novices encroaching on their practice, the market for oil paintings of popular tourist sites in the Lake District, the Peaks, Wales, and Scotland was strongly affected by the popularity of the picturesque. In 1800 when Turner exhibited as his Academy diploma piece his sublime view of Dolbadern Castle, in which picturesque variety of outline and form is sharply limited in favor of varied arrays of indistinct masses of shadow and light, one of the few critical comments it elicited in the press indicated the public to whom the writer perceived the work to be directed. The critic declared that it was "a Picture of the first merit, which the Gentlemen who draw for tours in Wales might very profitably study" ("Exhibition of Paintings, etc. at the Royal Academy," *St. James Chronicle*, 29 April–1 May 1800).

52. Lindsay Stainton, *British Landscape Watercolours 1600–1800* (British Museum exhib. cat., Cambridge: Cambridge University Press, 1985), pp. 42–3.

53. Gilpin is clearly keen to avoid practices associated with topographical drawing. See, for example, his *Observations Relative Chiefly to Picturesque Beauty*, 2 vols. (London, 1786), where he warns that a landscape painting which comprehends too much of a view threatens to turn a picture into a map (1, p. 146). For the move away from panoramic landscapes to more occluded views, around 1800, see John Murdoch, "Foregrounds and Focus: Changes in the Perception of Landscape *c.*1800," in *The Lake District: A Sort of National Property* (Cheltenham: Countryside Commission, 1986), pp. 43–59; and

Bermingham, "System, Order and Abstraction," pp. 79–86.

54. James Roberts, *Introductory Lessons, with Familiar Examples in Landscape, for the Use of Those Who Are Desirous of Gaining Some Knowledge of the Pleasing Art of Painting in Water-Colours* (London: W. Bulmer, 1800), p. 1.

55. Ibid., p. 2.

56. Ibid., p. 14.

57. See, for example, his effusive description of the light and color effects playing over the ocean in his *Observations on the Coasts of Hampshire, Sussex and Kent Relative to Picturesque Beauty* (London: Cadell and Davies, 1804), p. 4.

58. Gilpin, *Three Essays*, p. 88.

59. Roberts, pp. 6–7. Although Roberts most frequently cites as models older artists, such as Sandby, whose work relies upon form and outline more than color, at one point he also recommends that students study and copy the drawings of Turner and Girtin (p. 9). Unfortunately for the student, Roberts provides no instruction in the selection of materials or the use of the techniques necessary for the production of the transparent veils of color and bold light effects which these professional artists achieved. Students are offered models whom they can admire, but cannot hope to emulate.

60. Ann Pullan notes that this tendency to "caution" is also registered by the appearance of numerous essays and guides to perspective geared to amateurs. These attempted to regulate the visual field of landscape at precisely the moment when artists like Girtin and Turner were investigating new modes of representing space (Pullan, "Fashioning a Public for Art," pp. 183–4).

61. John Gage has carefully considered Turner's encounter with the picturesque in the decade of the 1790s in "Turner and the Picturesque," *Burlington Magazine* 107 (January–June 1965), Part 1, pp. 16–25; Part 2, pp. 75–81. For a discussion of Turner's reworking of the picturesque in the context of nationalist discourse in the 1830s see Elizabeth Helsinger, "Turner and the Representation of England," in *Landscape and Power*, ed. W. J. T. Mitchell (Chicago and London: University of Chicago Press, 1994), pp. 103–25.

62. Carrington Bowles, *The Art of Painting in Water Colours* (London: Laurie and Whittle, 1799), p. 7.

63. Carrington Bowles, *The Art of Painting in Oil: Rendered Familiar to Every Capacity*, 9th edn.

(London: Laurie and Whittle, 1817), p. 33. Bowles was not unique in recommending an extremely subdued palette. William Oram's *Precepts and Observations on the Art of Colouring in Landscape Painting* (London: White and Cochrane, 1810) places primary emphasis not on the brilliant effects which can be achieved through the use of color, but on the way in which "true" colors are subdued by various forms of "privation" – specifically, *"privation of light, the distance from the eye*, and the *species of medium"* (p. 3; emphasis in the original).

64. Bowles, *The Art of Painting in Oil*, p. 35.

65. *Ackermann's New Drawing Book*, Plate XXIV.

66. The text is most likely by W. H. Pyne, who, as previously noted, was known to have worked for Ackermann. In any event the writer of the *New Drawing Book* was certainly the same person who authored the series "Observations on the Rise and Progress of Water Colours," which appeared in the *Repository* in 1812–13, for these texts show close similarities in language and intent.

67. *Ackermann's New Drawing Book*, p. ii. Whereas modern accounts of the history of watercolor frequently cite the medium's transparency as one of its unique and distinguishing features, Sandby is credited in this text with introducing the translucence found in oil painting to the domain of watercolor. This is but one indication of the very complex relationship that was seen to exist between oil and watercolor painting by contemporary artists and writers. This relationship deserves a close and attentive study. What can be said with confidence is that there existed no contemporary consensus on the direction or the exact nature of the influence of the one medium upon the other.

68. Ibid.

69. Ibid.

70. These remarks echo a passage in "Observations on the Rise and Progress of Painting in Water Colour," which states that it is "to the honour of our enlightened countrywomen, that the great display of talent which the English artists have exhibited to the world, has been called forth by that love of the art which has so generally been shewn by the female part of the higher circles within the last twenty years" (*Repository of Arts*, March 1813, p. 147).

71. Hazlitt, *Complete Works*, 18, p. 35.

72. Ibid., pp. 36–7.

73. See William Spence, *Britain Independent of Commerce* (London, 1806); and James Mill, *Commerce Defended* (London: Baldwin, 1806).

For a discussion of the Orders in Council and the successful campaign to repeal them (effective in 1812) see J. E. Cookson, *The Friends of Peace: Anti-war Liberalism in England 1793–1815* (Cambridge: Cambridge University Press, 1982), pp. 65–8.

74. Malthus's *Essay on Population* (1798) was the most widely discussed and circulated of his writings at this time. For a brief and cogent analysis of Malthus's writings see Stefan Collini, Donald Winch, and John Burrow, *That Noble Science of Politics* (Cambridge: Cambridge University Press, 1983), pp. 70–89.

75. Hazlitt's *Commentary* was published first in an abbreviated form as letters which appeared in William Cobbett's *Political Register.*

76. Hazlitt, *Extracts from the "Essay on Population" with a Commentary and Notes* (originally published as *A Reply to the Essay on Population by T. R. Malthus*, London, 1807), in *Complete Works*, 1, p. 355.

77. Hazlitt and publishers like Ackermann shared a commitment to the professionalization of art criticism, regardless of their other ideological allegiances. Writ large, the change I am suggesting here is from powerful aristocratic connoisseurs like Lords Shaftesbury and Burlington, whose artistic pronouncements had an enormous impact on cultural production and art theory during the early years of the eighteenth century, to that of a middle-class intellectual like John Ruskin, who produced the most influential writing on art and architecture in England during the nineteenth century. For a further discussion of the professionalization of intellectuals and the increased importance they placed on intellectual "capital," see Andrew Hemingway, *Landscape Imagery and Urban Culture in Early Nineteenth Century Britain* (Cambridge: Cambridge University Press, 1992) p. 34.

78. *Ackermann's New Drawing Book*, Plate X, *Dulwich.*

79. Fuseli, Lecture VII, in *The Life and Writings of Henry Fuseli*, ed. John Knowles, 3 vols. (London, 1831), 2, p. 306.

80. See, for example, Joshua Reynolds, Discourse XI, p. 201; Fuseli, 2, p. 192, and John Opie, *The Lectures of John Opie* (orig. pub. 1809), in *Lectures on Painting by the Royal Academicians*, ed. Ralph Wornum (London, 1848), pp. 256–7.

81. Fuseli, 2, p. 217. It is worth recalling that James Barry shared Fuseli's opinion about portraiture, as evidenced both in his writings and in his use of a high-key color and

painterly effects in group portraits in the
Great Room of the Society of Arts. See
Chapter 1.

82. Fuseli initiated his course of lectures in March
1801; he resigned as Professor of Painting in
1804 to take up the position of Keeper, but
returned temporarily to the professorship in
1810; at this time he repeated his Academy
lectures.

83. Ibid.

84. Ibid., p. 192.

85. See ibid., pp. 193–6, for a discussion of epic,
dramatic, and historic subjects, which address
the intellect and/or human sympathy and
thus constitute varying types of viewing
public.

86. J. M. W. Turner, letter to John Britton,
November 1811, in *The Collected Correspondence of J. M. W. Turner*, ed. John Gage (Oxford: Clarendon 1980), pp. 50–1. In this
letter Turner expressed a desire to have a remark Britton had made privately concerning
Fuseli's attack on topography included in the
introduction to the engravings, "for it
[Britton's comment] espoused the part of
Elevated Landscape against the aspersions of
Map making criticism."

87. Britton, *Fine Arts*, pp. 65–6. Britton here
follows other contemporary writers on
Wilson by emphasizing not the classical harmony of his landscapes, but their atmospheric
effects. Such an emphasis accords with the
issue under examination here – the shift from
classical to empirical modes of knowing and
seeing.

88. Britton's sympathy for prosecuted radicals
such as Horne Tooke, Thomas Hardy, and
William Godwin is recorded in his autobiography [*The Autobiography of John Britton*,
2 vols. (London, 1850), 1, pp. 94–5].

89. On the appeal to custom in Reynolds's writings, see John Barrell, *The Political Theory of
Painting from Reynolds to Hazlitt: The Body of
the Public* (New Haven and London: Yale
University Press, 1986), pp. 158–62. On
changes in the theory and practice of landscape painting see Barrell, "The Public Prospect and the Private View: The Politics of
Taste in Eighteenth-Century Britain," in *The
Birth of Pandora and the Division of Knowledge*
(London: Macmillan, 1992), pp. 41–
61; Murdoch, "Foregrounds and Focus";
and Bermingham, "System, Order, and
Abstraction."

90. My conceptualization of "custom" is heavily
indebted to John Barrell's analysis of the
ideological function of the discourse on

custom in the political writings of Johnson,
Burke, and Coleridge (*Political Theory*,
pp. 136–41). Barrell argues that it was the
radicals' appropriation of the universalist discourse of civic humanism that spurred Joshua
Reynolds to endorse, albeit very hesitantly,
the inclusion of some aspects of the customary (such as specific types of ornament) in
painting.

91. Edmund Burke, *Reflections on the Revolution in
France*, ed. Thomas Mahoney (Indianapolis:
Bobbs-Merrill, 1955; orig. pub. 1790),
pp. 37–9.

92. David Simpson, *Romanticism, Nationalism, and
the Revolt against Theory* (Chicago and
London: University of Chicago Press, 1993),
pp. 40–63.

93. [Richard Payne Knight], review of *The
Works of James Barry Esq., Historical Painter*, in
Edinburgh Review 16 (August 1810), p. 316.

94. John Gage, *A Decade of English Naturalism
1810–20* (Norwich Castle Museum and
Victoria and Albert Museum exhib. cat.,
Norwich and London, 1969).

95. Hemingway, *Landscape Imagery*, pp. 216–19.

96. The Fawkes exhibition of Turner watercolors
is discussed in Chapter 5. A similar focus on
empirically observed atmospheric phenomena
is evident in the criticism that Turner's historical landscapes generated in the teens. See
for example contemporary reviews of *Snowstorm: Hannibal and his Army Crossing the Alps*
(RA, 1812) which are excerpted in Martin
Butlin and Evelyn Joll, *The Paintings of
J. M. W. Turner*, rev. edn., 2 vols. (New
Haven and London: Yale University Press,
1984), 1, p. 90.

97. See Solkin, *Richard Wilson*, pp. 56–76 for a
discussion of this relationship.

98. William Paley, *Natural Theology* (London,
1802). Paley's treatise went through twenty
editions by 1820. As Andrew Hemingway
notes, natural theology was ideologically conservative. It naturalized the inequalities of the
social order by asserting an analogical relationship between the natural order and the
social order, both of which were divinely
ordained (Hemingway, *Landscape Imagery*, pp.
63–4).

99. In making this distinction I do not wish to
minimize the complexity of the process by
which picturesque, topographical, and naturalist painting variously served to image a
nation which was in the midst of rapid social
and economic change. However, studies of
this issue tend to focus on the production of
a national identity for a certain class of patron

or viewer, rather than on the production of the artist as an ideal of Englishness. Elizabeth Helsinger comes the closest to engaging in this project in her essay, "Constable: The Making of a National Painter" [*Critical Inquiry* 15 (Winter 1989), pp. 253–79]. But while she astutely analyzes how Constable may have chosen to represent himself as a national painter, she does not address the problematic issue of how successfully this representation was received by Constable's contemporaries.

4   The Imaginative Genius, the "Poverty of Landscape," and Associated Pleasures

1. Coppin, cited in John Britton, *Fine Arts of the English School* (London: Longman and Hurst, 1812), p. 24.

2. Britton, ibid., p. 19.

3. John Hayes speculates that Coppin may have been an agent who purchased *The Cottage Door* for Mrs Harvey of Norwich, who owned the picture in 1807 when John Britton saw it and recommended that Sir John Fleming Leicester purchase it. See John Hayes, *The Landscape Paintings of Thomas Gainsborough*, 2 vols. (London: Sotheby Publications, 1982), 2, p. 477.

4. Britton, *Fine Arts*, p. 24.

5. For a history of associationism see Martin Kallich, *The Association of Ideas and Critical Theory in Eighteenth Century England* (The Hague and Paris: Mouton, 1970). More recently Andrew Hemingway has analyzed the development of associationist aesthetics within the philosophical tradition of the Scottish Enlightenment in "The 'Sociology' of Taste in the Scottish Enlightenment," *Oxford Art Journal* 12:2 (1989), pp. 3–35.

6. Helène Roberts, "'Trains of Fascinating and Endless Imagery': Associationist Art Criticism before 1850," *Victorian Periodicals Newsletter* 10:3 (September 1977), pp. 91–105.

7. Kathleen Nicholson, "Turner, Poetry, and the Transformation of History Painting," *Arts Magazine* 56 (April 1982), pp. 92–7. Shanes has pursued this theme in a number of books and articles; his most extended exploration of poetic associations can be found in *Turner's Human Landscape* (London: Heinemann, 1990), especially Part I: "The Association of Images and Ideas," pp. 47–138.

8. Andrew Hemingway, *Landscape Imagery and Urban Culture in Early Nineteenth Century Britain* (Cambridge: Cambridge University Press, 1992), pp. 62–78. On the ideological differences between associationist aesthetics and academic theory see also Hemingway, "Academic Theory versus Associationist Aesthetics: The Ideological Forms of a Conflict of Interests in the Early Nineteenth Century," *Ideas and Production* 5 (1985), pp. 18–42.

9. Peter Funnell, "Richard Payne Knight, 1751–1824: Aspects of Aesthetics and Art Criticism in Late Eighteenth and Early Nineteenth Century England" (Ph.D. diss., Oxford University, 1985), p. 14.

10. Archibald Alison, *Essays on the Nature and Principles of Taste*, 3rd edn., 2 vols. (Edinburgh, 1812), 1, p. 5.

11. Ibid., pp. 12, 34.

12. In fact the first edition is even more strongly oriented to landscape than later ones, for the major section on the human figure was added in the second edition. This raises the intriguing, if, at this point, unanswerable question of whether or not the author was requested to add the later material to redress a perceived overemphasis on landscape.

13. Alison, 3rd edn., 1, p. 27.

14. Thomas Whately, *Observations on Modern Gardening* (London, 1770), cited ibid., pp. 60–1.

15. Ibid., 2, pp. 425–6.

16. Ibid., p. 440.

17. Ibid., 1, pp. 63–7.

18. Ibid., pp. 66–7.

19. Ibid., pp. 38–9.

20. Ibid., pp. 125–6.

21. See, for example, Joshua Reynolds, Discourse IV, in *Discourses on Art*, ed. Robert Wark (New Haven and London: Yale University Press, 1959; orig. pub. 1797), pp. 58–9.

22. The picturesque also calls for the careful selection and rejection of features to be included in a composition; nonetheless, the picturesque requires a visual play of variety in forms and incidental details which is substantially different from the visually simplified and expressively unified production Alison is recommending here.

23. Alison, 1, pp.129–30.

24. John Prebble, *The Highland Clearances* (London: Secker and Warburg, 1963). One of the major art collectors of the early nineteenth century was the Marquis of Stafford who reaped immense profits from grazing sheep on Highland terrain which was cleared of between 5,000 and 10,000 crofters and small tenant farmers. Prebble reports that Stafford's income in these years averaged £300,000 per year (p. 57).

25. Turner and Girtin had no monopoly on such

innovative techniques. For example, John Sell Cotman, working at the same time in Norwich, was also producing watercolors which exploited the use of broad washes, bold brushwork and stopping out to "evoke" a mood rather than particularize the topography of a panoramic view. See for example his *Bedlam Furnace*, *c.*1802–3 (British Museum), reproduced as Plate 44 in *The Great Age of British Watercolours 1750–1880* (Royal Academy of Arts exhib. cat., Munich: Prestel, 1993).

26. Alison, 1, pp. 128–9.

27. Ann Bermingham analyzes Constable's landscape practice in the 1820s in terms of a similar conflation of the character of the artist and of nature. She argues that his sketch-like finish "functions as evidence of both a naturalistic observation and a subjective response. Its dual signification works to collapse the distinction between Constable and the landscape that he paints. In its most radical form, it makes it impossible for us to decide which is being represented" [Bermingham, "Reading Constable," *Art History* 10, p. 1 (March 1987), p. 39].

28. He does repeat Joseph Addison's often cited statement that artistic pleasures serve "to exalt the human Mind, from corporeal to intellectual pursuits" in the Introduction of the *Essays* (1, p. xii). And, as previously noted, in the conclusion he makes the equally commonplace assertion that the ability to derive intense pleasure from nature's magnificence awakens feelings for the Divine Creator (2, p. 445). But these are passing comments, rather than points presented for sustained discussion and analysis. For Addison's account of the moral pleasures of the imagination see his *Essays on the Pleasures of the Imagination* (London, 1812; orig. pub. *Spectator*, 1712), p. 6.

29. Jeffrey's review of Alison appeared in a modified form as the entry for "Beauty" in the supplement to the 1824 edition of the *Encyclopaedia Britannica*.

30. [Francis Jeffrey], review of *Essays on the Nature and Principles of Taste*, by Archibald Alison, in *Edinburgh Review* 18 (May 1811), pp. 8–9; hereafter cited by the review's title, "Alison on Taste."

31. Ibid., pp. 23–4.

32. Stewart occupied the chair of moral philosophy at the University of Edinburgh (previously held by Adam Smith) from 1785 to 1810 and had an immense impact on the intellectual thought of the editors of the *Edinburgh Review*. For an account of the intellec-

tual tradition of the journal see Biancamaria Fontana, *Rethinking the Politics of Commercial Society: the "Edinburgh Review," 1802–1832* (Cambridge: Cambridge University Press, 1985). The literature devoted to the Scottish Enlightenment is vast. I have found a most concise and insightful account to be Istvan Hont and Michael Ignatieff, ed., *Wealth and Virtue: The Shaping of Political Economy in the Scottish Enlightenment* (Cambridge: Cambridge University Press, 1983); for more bibliography see Hemingway, "The 'Sociology' of Taste," especially p. 32, n. 71.

33. Dugald Stewart, "Account of the Life and Writings of Adam Smith, L.L.D." (orig. pub. 1794), biographical memoir in Adam Smith, *The Theory of Moral Sentiments* (London: George Bell and Sons, 1887; orig. pub. 1759), p. xx.

34. Smith, p. 3.

35. This is a basic argument of Smith's *Theory of Moral Sentiments*; see for example, p. 497.

36. Dugald Stewart, *Lectures on Political Economy*, 2 vols., ed. William Hamilton (Edinburgh: Thomas Constable, 1855), 1, p. 23. These lectures were delivered between 1800 and 1810; the editor recounts that Francis Jeffrey made extensive notes of the lectures he attended in 1802.

37. As Maxine Berg has observed, by the second decade of the nineteenth century such economic liberalism had gained greater acceptance among a wide range of members of the propertied classes, including establishment Whigs and progressive Tories [Berg, *The Machinery Question and the Making of Political Economy, 1815–1848* (Cambridge: Cambridge University Press, 1980), p. 41].

38. [Francis Jeffrey], review of *The Speech of the Right Hon. William Windham*, in *Edinburgh Review* 17 (February 1811), pp. 266–7. The notion that the emotions (or "passions") rather than reason are the primary vehicles for determining the socio-political behavior of individuals was elaborated most fully in the eighteenth century by another intellectual associated with the Scottish Enlightenment, David Hume. See his *Treatise of Human Nature*, 2nd edn., ed. L.A. Selby-Bigge and P.H. Nidditch (Oxford: Clarendon, 1978; orig. pub. 1739 and 1740), especially Book II.

39. Raymond Williams, *Marxism and Literature* (Oxford: Oxford University Press, 1977), pp. 128–35.

40. [Jeffrey], "Alison on Taste," p. 21.

41. Ibid., pp. 8–9.

42. Ibid., p. 15.
43. According to Eric Shanes, the imprint date of 1819 is incorrect, as the *Views in Sussex* was not published until 1820. For a discussion of the difficulties Cooke encountered in publishing the volume see Shanes, *Turner's Rivers, Harbours and Coasts* (London: Chatto and Windus, 1981), pp. 8–9.
44. Ibid., p. 5.
45. See, for example, the letterpress for Philippe de Loutherbourg's *Romantic and Picturesque Scenery of England and Wales* (London, 1805), or the more elaborate *Description to the Plates of Thames Scenery* (London: Murray, 1818) which accompanied W.B. Cooke's engravings of *Thames Scenery* (London, 1814–29), based upon drawings by S. Owen, P. De Wint, R. Reinagle, and others.
46. An example of a typical guidebook description of the area around Hastings can be found in the opening passage of *The Hastings Guide; Containing a Description of that Ancient Town and Port, and its Environs* (London: J. Barry, 1815): "The Vicinity of Hastings abounds with the most delightful walks and rides, and it is impossible to select any road that does not lead to some rural scene: the views are as beautiful as extensive, and the sea exhibits a continual round of passing variety" (p. 1).
47. While topographical drawings were often consciously aestheticized by their producers, they were assessed largely in terms of their accuracy in representing a specific place. For a general discussion of visual conventions and codes governing topographical imagery in seventeenth-century Holland, see Svetlana Alpers, *The Art of Describing: Dutch Art in the Seventeenth Century* (Chicago: University of Chicago Press, 1983), pp. 119–68.
48. Shanes, *Turner's Rivers, Harbours and Coasts*, p. 20.
49. Ramsay Reinagle, "Scientific and Explanatory Notes," in *Views in Sussex, Consisting of the Most Interesting Landscape and Marine Scenery in the Rape of Hastings*, by Joseph William Mallord Turner (London: John Murray and W.B. Cooke, 1820), n. p.
50. Ibid.
51. Ibid.
52. Ibid.
53. I would like to thank Laurie Monahan for her thoughtful comments concerning the issue of boundaries in relation to this passage of Reinagle's text.
54. The watercolor upon which this engraving is based is untraced after 1908 [W.G. Rawlinson, *The Engraved Work of J.M.W.

Turner*, 2 vols. (London: Macmillan, 1908 and 1913), 1, p. 68].
55. Reinagle, "Scientific and Explanatory Notes."
56. As Christopher Hill has argued, this constitutionalist reading of history understood the Norman Conquest as the imposition of a foreign system of oppressive and absolutist rule on a society which, although ruled by monarchs, had been egalitarian and just. Although the notion of a "Norman yoke" had originated in radical circles in the late seventeenth century, it witnessed a resurgence a century later, being promoted by English Jacobins and parliamentary reformists as late as the mid-1790s. See Hill, *Puritanism and Revolution* (London: Secker and Warburg, 1958), pp. 50–122. For the association of the "Norman yoke" with English radicalism at the end of the eighteenth century see E.P. Thompson, *The Making of the English Working Class*, rev. edn. (Harmondsworth: Penguin, 1980), pp. 94–5.
57. W.B. Cooke, "Dedication," *Views in Sussex*.
58. For a classic Tory critique of the turning over of landed estates to managers, see William Marshall, *On the Landed Property of England* (London, 1804), p. 336. An anti-war liberal, writing in the *Monthly Magazine* in 1814, connected the lack of proprietors' involvement in local concerns to the pursuit of selfish interests rather than the national good ("Abuses on Letting Estates," *Monthly Magazine*, May 1814, pp. 310–12).
59. Shanes, *Turner's Rivers, Harbours and Coasts*, p. 5.
60. The first Martello towers were built in England in 1804.
61. Reinagle, "Scientific and Explanatory Notes."
62. See, for example, *The Two Pictures; or a View of the Miseries of France Contrasted with the Blessings of England* (London, 1810), p. 22, where an extended description of the English countryside is presented as evidence of English prosperity and political stability in stark contrast to the economic and political distress rampant in France: "The neat cottage, the substantial farm-house, the splendid villa, are constantly rising to the sight, surrounded by the most choice and poetical attributes of the landscape.... A picture of as much neatness, softness, and elegance, is exposed to the eye, as can be given to the imagination by the finest etching, or the most mellowed drawing. The vision is not more delightfully recreated by the rural scenery, than the moral

sense is gratified, and the understanding, elevated by the institutions of this great country." As Nigel Everett has demonstrated, however, the conceptualization of the nation as a country estate in the late eighteenth and early nineteenth centuries commonly related to internal political and economic conflicts between those who identified themselves with the landed interest and those promoting the interests of commerce and manufacture. See Everett, *The Tory View of Landscape* (New Haven and London: Yale University Press, 1994), especially pp. 151–82.

63. For an account of the successful campaign to revoke the Orders in Council by manufacturers see J.E. Cookson, *The Friends of Peace: Anti-War Liberalism in England 1793–1815* (Cambridge: Cambridge University Press, 1982), pp. 65–8. A concise and cogent discussion of the Luddite movement is provided by Thompson, pp. 569–659.

64. Thompson, p. 656.

65. Thompson reports that in the first two decades of the century minimum wages clauses, apprentice clauses, and the Arbitration Acts were repealed, while at the same time worker resistance to these actions in the form of organized trade unions was outlawed by the Combination Acts (ibid., p. 595).

66. Ibid., p. 617.

67. Harold Perkin argues that both the working class and the middle class became publicly recognized socio-political formations in the debates and agitation around the reform issue during the period between 1815 and 1820 [Perkin, *The Origins of Modern English Society 1780–1830* (London: Routledge and Kegan Paul, 1969), pp. 178–217]. E.P. Thompson suggests that it was not until the end of the 1820s that a working-class consciousness was developed. In either case, it is clear that in the years immediately following Waterloo inter-class conflict became a topic of public debate.

68. [J.E. Taylor], *Notes and Observations . . . on the Papers Relative to the Internal State of the Country Recently Presented to Parliament* (1820), quoted in Perkin, p. 213.

69. Elie Halévy notes that Ricardo was the first person to publish a complete treatise on political economy since Adam Smith in the 1770s [Halévy, *The Growth of Philosophical Radicalism* (1928), cited in Berg, p. 36].

70. David Ricardo, *The Principles of Political Economy and Taxation* (London: Dent, 1973; orig. pub. 1817), p. 225. These remarks on class conflict occur in Ricardo's section on

rent and the relationship between the price of grain and the wages of laborers. For a cogent discussion of Ricardo see Eric Roll, *A History of Economic Thought*, 4th edn., revised (London: Faber and Faber, 1973), especially pp. 171–205. Scholarly debate continues concerning the degree to which Ricardo's theories taken as a whole are an attack on landed proprietors [for an account contrary to Roll's which argues that Ricardo was not biased against landowners see Samuel Hollander, *The Economics of David Ricardo* (Toronto: University of Toronto Press, 1979), pp. 589–93]. Whether or not this issue is ever satisfactorily settled, it is clear that contemporary writers defending the landed interest (Thomas Malthus being foremost among them) interpreted Ricardo's theory of rent and labor as hostile to landowners and to a view of economics based upon a mutuality of social interests.

71. "Ricardo and the *Edinburgh Review*," *Blackwood's Edinburgh Magazine* 4 (1818), p. 59 (also cited in Perkin, p. 245). See previous note for the relevant section in Ricardo's *Principles.*

72. "On the Influences of Wages on the Rate of Profits," *Blackwood's Edinburgh Magazine* 5 (1819), pp. 171–2, cited in Perkin, p. 245.

73. "On the Analogy between the Growth of Individual and National Genius," *Blackwood's Edinburgh Magazine* 6 (January 1820), p. 376.

74. Ibid.

75. Associationism was the intellectual product of those philosophers of the Scottish Enlightenment who were identified with economic liberalism; it was promoted in the early 1800s by the *Edinburgh Review*, *Blackwood's* strongest rival among the quarterlies.

76. "On the Analogy between . . . Individual and National Genius," p. 379. Profoundly conservative and culturally isolationist in its ideological positioning, this essay ends with an impassioned (and prescient) warning about the consequences of imposing British traditions, both intellectual and cultural, upon the people of India at a time when British dominance of that country had increased with the conquest in 1817–18 of territories around Bombay: "Alas! our civilization, our knowledge, wars with her [India's] spirit; and subjugated as her strength is by our arms, her ancient mind will perhaps, be yet more prostrate under the ascendancy of our conquering intellect" (p. 381).

77. Ibid., p. 380.

78. Ibid., p. 376.

79. Timothy Mitchell, *Art and Science in German Landscape Painting 1770–1840* (Oxford: Clarendon, 1993), pp. 127–51; see also his "Bound by Time and Place: The Art of Caspar David Friedrich," *Arts Magazine* 61 (November 1986), pp. 48–53.

80. The Abbé Dubos and Montesquieu were the other two continental writers who aroused English anger in connecting climate to national character. For a brief discussion of the English response to Winckelmann, Dubos, and Montesquieu, see Morris Eaves, *The Counter-Arts Conspiracy: Art and Industry in the Age of Blake* (Ithaca, NY, and London: Cornell University Press, 1992), pp. 4–7.

81. William Gilpin, *Observations Relative Chiefly to Picturesque Beauty*, 2 vols. (London, 1786), 1, p. 10.

82. Joseph Pott, *An Essay on Landscape Painting* (London: J. Johnson, 1782), p. 57.

83. Kathleen Nicholson has carefully analyzed Turner's use of poetic glosses on many of his landscapes exhibited at the Royal Academy as a tactic designed to elevate landscape painting to the status of history painting (Nicholson, pp. 92–7). These tags were a direct attempt to control the types of association the spectator was to experience when viewing the artist's work.

84. Foremost among modern theorists who have considered the relationship between seeing and knowing is Michel Foucault. In *The Order of Things* he connects the development of botany and natural history in the seventeenth and eighteenth centuries to the increasing authority which visual evidence was to enjoy compared to that provided by the other senses [*The Order of Things* (New York: Vintage Books, 1973; orig. pub. in French 1966), pp. 132–8]. For a useful discussion of Foucault's conception of power, knowledge, and visibility see John Rajchman, "Foucault's Art of Seeing," *October* 44 (Spring 1988), pp. 89–117.

85. Reinagle, "Scientific and Explanatory Notes."

86. Jeffrey writes: "As the poet sees more of beauty in nature than ordinary mortals, just because he perceives more of these analogies and relations to social emotions, in which all beauty consists; so, other men see more or less of this beauty, exactly as they happen to possess that fancy, or those habits, which enable them readily to trace out these relations" ("Alison on Taste," p. 45).

87. Alison, 1, p. 6.

88. Ibid., p. 9.

5   Genius as Alibi

1. "Royal Academy," *London Chronicle*, 3–4 May 1814, p. 419. Other critics also remarked on the profusion of brilliantly colored portraits displayed at this exhibition. Unlike the writer for the *London Chronicle*, critics for the *Repository of Arts* (June 1814, p. 354) and the *Champion* (7 May 1814, p. 149) registered their concern that portraits were supplanting serious painting. The *Champion's* criticism appeared as introductory remarks to the exhibition, couched as a witty and extended satirical attack on the vulgarity of the public for portraits and on the artists who display a "servile acquiescence with the capricious dictates of frivolous ignorance."

2. Jon Klancher, *The Making of English Reading Audiences, 1790–1832* (Madison: University of Wisconsin Press, 1987), p. 151.

3. The critic goes on to praise specific artists and works: portraits by George Dawe, Thomas Lawrence, and Martin Archer Shee and "oriental" scenery (a view taken near Gungavapetta) by Thomas Daniell; later he comments briefly but favorably upon Constable's *Ploughing Scene* and *Cottage Window by Woodforde*. In a review published the following week Turner's *Dido and Aeneas* is praised for "the great facility and great knowledge of grouping evinced in the order and harmony with which a multitude of objects are here accumulated and distributed" (*London Chronicle*, 9 May 1814, p. 435).

4. Andrew Hemingway addresses the difficulties involved in analysing art criticism in a number of his publications, including his book *Landscape Imagery and Urban Culture in Early Nineteenth Century Britain* (Cambridge: Cambridge University Press, 1992) and most recently in an essay, "Art Exhibitions as Leisure-Class Rituals in Early Nineteenth-Century London," in *Towards a Modern Art World*, ed. Brian Allen (New Haven and London: Yale University Press, 1995), pp. 95–108.

5. Cf. reviews of the exhibition in the *Repository of Arts*, June 1814, pp. 350–4; *New Monthly Magazine*, 1 June 1814, pp. 468–9; Hazlitt's review in the *Champion*, 22 May 1814, p. 165 (augmented by individual essays on Wilson, Hogarth, and Gainsborough, but not Zoffany) can be found in *The Complete Works of William Hazlitt*, 21 vols., ed. P.P. Howe (London and Toronto: J.M. Dent, 1933), vol. 18. Robert Hunt in the *Examiner* (8 May

1814, p. 302) did have some words of praise for Zoffany's theatrical scenes.

6. Rüdiger Joppien, *Philippe Jacques de Loutherbourg, R.A. 1740–1812* (Greater London Arts Council exhib. cat., London: 1973), n. p.

7. For *Coalbrookdale*, see brief comments in the *Monthly Magazine*, June 1801, p. 439 and *St. James Chronicle*, 7–9 May 1801; for *Avalanche in the Alps* see *Monthly Mirror*, July 1804, p. 16, *Morning Post*, 5 May 1804, and *British Press*, 7 May 1804. John Leicester bought *Avalanche in the Alps*; his friend and fellow collector, Richard Colt Hoare, so admired it that he had watercolorist Francis Nicholson make him a copy of it.

8. Joseph Pott was an early proponent of a specifically English school of landscape painting based upon Dutch and Flemish models. In *An Essay on Landscape Painting* (London: J. Johnson, 1782) Pott declared that Loutherbourg's pictures were visionary, affected, and extravagant, and were "painted with all that French pomposity so unlike the truth of the Flemish, or the chaste elegance of the Italian manner" (p. 78).

9. "Exhibition of Paintings – Royal Academy," *Repository of Arts*, June 1809, p. 490.

10. This assessment is also advanced by Katharine Baetjer in her catalogue entry for the picture in the Mead Art Museum in *Glorious Nature: British Landscape Painting 1750–1850* (Denver Art Museum exhib. cat., New York: Hudson Hills Press, 1993), p. 140.

11. [Anthony Pasquin (John Williams)], "Royal Academy," *Morning Herald*, 11 May 1809.

12. [Leigh Hunt], "Remarks on the Past and Present State of the Arts in England," *Reflector* 1 (1812), p. 229. The *Reflector* was a short-lived journal devoted to literature, theater, and the visual arts. Edited and written largely by Hunt, it presented the same critique of materialism and governmental corruption as that of his more successful *Examiner*.

13. Loutherbourg was born in Strasbourg where he lived until he was fifteen; his family then moved to Paris, where he trained under the academic painter Carle van Loo (Joppien, unpaged).

14. "The Modern Spectator," *Repository of Arts*, October 1812, p. 206; [Leigh Hunt], "The English Considered as a Thinking People," *Reflector* 1 (1812), p. 1.

15. "The Dreadful Picture of France," *Repository of Arts*, June 1809, pp. 345–7.

16. [L. Hunt], "The English Considered as a Thinking People," p. 3.

17. This kind of "imperial" consciousness is evident in the many guidebooks and travel narratives published in England at this time, which professed a deep and intimate knowledge of the manners, morals, customs, and political structure of the countries in question. See, for example, John Scott's *A Visit to Paris in 1814* (London: Longmans, 1815), for an account that makes judgments about the essential differences between French and English society, politics, and cultures.

18. Andrew Wilton describes how Turner's application of pigment via tiny brushstrokes differs markedly from paint applied broadly and impressionistically in his catalogue, *Turner and the Sublime* (Art Gallery of Ontario and Yale Center for British Art exhib. cat., Chicago: University of Chicago Press, 1982), p. 123.

19. "Mr. Fawkes's Collection of Watercolour Drawings," *Champion*, 2 May 1819, p. 284.

20. "Mr. Fawkes' Pictures," *London Chronicle*, 10 April 1819, p. 347.

21. "Mr. Fawkes's Gallery," *Repository of Arts*, 1 May 1819, pp. 299–300.

22. Archibald Alison, *Essays on the Nature and Principles of Taste*, 3rd edn., 2 vols. (Edinburgh, 1812), 1, pp. 8–11.

23. For reviews praising Fawkes in 1819 see the *New Monthly Magazine*, 1 May, pp. 353–5; the *Champion*, 2 May, pp. 284–5; and the *Repository of Arts*, 2 May, pp. 297–301.

24. "Mr. Fawkes' Pictures," p. 347.

25. "Mr. Fawkes's Gallery," p. 297.

26. Ibid., p. 299.

27. The critic for the *Champion* referred directly to the private nature of collecting watercolors in his review of the exhibition: "Mr. Fawkes, we understand, has been long in the habit of indulging himself and his particular friends in the private luxury of the port-folio, till that liberal feeling, which upon all subjects does honour to his character, suggested that a gratification so high and so refined ought not to be restricted to a private circle; and that by transferring these treasures of the pencil from the portfolio to the frame – he should do a kindness to the lover, and promote the interests of the professor of one of those branches of the fine arts, in which our countrymen are admitted to excel" ("Mr. Fawkes's Collection of Watercolour Drawings," p. 284).

28. "On the Superiority of the Painter's Feelings," *Repository of Arts*, March 1817, p. 141.

29. Ibid., p. 140.

30. The classic study of the dichotomy between the notion of the countryside as locus of

moral purity and social harmony and the city as the setting for vice and conflict remains Raymond Williams's *The City and the Country* (New York: Oxford University Press, 1973). David Solkin addresses this issue in regard to eighteenth-century British landscape painting in *Richard Wilson: The Landscape of Reaction* (Tate Gallery exhib. cat., London, 1982); see especially pp. 56–76.

31. "On the Superiority of the Painter's Feelings," pp. 140–1.

32. Cited in Edith Fawkes, "Turner at Farnley," n. d. (*c.*1900), typescript, archives of the National Gallery, London.

33. Andrew Hemingway discusses a number of contemporary art critics who complained about the profusion of overdressed bodies and highly colored pictures at art exhibitions, especially the Royal Academy, in his essay, "Art Exhibitions as Leisure-Class Rituals in Early Nineteenth-Century London."

34. "Royal Academy," *British Press*, 9 May 1806.

35. "Monthly Retrospect of the Fine Arts," *Monthly Magazine*, June 1810, p. 430.

36. "Monthly Retrospect of the Fine Arts," *Monthly Magazine*, July 1810, p. 577.

37. *La Belle Assemblée*, 1810, p. 250 and *Public Ledger and Daily Advertiser*, 9 May 1810, quoted in Martin Butlin and Evelyn Joll, *The Paintings of J. M. W. Turner*, rev. edn., 2 vols. (New Haven and London: Yale University Press, 1984), 1, p. 80. Butlin suggests that the effects seen in the Petworth view were the result of Turner's attempt to achieve high-key color by using a white ground, which derived from his experiments with watercolor.

38. [Robert Hunt], "British Institution," *Examiner*, 14 April 1814, p. 254.

39. Peter de Bolla, *The Discourse of the Sublime: History, Aesthetics, and the Subject* (Oxford: Basil Blackwell, 1989), p. 170.

40. Ibid.

41. [W. H. Pyne?], "Observations on . . . Painting in Water Colours," *Repository of Arts*, February 1813, p. 92.

42. [L. Hunt], "Remarks on the Past and Present State of the Arts," p. 215.

43. [Robert Hunt], "Angelica Kaufmann [*sic*]," *Examiner*, 17 January 1808, p. 45.

44. [Robert Hunt], "Royal Academy Exhibition," *Examiner*, 17 June 1810, p. 379.

45. "Royal Academy," *London Chronicle*, 8 May 1812, p. 447.

46. For an account of Callcott's relationship with Turner, see David Blayney Brown, *Augustus Wall Callcott* (Tate Gallery exhib. cat., London, 1981), pp. 22–46.

47. "Royal Academy – Exhibition, 1807," *Star*, 22 May 1807. For other positive responses to *Cowboys* by artists and connoisseurs see Brown, p. 62.

48. Thomas Uwins, *The Memoirs of Thomas Uwins* (London, 1858), p. 44, quoted in Brown, p. 78.

49. "Exhibition of the Royal Academy," *Repository of Arts*, 1 June 1816, p. 358. The Cuyp referred to here is no doubt *The Fleet at Nijmegan*, which was listed under the title *Landing of Prince Maurice At Dort* (catalogue no. 142) in John Britton's *Catalogue Raisonné of the Pictures Belonging to the Most Honourable the Marquis of Stafford in the Gallery of Cleveland House* (London: Longman, Hurst, Rees, and Orme, 1808). A color plate of the painting appears in Julia Lloyd Williams, *Dutch Art and Scotland: A Reflection of Taste* (National Gallery of Scotland exhib. cat., Edinburgh, 1992).

50. Of course one cannot account for the success of *The Entrance to the Pool of London* without considering the site depicted, which was a (if not *the*) center of British maritime activity. As such it served as a potent symbol of national wealth and economic well-being at the end of a period when British maritime trade had been threatened by the continental wars and the French blockade of British ships.

51. [John Landseer], "Mr. Turner's Gallery," *Review of Publications of Art*, 1 (1808), pp. 163 and 164 (cited in Butlin and Joll, 1, p. 59). As Martin Butlin notes, Landseer's referencing of Cuyp in regard to *The Forest of Bere* is telling, since the work is much closer in composition and tonality to Rubens's landscapes (especially his *Landscape by Moonlight*, now in the Courtauld Institute Gallery). However, Turner himself indicated that Rubens provided a much less acceptable model for English landscape painters than Cuyp, even though both northern masters were popular with collectors.

52. Brown speculates that Callcott may have seen Cuyp's *Herdsmen with Cows* either when it went on sale in London in 1798, or subsequently in Sir Francis Bourgeois's collection, and may have produced *Cowboys* as a response to this work (Brown, p. 62).

53. "Descriptive and Critical Catalogues of the Most Splendid Collection of Works of Art in Great Britain – Dulwich College," *Annals of the Fine Arts*, 1816, p. 370.

54. In 1818 the critic for the *Annals of the Fine*

Arts declared that he would like to see two pictures in that year's Royal Academy exhibition, Callcott's *Mouth of the Tyne* and Turner's *The Dort Packet Boat for Rotterdam Becalmed,* placed in the same room with two or three works by the Dutch marine painter Van de Velde so that all the works could be compared ("Exhibition of the Royal Academy," *Annals of the Fine Arts,* 1818, p. 294).

55. "Royal Academy – Exhibition," *Star,* 14 May 1807. This critic is unique (as far as I can determine) in comparing Callcott to the Dutch landscape artist and engraver Anthonie Waterloo, who was known primarily for his prints.

56. *The Diary of Joseph Farington,* 16 vols., ed. Kenneth Garlick, Angus Macintyre, and Kathryn Cave (New Haven and London: Yale University Press, 1978–84), 9 April 1804.

57. "Exhibition of Paintings – Royal Academy,' *Repository of Arts,* June 1809, p. 409. [Robert Hunt], "British Institution," *Examiner,* 23 February 1817, p. 126.

58. For a discussion of Turner's perspective lectures and a transcript of the final lecture, see Jerrold Ziff, "'Backgrounds, Introduction of Architecture and Landscape': A Lecture by J. M. W. Turner," *Journal of the Warburg and Courtauld Institutes* 26 (1963), pp. 124–47.

59. J. M. W. Turner, "Backgrounds, Introduction of Architecture and Landscape," quoted ibid., p. 145.

60. Ibid., pp. 145–6.

61. [Robert Hunt], "Royal Academy", *Examiner,* 8 May 1808, p. 300.

62. "Remarks on the Exhibition of the Royal Academy," *Monthly Mirror,* May 1802, p. 378.

63. Ibid., p. 379.

64. "The Exhibition of the Royal Academy," *New Monthly Magazine,* 1 June 1820, p. 716.

65. "Exhibition of Paintings – Royal Academy," *Repository of Arts,* June 1809, p. 490.

66. For other illustrations of Callcott's work see Brown, especially Plates 3, 4, 6, and 15.

67. "Exhibition of the Society of Painters in Oil and Water Colours," *Champion,* 9 May 1819, p. 300. For another example of Fielding's "pictures of nothing," see his *Coast Scene with a Beached Boat* (Yale Center for British Art), reproduced as Plate 111 in *Presences of Nature. British Landscape 1780–1830* by Louis Hawes (Yale Center for British Art exhib. cat., New Haven, 1982).

68. William Hazlitt, "British Institution" (orig. pub. in the *Champion,* February 1815), reprinted in *Complete Works,* 18, pp. 94–5.

69. See Ann Bermingham, "System, Order and Abstraction: The Politics of English Landscape Drawing around 1795," in *Landscape and Power,* ed. W. J. T. Mitchell (Chicago and London: University of Chicago Press, 1994), pp. 77–102, for a discussion of fears about the uncoupling of the signifier from the referent (the "imitation from the thing imitated") in art, language, and politics at the turn of the century.

70. See Chapter 3, p. 73 for a discussion of this passage in the essay, "On Gainsborough's Pictures," which appeared in the *Champion* in 1814.

71. William Hazlitt, "On Imitation" (orig. pub. 1816), reprinted in *Complete Works,* 4, pp. 73–4.

72. Ibid., pp. 75 and 76.

73. Ibid., p. 76 n.

74. Ibid., pp. 76–7.

75. For Hazlitt's position on the public function of art and public patronage of the arts see John Barrell, *The Political Theory of Painting from Reynolds to Hazlitt: The Body of the Public* (New Haven and London: Yale University Press, 1986), pp. 333–8.

76. John Murdoch discusses the shift in emphasis from panoramic views to those with a lowered viewpoint and a heightened emphasis on foregrounds in connection with the popularity of the picturesque [Murdoch, "Foregrounds and Focus: Changes in the Perception of Landscape *c.*1800," in *The Lake District: A Sort of National Property* (Cheltenham: Countryside Commission, 1986), pp. 43–59].

77. De Bolla, pp. 195–6.

78. Edmund Burke, *A Philosophical Enquiry into the Origin of Our Ideas of the Sublime and Beautiful,* 2nd edn., ed. and intro. by J. T. Boulton (London: Routledge and Kegan Paul, 1958; orig. pub. 1759), p. 60; Alexander Gerard, *An Essay on Taste,* 2nd edn. (London, 1764), p. 4.

79. William Gilpin, *Three Essays on Picturesque Beauty; on Picturesque Travel; and on Sketching Landscapes* (London, 1792), p. 62 (emphases in the original).

80. John Barrell also argues that the indeterminacy of the sketch was deemed appropriate only as a form of leisure for the private individual, but does not stress the perceived need for the private viewer to have a highly controlled and cultivated taste. See his "The

Private Comedy of Thomas Rowlandson," *Art History* 6:4 (December 1983), pp. 423–41 (especially pp. 429–31). He also takes up the issue of the sketch as a private art form in *The Political Theory of Painting*, pp. 112–16.

81. Joshua Reynolds, *Discourses on Art*, ed. Robert Wark (New Haven and London: Yale University Press, 1959; orig. pub. 1797), Discourse VIII, p. 164.

82. See, for example, exhibition reviews of Turner's early works in the *London Packet*, 1 May 1799, 14–16 May 1800, and the *Sun*, 13 May 1799 and 17 May 1802. Girtin also received his share of criticism for his indistinctness; see the *Monthly Mirror*'s otherwise adulatory review of his *Bolton Bridge*, June 1801, p. 376, and the *London Packet's* critique of his *St Nicholas Church*, 14–16 May 1798, and the *Whitehall Evening Post*'s savage attack on his slovenliness of his *Rievaulx Abbey* in the 31 May–1 June issue.

83. See, for example, the exhibition reviews for the Royal Academy of 1806 in the *Sun* on 5 May, 21 May, and 23 May of that year.

84. [John Landseer], "Landscape Scenery of Scotland" (review), *Review of Publications of Art* 1 (1808), p. 67. Although the writer did not elaborate on this statement, from other comments he makes in his journal it seems likely that the theory he referred to is grounded in associationism. For example, in discussing Turner's *Margate* (reproduced as Plate 88 in Butlin and Joll), exhibited in Turner's Gallery in 1808, Landseer remarks that the artist is a master of the philosophy of art, and then goes on to praise the mistiness of the scene, which permits the viewer to associate the greater forms of the city with Greek temples: "Mr. Turner delights to paint to the imagination: and sometimes he even apparently paints with a view to calling up distant, but still associated, trains of ideas"("Mr. Turner's Gallery," p. 166). Helène Roberts discusses the impact of associationism on Landseer's criticism in her article, "'Trains of Fascinating and Endless Imagery': Associationist Art Criticism before 1850," *Victorian Periodicals Newsletter* 10:3 (September 1977), pp. 91–105.

85. [Landseer], "Mr. Turner's Gallery," pp. 151–69.

86. Ibid., p. 160.

87. Ibid., p. 161.

88. [John Landseer], "British Institution," *Review of Publications of Art* 1 (1808), p. 82.

89. In addition to the analysis of Alison and Jeffrey in Chapter 3, see also Jeffrey's discussion of indistinctness and Scott's poetry in his review of *Essays on the Nature and Principles of Taste*, by Archibald Alison, in *Edinburgh Review* 18 (May 1811), p. 28.

90. Richard Payne Knight, *The Progress of Civil Society* (London, 1796), pp. 80–1.

91. Ibid., p. 148.

92. Ibid., pp. xi–xii.

93. See, for example, *Political Essays on Popular Subjects, Containing Dissertations on First Principles; Liberty; Democracy and the Party Denominations of Whig and Tory*, 3rd edn. (London, 1801). A passage from this text which describes French principles in terms of glaring colors and tinsel displays is discussed in Chapter 2, p. 52.

94. Richard Payne Knight, *An Analytical Inquiry into the Principles of Taste* (London, 1805), p. 361.

95. See ibid., pp. 192–4, for Knight's discussion of the superior aesthetic capacity and pleasure accruing to the "learned beholder" compared to the ignorant, whose mind is "wholly unprovided with correct ideas." The choice of the word "correct" indicates the legislative activity involved in this formulation of a socially elevated (and elevating) taste.

96. [Richard Payne Knight], preface to *Catalogue of the Pictures by the Late Sir Joshua Reynolds* (British Institution exhib. cat., London: Bulmer, 1813), p. 10. The attribution of the preface to Knight is given by the anonymous author of *A Catalogue Raisonné of the Pictures Now Exhibiting in Pall Mall* (London, 1816), p. iv. It is possible that this attack on genius was leveled specifically at history painter Benjamin Robert Haydon, who complained bitterly about the lack of support of English genius on the part of connoisseurs like Knight. In any event, Haydon wrote in his *Diary* that he felt the attack was directed at him [*The Diary of Benjamin Robert Haydon*, 5 vols., ed. W.B. Pope (Cambridge, MA: Harvard University Press, 1960–3), 1, p. 398].

97. Knight, *The Progress of Civil Society*, p. 65.

98. The degree to which Knight did or did not support artists, both financially and in his writings, remains vigorously contested even now. In a review of *The Arrogant Connoisseur: Richard Payne Knight 1751–1824*, which deals with Knight as a collector, connoisseur, and aesthetician, Alex Potts presents a strong case for concluding that Knight indeed supported a devaluation of the economic and cultural

status of painters. This review (and this particular issue of Knight's artistic support) provoked a heated exchange between Potts and
Nicholas Penny, one of the catalogue's
editors [the review and responses were
published together in *Oxford Art Journal*,
5:1 (1982), pp. 70–6]. As Potts notes in his
response to Penny, the source of their
disagreement rests on their political values,
not simply their personal tastes. To attack or
defend Knight as a privileged member of the
upper class whose views on culture reinforced
that privilege, is to take a position on contemporary relations of political power and
cultural hegemony.

99. Preface to the *Exhibition of Paintings of
    Hogarth, Wilson, Gainsborough and Zoffany*
    (British Institution exhib. cat., London,
    1814), p. 10.

100. Dayes's attack on Girtin is cited in full in
     Chapter 1, p. 22.

101. *The Works of the Late Edward Dayes* (London:
     E. W. Brayley, 1805), p. 270. This passage is
     discussed in Chapter 1, pp. 25–6.

102. *Dictionary of National Biography*, 22 vols., ed.
     Leslie Stephen and Sidney Lee (London,
     1885–1901), s. v. John Foster.

103. John Foster, "On the Application of the
     Epithet Romantic," in *Essays in a Series of
     Letters on the Following Subjects . . .* , 7th edn.
     (Andover: Mark Newton, 1826; orig. pub. as
     Essays in a Series of Letters to a Friend, London,
     1805), p. 114. All further references are to
     the 7th edition.

104. Ibid., pp. 117–18.

105. Ibid., p. 116.

106. Ibid., p. 117.

107. Ibid., p. 122.

108. Ibid.

109. Ibid., p. 124.

110. Jürgen Habermas, *The Structural Transformation
     of the Public Sphere* (Cambridge: Polity Press,
     1989; orig. pub. in German, 1962), p. 49.

111. [L. Hunt], "Remarks on the Past and Present
     State of the Arts," p. 230. Like the author of
     the *New Drawing Book*, Hunt linked the prac-
     tice of amateur drawing by women to the rise
     of male landscape watercolorists such as
     Girtin and Varley. Nonetheless, he relegated
     watercolor to an inferior position with re-
     spect to oil painting because of the latter's
     durability (p. 229).

112. This seems to be the position of Reinagle in
     his commentary on Turner's Sussex views
     as well as Francis Jeffrey, in his review of
     Alison's *Essays*. Jeffrey, recall, differentiated

between the ordinary viewer's experience of
natural scenery and the artist's superior, but
not constitutionally different, ability to feel
and represent the social sentiments that form
the character of the domestic landscape.

113. "The Cogitations of Scriblerius," *Repository of
     Arts*, June 1814, p. 334.

114. John Landseer, quoted by Robert Hunt in
     "Royal Academy Exhibition," *Examiner*, 5
     June 1814, p. 356.

Conclusion

1. Raymond Williams's account of poetic
   genius as evidenced in the writings of
   Shelley, Wordsworth, and Blake centers on
   the poet's opposition to a market economy
   hostile to the realm of the imagination and
   human creativity [*Culture and Society 1780–
   1850* (New York: Columbia University
   Press, 1983; orig. pub. 1958), pp. 30–48].
   Carole Fabricant, writing of Wordsworth,
   presents the poet's turn to nature as embodying an "altered conception of power – no
   longer a power *over*, but rather a power
   through, in conjunction with, outside forces of
   nature and divinity" ["The Aesthetics and
   Politics of Landscape in the Eighteenth Century," in *Studies in Eighteenth Century British
   Art and Aesthetics*, ed. Ralph Cohen
   (Berkeley: University of California Press,
   1985), p. 80]. It is not my intention to dispute these accounts, but rather to suggest that
   in the domain of landscape painting, genius
   was also marshalled in support of a market
   society and of social interests wielding power
   "over" nature (and other people).

2. This passage is discussed in Chapter 5, p. 110.

3. "Mr. Fawkes' Pictures," *London Chronicle*, 10
   April 1819, p. 347.

4. Although writings by academic history painters about the relationship of artists to their
   societies include references to artists' lives,
   these accounts rely most heavily upon the
   rise to historical prominence (and inevitable
   fall) of the societies in question. See for
   example James Barry's account of art in
   Greece in his *Inquiry into the Real and Imaginary Obstructions to the Acquisition of the Arts
   in England* (London, 1775); reprinted in
   The Works of James Barry, Esq., 2 vols.
   (London: Cadell and Davies, 1809), 2, pp.
   167–299.

5. For the increasing importance of biography
   in the construction of the landscape artist as a
   bearer of local and/or national identity in the

1820s and succeeding decades see Adèle Holcomb, "More Matter with Less Art: Romantic Attitudes toward Landscape Painting," *Art Journal* 36 (Summer 1977), pp. 303–6. Ann Bermingham has considered the

function of autobiography in the context of Constable's artistic practice; see *Landscape and Ideology: The English Rustic Tradition, 1740–1860* (Berkeley: University of California Press, 1986), pp. 87–155.

Bibliography

Primary Sources

Reviews of individual Royal Academy exhibitions are not listed below; they appear in the notes. The following periodicals contain at least one review cited in the body of the text: *Annals of the Fine Arts*; *British Press*; *Champion*; *Daily Advertiser, Oracle and True Briton* (later published under the title *True Briton*); *Examiner* (most reviews by Robert Hunt); *London Chronicle*; *London Packet*; *Monthly Magazine*; *Monthly Mirror*; *Morning Chronicle*; *Morning Herald*; *Morning Post*; *New Monthly Magazine*; *Repository of Arts*; *St. James Chronicle*; *Star*; *Sun*; *Whitehall Evening Post*.

"Abuses in Letting Estates." *Monthly Magazine*, May 1814, pp. 310–12.

Ackermann's New Drawing Book of Light and Shadow. London: Ackermann's, 1812.

Addison, Joseph. *Essays on the Pleasures of the Imagination*. London, 1812; originally published in the *Spectator*, 1712.

Alison, Archibald. *Essays on the Nature and Principles of Taste*. 3rd edn. 2 vols. Edinburgh, 1812.

"The Baring Fête." *True Briton*, 8 May 1806.

Barry, James. *The Works of James Barry, Esq*. 2 vols. London: Cadell and Davies, 1809.

Bowles, Carrington. *The Art of Painting in Oil: Rendered Familiar to Every Capacity*. 9th edn. London: Laurie and Whittle, 1817.

——*The Art of Painting in Water Colours*. London: Laurie and Whittle, 1799.

"British Gallery." *Champion*, 28 February 1819, p. 140.

"British Gallery of Pictures." *Morning Post*, 18 June 1813.

Britton, John. *The Autobiography of John Britton*. 2 vols. London, 1850.

——*Catalogue Raisonné of the Pictures Belonging to the Most Honourable the Marquis of Stafford in the Gallery of Cleveland House*. London: Long, Hurst, Rees, and Orme, 1808.

——*Fine Arts of the English School*. London: Longman and Hurst, 1812.

Buchanan, William. *William Buchanan and the Nineteenth Century Art Trade: One Hundred Letters to his Agents in London and Italy*. Edited by Hugh Brigstocke. London: Paul Mellon Centre, 1982.

Burke, Edmund. *A Philosophical Enquiry into the Origin of Our Ideas of the Sublime and Beautiful*. 2nd edn. Edited and introduced by J. T. Boulton. London: Routledge and Kegan Paul, 1958; originally published 1759.

——*Reflections on the Revolution in France*. Edited by Thomas Mahoney. Indianapolis: Bobbs-Merrill, 1955; originally published 1790.

A Catalogue Raisonnée of the Pictures Now Exhibiting at the British Institution. London, 1815.

A Catalogue Raisonné of the Pictures Now Exhibiting in Pall Mall. London, 1816.

"Claudius." "On the Patronage of the Fine Arts." *New Monthly Magazine*, 1 March 1814, pp. 121–2.

"The Cogitations of Scriblerius." *Repository of Arts*, June 1814, p. 334.

Cooke, W.B. *Description to the Plates of Thames Scenery.* London: Murray, 1818.

Dayes, Edward. *The Works of the Late Edward Dayes.* London: E.W. Brayley, 1805.

"Descriptive and Critical Catalogues of the Most Splendid Collections of Works of Art in Great Britain – Dulwich College." *Annals of the Fine Arts*, 1816, pp. 370–401.

"The Dreadful Picture of France." *Repository of Arts*, June 1809, pp. 345–51.

Edwards, Edward. *Anecdotes of Painters Who Have Resided or Been Born in England.* London: Leigh and Sotheby, 1808.

Exhibition of Paintings of Hogarth, Wilson, Gainsborough and Zoffany. British Institution exhibition catalogue. London, 1814.

"Exhibition of the British Institution." *Repository of Arts*, 1 March 1819, pp. 169–74.

"Exhibition of the Society of Painters in Oil and Water Colours." *Champion*, 9 May 1819, p. 300.

Farington, Joseph. *The Diary of Joseph Farington.* Edited by Kenneth Garlic, Angus Macintyre, and Kathryn Cave. 16 vols. New Haven and London: Yale University Press, 1978–84.

"Fine Arts." *Le Beau Monde*, 7 January 1807, pp. 163–4.

Foster, John. "On the Application of the Epithet Romantic." In *Essays in a Series of Letters on the Following Subjects* . . . 7th edn. Andover: Mark Newton, 1826; originally published as *Essays in a Series of Letters to a Friend*, London, 1805.

Fuseli, Henry. *The Life and Writings of Henry Fuseli.* Edited by John Knowles. 3 vols. London, 1831.

Gerard, Alexander. *An Essay on Taste.* 2nd edn. London, 1764.

Gilpin, William. *Moral Contrasts.* London, 1798.

—— *Observations on the Coasts of Hampshire, Sussex and Kent Relative to Picturesque Beauty.* London: Cadell and Davies, 1804.

—— *Observations on the River Wye.* London, 1782.

—— *Observations Relative Chiefly to Picturesque Beauty.* 2 vols. London, 1786.

—— *Three Essays on Picturesque Beauty; on Picturesque Travel; and on Sketching Landscapes.* London, 1792.

Gisborne, Thomas. *An Enquiry into the Duties of Men.* 2 vols. London, 1794.

—— *An Enquiry into the Duties of the Female Sex.* London, 1797.

—— *Walks in a Forest.* 4th edn. London, 1799; originally published 1794.

The Hastings Guide; Containing a Description of that Ancient Town and Port, and its Environs. London: J. Barry, 1815.

Haydon, Benjamin Robert. *The Diary of Benjamin Robert Haydon.* 5 vols. Edited by W.B. Pope. Cambridge, MA: Harvard University Press, 1960–3.

Hazlitt, William. *The Complete Works of William Hazlitt.* 21 vols. Edited by P.P. Howe. London and Toronto: J.M. Dent, 1933.

Hoare, Prince. *Inquiry into the Requisite Cultivation and Present State of the Arts of Design in England.* London, 1806.

[Hoppner, John]. Review of *Anecdotes of Painters* by Edward Edwards. *Quarterly Review* 1:1 (February 1809), pp. 36–49.

Hume, David. *A Treatise of Human Nature.* 2nd edn. Edited by L.A. Selby-Bigge and P. H.

Nidditch. Oxford: Clarendon, 1978; originally published 1739 and 1740.

[Hunt, Leigh]. "The English Considered as a Thinking People." *Reflector* 1 (1812), pp. 1–17.

[——] "Remarks on the Past and Present State of the Arts in England." *Reflector* 1 (1812), pp. 207–32.

[——] "The Round Table, no. 8." *Examiner*, 19 February 1815, p. 123.

H[unt], R[obert]. "Angelica Kaufman [*sic*]." *Examiner*, 17 January 1808, p. 45.

[——] "British Institution." *Examiner*, 1814–17, *passim*.

[Jeffrey, Francis]. Review of *Essays on the Nature and Principles of Taste*, by Archibald Alison. *Edinburgh Review* 18 (May 1811), pp. 1–46.

[——] Review of *The Speech of the Right Hon. William Windham*, by William Windham. *Edinburgh Review* 17 (February 1811), pp. 253–90.

Knight, Richard Payne. *An Analytical Inquiry into the Principles of Taste*. London, 1805.

—— *The Landscape*. 2nd edn. London, 1795; originally published 1794.

[——?] Preface to *Catalogue of the Exhibition of Paintings from the Dutch and Flemish Schools*. British Institution exhibition catalogue. London: Bulmer, 1815.

[——] Preface to *Catalogue of the Pictures by the Late Sir Joshua Reynolds*. British Institution exhibition catalogue. London: Bulmer, 1813.

—— *The Progress of Civil Society*. London, 1796.

—— Review of *The Life of Sir Joshua Reynolds*, by James Northcote. *Edinburgh Review* 23 (September 1814), pp. 263–92.

[——] Review of *The Works of James Barry Esq., Historical Painter*, by James Barry. *Edinburgh Review* 16 (August 1810), pp. 293–326.

[Landseer, John]. "British Institution." *Review of Publications of Art* 1 (1808).

[——] "Landscape Scenery of Scotland." *Review of Publications of Art* 1 (1808).

[——] "Mr. Turner's Gallery." *Review of Publications of Art* 1 (1808).

Loutherbourg, Philippe de. *Romantic and Picturesque Scenery of England and Wales*. London, 1805.

Mandeville, Bernard. *The Fable of the Bees: Or Private Vices, Publick Benefits*. 2 vols. Introduction by F. B. Kaye. Oxford: Clarendon, 1957; originally published 1732.

Marshall, William. *On the Landed Property of England*. London, 1804.

Mill, James. *Commerce Defended*. London: Baldwin, 1806.

"The Modern Spectator." *Repository of Arts*, October 1812, pp. 204–9.

"Mr. Fawkes's Collection of Watercolour Drawings." *Champion*, 2 May 1819, pp. 284–5.

"Mr. Fawkes's Gallery." *Repository of Arts*, 1 May 1819, pp. 297–301.

"Mr. Fawkes' Pictures." *London Chronicle*, 10 April 1819, pp. 347–8.

"On the Analogy between the Growth of Individual and National Genius." *Blackwood's Edinburgh Magazine* 6 (January 1820), pp. 375–81.

"On the Superiority of the Painter's Feelings." *Repository of Arts*, March 1817, pp. 140–3.

Opie, John. *The Lectures of John Opie* (1809). In *Lectures on Painting by the Royal Academicians*, ed. Ralph Wornum. London, 1848.

Oram, William. *Precepts and Observations on the Art of Colouring in Landscape Painting*. London: White and Cochrane, 1810.

Paine, Thomas. *The Rights of Man*. Edited by M. Conway. New York and London: G. P. Putnam, 1894; originally published 1791.

Paley, William. *Natural Theology*. London, 1802.

Pasquin, Anthony [John Williams]. *Critical Guide to the Royal Academy Exhibition of 1796*. London, 1796.

Plumptre, James. *The Lakers*. London, 1797.

Political Essays on Popular Subjects, Containing Dissertations on First Principles: Liberty; Democracy and the Party Denominations of Whig and Tory. 3rd edn. London, 1801.

Pott, Joseph. *An Essay on Landscape Painting*. London: J. Johnson, 1782.

Price, Uvedale. *Dialogue on the Distinct Characters of the Picturesque and the Beautiful*. London, 1801.

——*Essays on the Picturesque*. 2nd edn. 3 vols. London, 1810; originally published 1794.

[Pyne, W.H.?]. "Observations on the Rise and Progress of Painting in Water Colours," *Repository of Arts*, November 1812–March 1813, *passim*.

Reinagle, Ramsay. "Scientific and Explanatory Notes." In *Views in Sussex, Consisting of the Most Interesting Landscape and Marine Scenery in the Rape of Hastings* by J.M.W. Turner. London: John Murray and W.B. Cooke, 1820.

"Retrospect of the Fine Arts." *La Belle Assemblée*, December 1810, p. 340.

Reynolds, Joshua. *Discourses on Art*. Edited by Robert Wark. New Haven and London: Yale University Press, 1959; originally published 1797.

"Ricardo and the *Edinburgh Review*." *Blackwood's Edinburgh Magazine* 4 (1818), pp. 58–62.

Ricardo, David. *The Principles of Political Economy and Taxation*. London: Dent, 1973; originally published 1817.

Roberts, James. *Introductory Lessons with Familiar Examples in Landscapes for . . . Painting in Water-Colours*. London: Bulmer, 1800.

[Scott, John]. "Reflections on the Patronage of the Fine Arts." *Champion*, 14 May 1815, p. 159.

——*A Visit to Paris in 1814*. London: Longmans, 1815.

Shee, Martin Archer. *Elements of Art*. In *Elements of Art . . . and Rhymes on Art*. London: William Miller, 1809.

——*Rhymes on Art*. London, 1805.

Smith, Adam. *The Theory of Moral Sentiments*. London: George Bell and Sons, 1887; originally published 1759.

Spence, William. *Britain Independent of Commerce*. London, 1806.

Stewart, Dugald. "Account of the Life and Writings of Adam Smith, L.L.D." Biographical memoir in *The Theory of Moral Sentiments* by Adam Smith. London: George Bell and Sons, 1887; originally published 1759.

——*Lectures on Political Economy*. 2 vols. Edited by William Hamilton. Edinburgh: Thomas Constable, 1855.

Turner, J.M.W. *The Collected Correspondence of J.M.W. Turner*. Edited by John Gage. Oxford: Clarendon, 1980.

——*Views in Sussex, Consisting of the Most Interesting Landscape and Marine Scenery in the Rape of Hastings*. London: John Murray and W.B. Cooke, 1820.

The Two Pictures: or a View of the Miseries of France Contrasted with the Blessings of England. London, 1810.

"Water-colour Exhibitions." *Repository of Arts*, June 1810, supplement.

Secondary Sources

Allan, D.G.C. "The Society of Arts and Government, 1754–1800: Public Encouragement of Arts, Manufactures, and Commerce in Eighteenth-Century England." *Eighteenth-Century Studies* 7:4 (1974), pp. 434–52.

Allan, D. G. C. and John L. Abbott, eds. *The Virtuoso Tribe of Arts and Sciences: Studies in the Eighteenth-Century Work and Membership of the London Society of Arts*. Athens, GA and London: University of Georgia Press, 1992.

Allen, Brian. "The Society of Arts and the First Exhibition of Contemporary Art in 1770." *Royal Society of Arts Journal* 139 (March 1991), pp. 265–9.

——ed. *Towards a Modern Art World*. New Haven and London: Yale University Press, 1995.

Alpers, Svetlana. *The Art of Describing: Dutch Art in the Seventeenth Century*. Chicago: University of Chicago Press, 1983.

Altick, Richard. *The Shows of London*. Cambridge, MA: Harvard University Press, 1978.

Baetjer, Katharine. *Glorious Nature: British Landscape Painting 1750–1850*. Denver Art Museum exhibition catalogue. New York: Hudson Hills Press, 1993.

Barrell, John. "'The Dangerous Goddess': Masculinity, Prestige, and the Aesthetic in Early Eighteenth-Century Britain." *Cultural Critique* 12 (Spring 1989), pp. 101–31.

——*The Dark Side of the Landscape: The Rural Poor in English Painting 1730–1840*. Cambridge: Cambridge University Press, 1980.

——ed. *Painting and the Politics of Culture: New Essays on British Art 1700–1850*. Oxford and London: Oxford University Press, 1992.

——*The Political Theory of Painting from Reynolds to Hazlitt: The Body of the Public*. New Haven and London: Yale University Press, 1986.

——"The Private Comedy of Thomas Rowlandson." *Art History* 6:4 (December 1983), pp. 423–41.

——"The Public Prospect and the Private View: The Politics of Taste in Eighteenth-Century Britain." In *The Birth of Pandora and the Division of Knowledge*, pp. 41–61. London: Macmillan, 1992.

——"Sir Joshua Reynolds and the Englishness of English Art." In *Nation and Narration*, ed. Homi Bhabha, pp. 154–76. London: Routledge, 1990.

Bell, C. F. "Fresh Light on Some Water-colour Painters of the Old British School, Derived from the Collections and Papers of James Moore, F.S.A." *Walpole Society* 5 (1917), pp. 47–83.

Bennett, Shelley. "Anthony Pasquin and the Function of Art Journalism in Late Eighteenth-Century England." *British Journal for Eighteenth Century Studies* 8:2 (1985), pp. 197–207.

Berg, Maxine. *The Machinery Question and the Making of Political Economy, 1815–1848*. Cambridge: Cambridge University Press, 1980.

Bermingham, Ann. "The Aesthetics of Ignorance: The Accomplished Woman in the Culture of Connoisseurship." *Oxford Art Journal* 16:2 (1993), pp. 3–20.

——"'An Exquisite Practice': The Institution of Drawing as a Polite Art in Britain." In *Towards a Modern Art World* ed. Brian Allen, pp. 47–66. New Haven and London: Yale University Press, 1995.

——*Landscape and Ideology: The English Rustic Tradition, 1740–1860*. Berkeley: University of California Press, 1986.

——"The Origins of Painting and the End of Art: Wright of Derby's *Corinthian Maid*." In *Painting and the Politics of Culture: New Essays on British Art, 1700–1850*, ed. John Barrell, pp. 135–64. Oxford and London: Oxford University Press, 1992.

——"The Picturesque and Ready-to-wear Femininity." In *The Politics of the Picturesque: Literature, Landscape and Aesthetics since 1770*, ed. Stephen Copley and Peter Gartside, pp. 81–119. Cambridge: Cambridge University Press, 1994.

——"Reading Constable." *Art History* 10:1 (March 1987), pp. 39–58.

——"System, Order and Abstraction: The Politics of English Landsape Drawing around 1795." In *Landscape and Power*, ed. W.J.T. Mitchell, pp. 77–102. Chicago and London: University of Chicago Press, 1994.

Bicknell, Peter and Janet Munro. *Gilpin to Ruskin: Drawing Masters and Their Manuals, 1800–1860.* Fitzwilliam Museum exhibition catalogue. Cambridge, 1988.

Boase, T.S.R. "Macklin and Bowyer." *Journal of the Warburg and Courtauld Institutes* 26 (1963), pp. 148–77.

Brenneman, David. "The Critical Response to Gainsborough's Painting." Ph.D. dissertation, Brown University, 1994.

Brown, David Blayney. *Augustus Wall Callcott.* Tate Gallery exhibition catalogue. London, 1981.

——"Edward Dayes: Historical Draughtsman." *Old Water-Colour Society's Club* 62 (1991), pp. 9–21.

Bruntjen, Sven. *John Boydell, 1719–1804: A Study of Art Patronage and Publishing in Georgian London.* New York: Garland, 1985.

Buchwald, Emilie. "Gainsborough's 'Prospect, Animated Prospect.'" In *Studies in Criticism and Aesthetics, 1660–1800: Essays in Honor of Samuel Monk*, ed. Howard Anderson and John Shea, pp. 358–79. Minneapolis: University of Minnesota Press, 1967.

Butlin, Martin and Evelyn Joll. *The Paintings of J.M.W. Turner.* Rev. edn. 2 vols. New Haven and London: Yale University Press, 1984.

Campbell, Colin. *The Romantic Ethic and the Spirit of Modern Consumerism.* Oxford: Basil Blackwell, 1987.

Cannadine, David. *Lords and Landlords: The Aristocracy and the Towns, 1774–1967.* Leicester: Leicester University Press, 1980.

Checkland, Sydney. *British Public Policy 1776–1939.* Cambridge: Cambridge University Press, 1983.

Clarke, Michael and Nicholas Penny, eds. *The Arrogant Connoisseur: Richard Payne Knight 1751–1824.* Whitworth Art Gallery exhibition catalogue. Manchester: Manchester University Press, 1982.

Clay, Mary Rotha. *Julius Caesar Ibbetson, 1759–1817.* London: Country Life, 1948.

Colley, Linda. *Britons: Forging the Nation, 1707–1837.* New Haven and London: Yale University Press, 1992.

——"Whose Nation? Class and National Consciousness in Britain, 1750–1830." *Past and Present* 113 (November 1986), pp. 97–117.

Collini, Stefan, Donald Winch, and John Burrow. *The Noble Science of Politics.* Cambridge: Cambridge University Press, 1983.

Constable, W.G. *Richard Wilson.* Cambridge, MA: Harvard University Press, 1953.

Cookson, J.E. *The Friends of Peace: Anti-War Liberalism in England 1793–1815.* Cambridge: Cambridge University Press, 1982.

Copley, Stephen. "William Gilpin and the Black-lead Mine." In *The Politics of the Picturesque: Literature, Landscape and Aesthetics since 1770*, ed. Stephen Copley and Peter Gartside, pp. 42–61. Cambridge: Cambridge University Press, 1994.

Daniels, Stephen. *Fields of Vision: Landscape Imagery and National Identity in England and the United States.* Princeton: Princeton University Press, 1993.

——"The Political Iconography of Woodland in Later Georgian England." In *The Iconography of Landscape*, ed. Denis Cosgrove and Stephen Daniels, pp. 43–82. Cambridge: Cambridge University Press, 1988.

Daniels, Stephen and Charles Watkins. "Picturesque Landscaping and Estate Management: Uvedale Price and Nathaniel Kent at Foxley." In *The Politics of the Picturesque: Literature, Landscape and Aesthetics since 1770*, ed. Stephen Copley and Peter Gartside, pp. 13–41. Cambridge: Cambridge University Press, 1994.

Dayes, J. "Edward Dayes." *Old Water-Colour Society's Club* 19 (1964), pp. 45–55.

de Bolla, Peter. *The Discourse of the Sublime: History, Aesthetics and the Subject*. Oxford: Basil Blackwell, 1989.

Dictionary of National Biography. Edited by Leslie Stephen and Sidney Lee. 22 vols. London, 1885–1901.

Divinsky, Pamela. "The Visual and Conceptual Category of the Public." Review of *The Political Theory of Painting from Reynolds to Hazlitt: The Body of the Public*, by John Barrell. *Oxford Art Journal* 10:1 (1987), pp. 92–8.

Eaves, Morris. *The Counter-Arts Conspiracy: Art and Industry in the Age of Blake*. Ithaca, NY, and London: Cornell University Press, 1992.

Everett, Nigel. *The Tory View of Landscape*. New Haven and London: Yale University Press, 1994.

Fabricant, Carole. "The Aesthetics and Politics of Landscape in the Eighteenth Century." In *Studies in Eighteenth Century British Art and Aesthetics*, ed. Ralph Cohen, pp. 49–81. Berkeley: University of California Press, 1985.

——"The Literature of Domestic Tourism and the Public Consumption of Private Property." In *The New Eighteenth Century: Theory, Politics, Literature*, ed. Felicity Nussbaum and Laura Brown, pp. 254–75. London and New York: Methuen, 1987.

Fawkes, Edith. "Turner at Farnley." n. d. (*c.*1900). Typescript. Archives of the National Gallery, London.

Fontana, Biancamaria. *Rethinking the Politics of Commercial Society: The "Edinburgh Review", 1802–1832*. Cambridge: Cambridge University Press, 1985.

Ford, John. *Ackermann 1783–1983: The Business of Art*. London: Ackermann, 1983.

Foucault, Michel. *The Order of Things*. New York: Vintage Books, 1973; originally published in French, 1966.

——"The Subject and Power." In *Michel Foucault: Beyond Structuralism and Hermeneutics*, by Herbert Dreyfus and Paul Rabinow, pp. 208–26. Brighton: Harvester, 1982.

Friedman, Winifred. *Boydell's Shakespeare Gallery*. New York: Garland, 1976.

Fullerton, Peter. "Patronage and Pedagogy: The British Institution in the Early Nineteenth Century." *Art History* 5:1 (March 1982), pp. 59–72.

Funnell, Peter. "Richard Payne Knight 1751–1824: Aspects of Aesthetics and Art Criticism in Late Eighteenth and Early Nineteenth Century England." Ph.D. dissertation. Oxford University, 1985.

——"'Visible Appearances.'" In *The Arrogant Connoisseur: Richard Payne Knight 1751–1824*, ed. Michael Clarke and Nicholas Penny, pp. 82–92. Whitworth Art Gallery exhibition catalogue. Manchester: Manchester University Press, 1982.

——"William Hazlitt, Prince Hoare, and the Institutionalisation of the British Art World." In *Towards a Modern Art World*, ed. Brian Allen, pp. 145–55. New Haven and London: Yale University Press, 1995.

Gage, John. *A Decade of English Naturalism 1810–20*. Norwich Castle Museum and Victoria and Albert Museum exhibition catalogue. Norwich and London, 1969.

——"Turner and the Picturesque." *Burlington Magazine* 107 (January–June 1965), Part 1, pp. 16–25; Part 2, pp. 75–81.

The Great Age of British Watercolours 1750–1880. Royal Academy of Arts exhibition catalogue. Munich: Prestel, 1993.

Habermas, Jürgen. *The Structural Transformation of the Public Sphere*. Cambridge: Polity Press, 1989; originally published in German, 1962.

Hardie, Martin. *Water-colour Painting in Britain*. 3 vols. New York: Barnes and Noble, 1967.

Haskell, Francis. *Rediscoveries in Art: Some Aspects of Taste, Fashion and Collecting in England and France*. London: Phaidon, 1976.

Hawes, Louis. *Presences of Nature: British Landscape 1780–1830*. Yale Center for British Art exhibition catalogue. New Haven and London, 1982.

Hayes, John. *The Landscape Paintings of Thomas Gainsborough*. 2 vols. London: Sotheby Publications, 1982.

Helsinger, Elizabeth. "Constable: The Making of a National Painter." *Critical Inquiry* 15 (Winter 1989), pp. 253–79.

——"Turner and the Representation of England." In *Landscape and Power*, ed. W.J.T. Mitchell, pp. 103–25. Chicago and London: University of Chicago Press, 1994.

Hemingway, Andrew. "Academic Theory versus Associationist Aesthetics: The Ideological Forms of a Conflict of Interests in the Early Nineteenth Century." *Ideas and Production* 5 (1985), pp. 18–42.

——"Art Exhibitions as Leisure-Class Rituals in Early Nineteenth-Century London." In *Towards a Modern Art World*, ed. Brian Allen, pp. 95–108. New Haven and London: Yale University Press, 1995.

——*Landscape Imagery and Urban Culture in Early Nineteenth Century Britain*. Cambridge: Cambridge University Press, 1992.

——"The Political Theory of Painting without the Politics." Review of *The Political Theory of Painting from Reynolds to Hazlitt: The Body of the Public*, by John Barrell. *Art History* 10:3 (September 1987), pp. 381–95.

——"The 'Sociology' of Taste in the Scottish Enlightenment." *Oxford Art Journal* 12:2 (1989), pp. 3–35.

Hill, Bridget. *Eighteenth Century Women: An Anthology*. London: Allen and Unwin, 1987.

Hill, Christopher. *Puritanism and Revolution*. London: Secker and Warburg, 1958.

Holcomb, Adèle. "More Matter with Less Art: Romantic Attitudes toward Landscape Painting." *Art Journal* 36 (Summer 1977), pp. 303–6.

Hollander, Samuel. *The Economics of David Ricardo*. Toronto: University of Toronto Press, 1979.

Hont, Istvan and Michael Ignatieff, eds. *Wealth and Virtue: The Shaping of Political Economy in the Scottish Enlightenment*. Cambridge: Cambridge University Press, 1983.

Hussey, Christopher. *The Picturesque*. London: Cass, 1967; originally published 1927.

Joppien, Rüdiger. *Philippe Jacques de Loutherbourg, R.A., 1740–1812*. Greater London Arts Council exhibition catalogue. London, 1973.

Kallich, Martin. *The Association of Ideas and Critical Theory in Eighteenth Century England*. The Hague and Paris: Mouton, 1970.

Klancher, Jon. *The Making of English Reading Audiences, 1790–1832*. Madison: University of Wisconsin Press, 1987.

——"Reading the Social Text: Power, Signs and Audience in Nineteenth Century Prose." *Studies in Romanticism* 23 (Summer 1984), pp. 183–204.

Kriedte, Peter. *Peasants, Landlords and Merchant Capitalists: Europe and the World Economy, 1500–1800*. Leamington Spa: Berg, 1980.

Lichtenstein, Jaqueline. *The Eloquence of Color: Rhetoric and Painting in the French Classical Age*. Berkeley: University of California Press, 1993; originally published in French, 1989.

——"Making Up Representation: The Risks of Femininity." *Representations* 20 (Fall 1987), pp. 77–87.

Lightbown, R. W. Introduction to reprint edition of *The Works of the Late Edward Dayes*. London: Cornmarket, 1971; originally published 1805.

Lloyd Williams, Julia. *Dutch Art and Scotland: A Reflection of Taste*. National Gallery of Scotland exhibition catalogue. Edinburgh, 1992.

McKendrick, Neil, John Brewer, and J. H. Plumb. *The Birth of a Consumer Society*. London: Hutchinson, 1983.

Mee, Jon. *Dangerous Enthusiasm: William Blake and the Culture of Radicalism in the 1790s*. Oxford: Clarendon, 1992.

Messmann, Frank. *Richard Payne Knight: The Twilight of Virtuosity*. The Hague and Paris: Mouton, 1974.

Michasiw, Kim Ian. "Nine Theses on the Picturesque." *Representations* 38 (Spring 1992), pp. 76–100.

Mitchell, Timothy. *Art and Science in German Landscape Painting 1770–1840*. Oxford: Clarendon, 1993.

——"Bound by Time and Place: The Art of Caspar David Friedrich." *Arts Magazine* 61 (November 1986), pp. 48–53.

Moir, Esther. *The Discovery of Britain*. London: Routledge and Kegan Paul, 1964.

Monk, Samuel. *The Sublime: A Study of Critical Theories in Eighteenth-Century England*. New York: Modern Language Association, 1935.

Murdoch, John. "Foregrounds and Focus: Changes in the Perception of Landscape *c*.1800." In *The Lake District: A Sort of National Property*. Cheltenham: Countryside Commission, 1986.

Newman, Gerald. *The Rise of English Nationalism: A Cultural History 1740–1830*. New York: St. Martin's, 1987.

Nicholson, Benedict. "Thomas Gisborne and Wright of Derby." *Burlington Magazine* 107 (1965), pp. 58–62.

Nicholson, Kathleen. "Turner, Poetry, and the Transformation of History Painting." *Arts Magazine* 56 (April 1982), pp. 92–7.

Owen, Felicity and David Blayney Brown. *Collector of Genius: A Life of Sir George Beaumont*. New Haven and London: Yale University Press, 1988.

Paulson, Ronald. *Hogarth*. 3 vols. New Brunswick, NJ: Rutgers University Press, 1991–3.

Pears Iain. *The Discovery of Painting: The Growth of Interest in the Arts in England 1680–1768*. New Haven and London: Yale University Press, 1988.

Penny, Nicholas. "Richard Payne Knight: A Brief Life." In *The Arrogant Connoisseur: Richard Payne Knight 1751–1824*, ed. Michael Clarke and Nicholas Penny, pp. 1–18. Whitworth Art Gallery exhibition catalogue. Manchester: Manchester University Press, 1982.

Perkin, Harold. *The Origins of Modern English Society 1780–1830*. London: Routledge and Kegan Paul, 1969.

Pocock, J. G. A. *The Machiavellian Moment: Florentine Political Thought and the Atlantic Republican Tradition*. Princeton: Princeton University Press, 1975.

—— *Virtue, Commerce and History*. Cambridge: Cambridge University Press, 1985.

Potts, Alex. "A Man of Taste's Picturesque." Review of *The Arrogant Connoisseur*, ed. Michael Clarke and Nicholas Penny. *Oxford Art Journal* 5:1 (1982), pp. 70–6.

Prebble, John. *The Highland Clearances*. London: Secker and Warburg, 1963.

Pressly, William. *James Barry: The Artist as Hero*. Tate Gallery exhibition catalogue. London, 1983.

——*The Life and Art of James Barry*. New Haven and London: Yale University Press, 1981.

Pullan, Ann. "'Conversations on the Arts': Writing a Space for the Female Viewer in the *Repository of Arts* 1809–15." *Oxford Art Journal* 15:2 (1992), pp. 15–26.

——"Fashioning a Public for Art: Ideology, Gender and the Fine Arts in the English Periodical *c.*1800–25." Ph.D. dissertation. University of Cambridge, 1992.

Raines, Robert. "Watteaus and 'Watteaus' in England before 1760." *Gazette des Beaux Arts* 6th series, 86 (February 1977), pp. 51–64.

Rajchman, John. "Foucault's Art of Seeing." *October* 44 (Spring 1988), pp. 89–117.

Rawlinson, W. G. *The Engraved Works of J. M. W. Turner*. 2 vols. London: Macmillan, 1908 and 1913.

Redgrave, Richard and Samuel Redgrave. *A Century of British Painters*. Ithaca, NY: Cornell University Press, 1981; originally published 1866.

Reitlinger, Gerald. *The Economics of Taste: The Rise and Fall of Picture Prices 1760–1960*. London: Barrie and Rockliff, 1961.

Roberts, Helène. "'Trains of Fascinating and Endless Imagery': Associationist Art Criticism before 1850." *Victorian Periodicals Newsletter* 10:3 (September 1977), pp. 91–105.

Roll, Eric. *A History of Economic Thought*. 4th edn. Revised. London: Faber and Faber, 1973.

Rosenthal, Michael. *Constable: The Painter and his Landscape*. New Haven and London: Yale University Press, 1983.

——"Landscape as High Art." In *Glorious Nature: British Landscape Painting 1750–1850*, catalogue by Katharine Baetjer, pp. 13–30. Denver Art Museum exhibition catalogue. New York: Hudson Hills Press, 1993.

Shanes, Eric. *Turner's Human Landscape*. London: Heinemann, 1990.

——*Turner's Rivers, Harbours and Coasts*. London: Chatto and Windus, 1981.

Simpson, David. *Romanticism, Nationalism, and the Revolt against Theory*. Chicago and London: University of Chicago Press, 1993.

Sloan, Kim. "Drawing – A 'Polite Recreation' in Eighteenth-Century England." *Studies in Eighteeth Century Culture* 2 (1982), pp. 217–40.

Smiles, Sam. *The Image of Antiquity: Ancient Britain and the Romantic Imagination*. New Haven and London: Yale University Press, 1994.

——"'Splashers,' 'Scrawlers' and 'Plasterers': British Landscape Painting and the Language of Criticism, 1800–40." *Turner Studies* 10:1 (Summer 1990), pp. 5–11.

Solkin, David. *Painting for Money: The Visual Arts and the Public Sphere in Eighteen Century England*. New Haven and London: Yale University Press, 1993.

——*Richard Wilson: The Landscape of Reaction*. Tate Gallery exhibition catalogue. London, 1982.

Stainton, Lindsay. *British Landscape Watercolours 1600–1800*. British Museum exhibition catalogue. Cambridge: Cambridge University Press, 1985.

Sykes, Christopher. *Private Palaces: Life in the Great London Houses*. New York: Viking, 1986.

Thompson, Edward P. *The Making of the English Working Class*. Rev. edn. Harmondsworth: Penguin, 1980.

Uphaus, Robert. "The Ideology of Reynolds' *Discourses on Art*." *Eighteenth Century Studies* 21:1 (Fall 1978), pp. 59–73.

Voloshinov, V.N. *Marxism and the Philosophy of Language*. New York: Academic Press, 1973.

Von Erffa, Helmut and Allen Staley. *The Paintings of Benjamin West*. New Haven and London: Yale University Press, 1986.

Waterfield, Giles. "'That White-Faced Man': Sir Francis Bourgeois, 1756–1811." *Turner Studies* 9:2 (Winter 1989), pp. 36–48.

Westall, Richard. "The Westall Brothers." *Turner Studies* 4:1 (Summer 1984), pp. 23–38.

White, Christopher. *English Landscape 1630–1850*. Yale Center for British Art exhibition catalogue. New Haven, 1977.

Whitley, William. *Art in England 1800–1820*. New York: Macmillan, 1928.

——*Artists and Their Friends in England 1700–1799*. 2 vols. New York and London: Benjamin Blom, 1968; originally published 1928.

Whittingham, Selby. "What You Will; or Some Notes Regarding the Influence of Watteau on Turner and Other British Artists," Parts I and II. *Turner Studies* 5:1 (Summer 1985), pp. 2–24 and 5:2 (Winter 1985), pp. 28–48.

Williams, Raymond. *The City and the Country*. New York: Oxford University Press, 1973.

——*Culture and Society 1780–1850*. New York: Columbia University Press, 1983; originally published 1958.

——*Marxism and Literature*. Oxford: Oxford University Press, 1977.

Wilton, Andrew. *Turner and the Sublime*. Art Gallery of Ontario and the Yale Center for British Art exhibition catalogue. Chicago: University of Chicago Press, 1982.

Ziff, Jerrold. "'Backgrounds, Introduction of Architecture and Landscape': A Lecture by J.M.W. Turner." *Journal of the Warburg and Courtauld Institutes* 26 (1963), pp. 124–47.

Index